Volume of Celebrant's Voice	Location of Celebrant	R L	Actions of the Celebrant or ❋ Sounds, Gestures and Ot[…]		
silent	center of altar		The Celebrant bows low over the altar and speaks the words of the Consecration slowly and silently.	**Consecration of the Host**	37
silent	center of altar		The Celebrant elevates the Sacred Host for all to adore.	**Elevation of the Host**	37
silent	center of altar		The Celebrant bows low over the Chalice and speaks the words of the Consecration slowly and silently.	**Consecration of the Wine**	39
silent	center of altar		The Celebrant elevates the Chalice for all to adore.	**Elevation of the Chalice**	39
raised	center of altar		The Celebrant strikes his breast as he says aloud, *"Nobis quoque peccatoribus."*	**Nobis quoque peccatoribus**	43
raised	center of altar		At High Mass, the Celebrant chants aloud the *Pater Noster.*	**Pater Noster**	45
normal	center of altar		Listen closely and you may hear the sound of the Priest breaking the Sacred Host.	**Breaking of the Host**	47
raised	center of altar		The Priest bows and strikes his breast three times. At High Mass, the *Agnus Dei* is sung by the choir.	**Agnus Dei**	49
raised	center of altar		The Priest strikes his breast thrice, each time repeating the words *"Domine non sum dignus..."*	**Communion of the Priest**	51
normal	center of altar		As the Priest finishes his Communion, the server bows low and again recites the *Confiteor.*	**Confiteor**	51
raised	center of altar		The Celebrant displays the Sacred Host, saying *"Ecce Agnus Dei..."* We repeat *"Domine non sum dignus..."*	**Communion of the Faithful**	53
normal	left side of altar (our right)		After completing the ablutions and the Communion Prayer in silence, the Celebrant now reads the Postcommunion aloud.	**Post-communion Prayer**	57
raised	center of altar		The Celebrant turns to the people and blesses them with the Sign of the Cross.	**Ite Missa Est/ Final Blessing**	59
raised	right side of altar (our left)		The Celebrant reads the beginning of John's Gospel, genuflecting at the words *"Et Verbum Caro Factum Est."*	**Last Gospel**	61
raised	foot of the altar		The Priest kneels at the foot of the altar and recites several prayers.	**Prayers after Low Mass**	63

"And this is written deep in the nature of man: We must have sensible signs and figures, for we are partly spiritual and partly corporal...And the truths of religion are spiritual, and the rites and ceremonies are corporal; yet as the soul is contained in the body, so the truths of religion are contained in the rites and ceremonies of the Church... show me a religion without rites and ceremonies, and I will show you a people drifting rapidly toward infidelity and the denial of all religion."

—Rev. James Luke Meagher,
Teaching Truth by Signs and Ceremonies

BOOKMARKS

It is not unusual to lose your place during the Mass, especially since much of it is in reverent silence. If this should happen, listen and watch for the clues in this chart to help you find the right page. ***Keep in mind that the sides of Christ's altar are determined by His Right and Left, not ours.*** See page xxv for an explanation of the sides of the altar.

Volume of Celebrant's Voice	Location of Celebrant	R L	Actions of the Celebrant or Ministers ❈ Sounds, Gestures and Other Cues ❈	Part of Mass	See Page #
normal	foot of the altar		The Celebrant bows low to recite the *Confiteor*, then the server or ministers do likewise.	**Confiteor**	5
raised	center of altar		At High Mass, the *Kyrie* is sung by the choir. At Low Mass, it is recited aloud by the Priest.	**Kyrie**	9
raised	center of altar		At High Mass, the Celebrant intones, "*Gloria in Excelsis Deo*," followed by the choir.	**Gloria**	11
raised	left side of altar (our right)		At High Mass, the Subdeacon reads the Epistle. At Low Mass, the Priest reads the Epistle aloud.	**Epistle**	13
raised	right side of altar (our left)		At High Mass, the Deacon reads the Gospel. At Low Mass, the Priest reads the Gospel aloud.	**Gospel**	15
raised	center of altar		At High Mass, the Celebrant intones, "*Credo in unum Deum*," followed by the choir. All kneel at the words "*Et incarnatus est*."	**Credo**	17
normal	left side of altar (our right)		The Celebrant pours wine and a drop of water into the Chalice.	**Mixing of Water and Wine**	21
normal	both sides of altar		At Solemn High Mass, the Celebrant will incense the offerings, the altar, and all those present.	**Incensing**	23
normal	left side of altar (our right)		The Celebrant washes his hands.	**Lavabo**	25
raised	center of altar		The Celebrant turns to the people with his hands raised in front of his body.	**Orate Fratres**	27
raised	center of altar		As we approach the Preface, a responsory is sung (or spoken at Low Mass), ending with the phrase, "*Dignum et Justum est*."	**Preface**	29
raised	center of altar		At High Mass, the choir sings the *Sanctus*.	**Sanctus**	29
silent	center of altar		The Celebrant imposes his hands over the offerings, symbolizing the placing of our sins upon the sacrificial Lamb.	**Hanc Igitur**	35

Volume of Celebrant's Voice	Location of Celebrant	R	L	Actions of the Celebrant or Ministers ❁ Sounds, Gestures and Other Cues ❁	Part of Mass	See Page #
silent	center of altar			The Celebrant bows low over the altar and speaks the words of the Consecration slowly and silently.	**Consecration of the Host**	37
silent	center of altar			The Celebrant elevates the Sacred Host for all to adore.	**Elevation of the Host**	37
silent	center of altar			The Celebrant bows low over the Chalice and speaks the words of the Consecration slowly and silently.	**Consecration of the Wine**	39
silent	center of altar			The Celebrant elevates the Chalice for all to adore.	**Elevation of the Chalice**	39
raised	center of altar			The Celebrant strikes his breast as he says aloud, *"Nobis quoque peccatoribus."*	**Nobis quoque peccatoribus**	43
raised	center of altar			At High Mass, the Celebrant chants aloud the *Pater Noster.*	**Pater Noster**	45
normal	center of altar			Listen closely and you may hear the sound of the Priest breaking the Sacred Host.	**Breaking of the Host**	47
raised	center of altar			The Priest bows and strikes his breast three times. At High Mass, the *Agnus Dei* is sung by the choir.	**Agnus Dei**	49
raised	center of altar			The Priest strikes his breast thrice, each time repeating the words *"Domine non sum dignus..."*	**Communion of the Priest**	51
normal	center of altar			As the Priest finishes his Communion, the server bows low and again recites the *Confiteor.*	**Confiteor**	51
raised	center of altar			The Celebrant displays the Sacred Host, saying *"Ecce Agnus Dei..."* We repeat *"Domine non sum dignus..."*	**Communion of the Faithful**	53
normal	left side of altar (our right)			After completing the ablutions and the Communion Prayer in silence, the Celebrant now reads the Postcommunion aloud.	**Post-communion Prayer**	57
raised	center of altar			The Celebrant turns to the people and blesses them with the Sign of the Cross.	**Ite Missa Est/ Final Blessing**	59
raised	right side of altar (our left)			The Celebrant reads the beginning of John's Gospel, genuflecting at the words *"Et Verbum Caro Factum Est."*	**Last Gospel**	61
raised	foot of the altar			The Priest kneels at the foot of the altar and recites several prayers.	**Prayers after Low Mass**	63

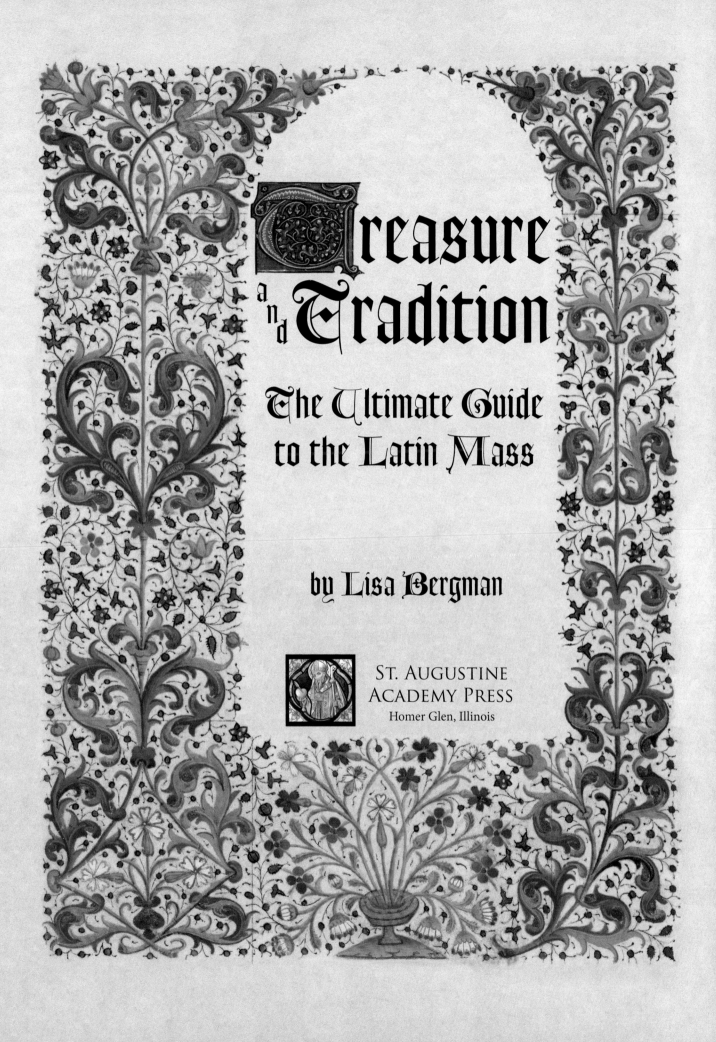

Treasure and Tradition

The Ultimate Guide to the Latin Mass

by Lisa Bergman

ST. AUGUSTINE
ACADEMY PRESS
Homer Glen, Illinois

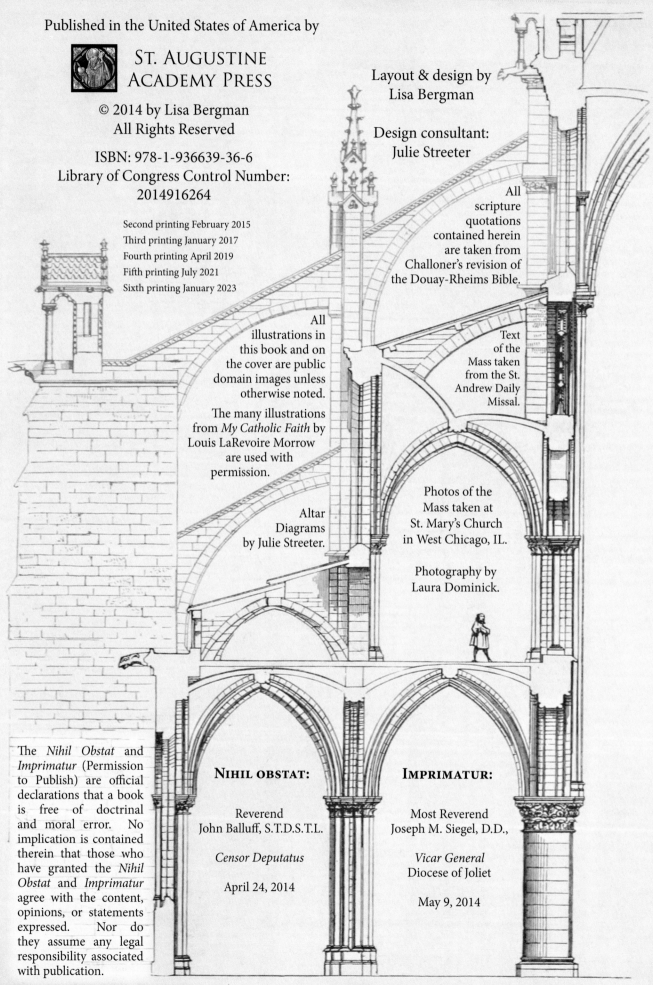

Published in the United States of America by

ST. AUGUSTINE
ACADEMY PRESS

© 2014 by Lisa Bergman
All Rights Reserved

ISBN: 978-1-936639-36-6
Library of Congress Control Number:
2014916264

Second printing February 2015
Third printing January 2017
Fourth printing April 2019
Fifth printing July 2021
Sixth printing January 2023

Layout & design by
Lisa Bergman

Design consultant:
Julie Streeter

All
scripture
quotations
contained herein
are taken from
Challoner's revision of
the Douay-Rheims Bible.

All
illustrations in
this book and on
the cover are public
domain images unless
otherwise noted.

The many illustrations
from *My Catholic Faith* by
Louis LaRevoire Morrow
are used with
permission.

Text
of the
Mass taken
from the St.
Andrew Daily
Missal.

Altar
Diagrams
by Julie Streeter.

Photos of the
Mass taken at
St. Mary's Church
in West Chicago, IL.

Photography by
Laura Dominick.

NIHIL OBSTAT:

Reverend
John Balluff, S.T.D.S.T.L.

Censor Deputatus

April 24, 2014

IMPRIMATUR:

Most Reverend
Joseph M. Siegel, D.D.,

Vicar General
Diocese of Joliet

May 9, 2014

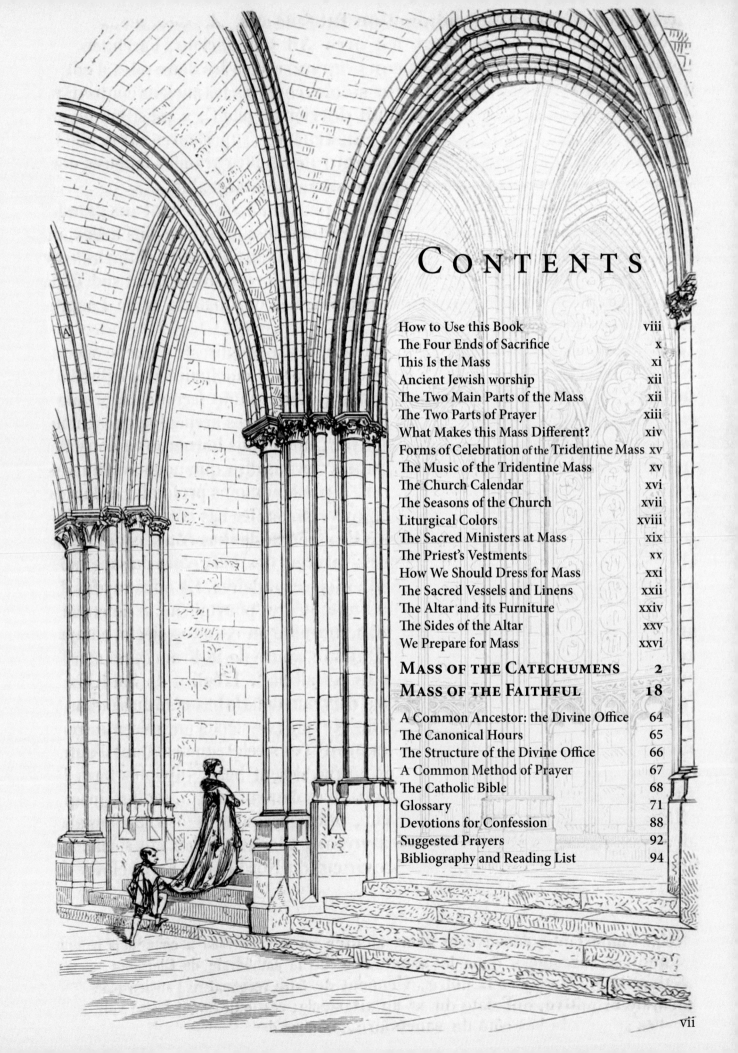

CONTENTS

How to Use this Book

This Missal is unlike any you have seen before. Here's an introduction to its parts.

Bookmark Chart

Any time you lose your place during the Mass, consult this chart at the front of the book and listen or look for cues that will help you find the right page.

normal	foot of the altar		The Celebrant bows low to recite the *Confiteor*, then the server or ministers do likewise.	Confiteor	5
raised	center of altar		At High Mass, the *Kyrie* is sung by the choir. At Low Mass, it is recited aloud by the Priest.	Kyrie	9
raised	center of altar		At High Mass, the Celebrant intones, "*Gloria in Excelsis Deo*," followed by the choir.	Gloria	11
raised	left side of altar (our right)		At High Mass, the Subdeacon reads the Epistle. At Low Mass, the Priest reads the Epistle aloud.	Epistle	13
raised	right side of altar (our left)		At High Mass, the Deacon reads the Gospel. At Low Mass, the Priest reads the Gospel aloud.	Gospel	15

A Crash Course in Black and White

The first 18 pages of this book are dedicated to laying the foundation you need for understanding the differences between the Ordinary Form and the Extraordinary Form. Learn about the structure of the Mass, its whys and wherefores, its music, its calendar (and why it is different from the one we use today), how to tell the difference between Low Mass and High Mass, and how to figure out who all those people are up on the altar (including what they are wearing and carrying). We also discuss what you can do to prepare yourself for Mass.

The Mass

Each double-page spread explores the themes and history of one part of the Mass, providing the text in Latin with English subtitles, as well as in plain English. Photographs and diagrams help to show what the Priest is doing at each point, and copious notes explain the various prayers and actions, when parts are omitted, and when parts are sung by the choir or cantor.

Photographs showing the actions of the Priest during High Mass

Notes explaining the prayers and actions of the Mass

Exploration of the themes and history of the Mass

The Mass in Latin with subtitles

Cues to the music of the Mass

The Mass in English

The propers of the Mass are set apart in a box (the ones included here are those for Trinity Sunday)

Diagrams showing the position of the Priest at Low Mass

Parts of the Mass which are sometimes omitted are shown in brackets or with this icon

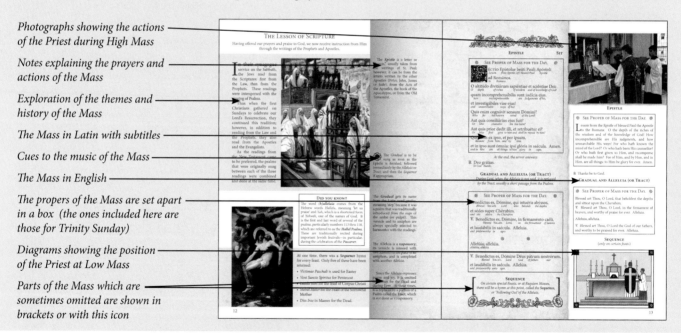

Appendix

Even more about the Mass can be found here. We compare its development with its sister liturgy, the Divine Office (also known as the Liturgy of the Hours); we explain the history of the various English translations of the Bible; we include a glossary (and a suggested reading list) to help you to discover more about the concepts you have learned; and lastly, we provide various prayers and a preparation for confession.

Introduction

BARQUE DE L'EGLISE

Most Catholics today are vaguely aware that at one time, Mass was said in Latin while the Priest faced the altar. However, most quite simply can't imagine sitting through a ceremony performed in a dead language by a man who has his back turned to them. Mention the fact that the most crucial parts of this rite are inaudible, and that the singing of the propers at High Mass obscures much of the rest, and suddenly this Mass seems less like the "Extraordinary Form" (*as in, thank heaven it's not the Ordinary Form!*) and more like a ritual that is hopelessly anachronistic, inaccessible and forbidding—in a word, *dead.*

But these are merely the human limitations of a liturgy which, through its thousands of years of usage, comes down to us directly from Christ Himself, and from the religious practices He followed in temple and synagogue. In fact, we may look back as far as Adam and Abel for the earliest ancestor of the sacrifice we offer on our altars. The practices handed down to Abraham, Isaac and Jacob were perfected by Moses and the Prophets. David wrote the Psalms to accompany the Temple services. All of them were shaping a Divinely inspired heritage of worship. And while Christ's death replaced the bloody sacrifices of the Old Covenant with His own, the Apostles changed little of the ancient practices of their faith in celebrating the early Mass, except to add the rite instituted by Christ at the Last Supper.

Thus, as we explore fully the treasures the Mass holds, we discover that this is no mere vestige of the pomp of medieval clerics, but a living tradition that incorporates the entire history of salvation. This book seeks to pull back the veil of time and disuse and reveal this rich ancestry, so that no barrier of language, custom or understanding can hinder us from glorying in its splendor.

"Picture then the High Priest Christ leaving the sacristy of heaven for the altar of Calvary. He has already put on the vestment of our human nature, the maniple of our suffering, the stole of priesthood, the chasuble of the Cross. Calvary is his cathedral; the rock of Calvary is the altar stone; the sun turning to red is the sanctuary lamp; Mary and John are the living side altars; the Host is His Body; the wine is His Blood. He is upright as Priest, yet He is prostrate as Victim. His Mass is about to begin."

—Bishop Fulton Sheen, *Calvary and the Mass.*

THE FOUR ENDS OF SACRIFICE

HOLY MASS IS THE MOST PERFECT FULFILLMENT OF THESE FOUR ENDS:

ADORATION

The sacrifice of God's only Son is the only truly worthy gift we can offer Him in honor and adoration.

THANKSGIVING

Through Christ we offer most efficiently our thanks and praise for all the many benefits we receive.

THE SACRIFICE OF THE MASS IS OFFERED FOR FOUR ENDS

ATONEMENT

Through the Sacrifice of the Mass, we apply the Blood of Christ for the forgiveness of our sins.

PETITION

Through Christ's intercession, we hope to obtain the assistance of God's grace for our intentions.

Under the old Law, different sacrifices were prescribed for each of these ends.

These were replaced by Christ's Perfect Sacrifice on the Cross.

This Perfect Sacrifice is renewed in the Mass, where Christ is both Priest and Victim.

THIS IS THE MASS

This is not a "religious service" or a scripture class;
this is Heaven on Earth: it is where our God comes to us.

When we speak of the Latin Mass (or the Extraordinary Form of the Mass), we are referring to what is known as the **Tridentine Mass**. It was promulgated in 1570 by Pope Pius V as part of the reforms of the Council of Trent, in order to standardize a liturgy that had become varied according to local traditions, as well as to safeguard it from the introduction of any Protestant errors. Careful study of ancient manuscripts was undertaken in order to restore the liturgy as closely as possible to "the pristine form and rite of the holy Fathers." (*Quo Primum*, 1570) Since that time, revised editions of the Missal were issued in 1604, 1634, 1884, 1920 and 1962.

Extraordinary is a good word for the Tridentine Mass, for it has three layers of mystery that set it apart: First, it is celebrated in a language that is no longer spoken. Next, the Priest faces the altar rather than the people. And third, the most important parts are spoken too quietly for anyone to hear! Yet the wisdom of all this mystery can be found in the illustration above.

"And all the angels stood round about the throne, and the ancients, and the four living creatures; and they fell down before the throne upon their faces, and adored God, saying: Amen. Benediction, and glory, and wisdom, and thanksgiving, honour, and power, and strength to our God for ever and ever. Amen."

(Apocalypse 7:11-12)

Here, upon the altar, is the Most Holy. As the Priest elevates the Host—which is now Christ's body—angels, saints and men hasten to adore Him just as on that first Christmas, when He became man for our sake. At every Mass, we experience this great privilege of being in His presence. And it is these layers of mystery and solemn beauty within the liturgy that serve to remind us that, for this brief moment, we are experiencing Heaven on Earth.

THE TWO MAIN FORMS OF ANCIENT JEWISH WORSHIP:

PRAYER AND PRAISE

Sacrifices could only be offered before the Temple in Jerusalem, but for many Jews, this was too far to travel. Most came only once a year, to fulfill their Passover duty. However, a faith which is practiced only once a year is too easily forgotten. Therefore any village large enough had a **synagogue** (from the Greek *synagōgē*, meaning assembly). This was a meeting place where devout Jews could gather to chant the Psalms and learn from the holy scriptures.

SACRIFICES AND OFFERINGS

Bread, wine, oil and incense were offered to God in the Temple in Jerusalem. However, in the old covenant, only the shedding of blood could remove the guilt of sin, so the blood of animals was offered to God in place of the blood of sinners. These **holocausts**, especially the yearly renewal of the Passover sacrifice, were the necessary mark of an observant Jew, like the blood on the lintels that had saved them from the Angel of Death in Egypt.

> Both these forms of worship emphasized the figure of the Messiah who was to come. In the Mass, we see the completion and fulfillment of that promise in everything we do.

THESE ARE FULFILLED IN THE TWO MAIN PARTS OF THE MASS:

MASS OF THE CATECHUMENS

From the Prayers at the Foot of the Altar to the Creed

THIS IS THE MASS OF **PREPARATION**:

Based on the practice of the Synagogue

Here we offer *prayers and praise* to God and receive instructon from Him.

Catechumens (those being instructed in the faith) were welcome for this portion of the Mass.

MASS OF THE FAITHFUL

From the Offertory to the Last Gospel

THIS IS THE MASS OF **FULFILLMENT**:

Based on the celebration of the Passover

Here we *recreate the sacrifice* of Calvary and receive our Lord in Communion.

Only the baptized were permitted to be present for the Mass of the Faithful.

EVERY PRAYER HAS TWO PARTS:

WE GIVE TO GOD

Prayer is the means by which we communicate with God; thus, like any conversation, it must go back and forth between us and Him. God created us to know Him, love Him and serve Him, and we do this best by offering Him the glory that is His due.

GOD GIVES TO US

Once we have fulfilled this duty, we humbly ask God for the things we need. Our Lord gave us the ideal model for this conversation in the *Our Father*. In each of the prayers of the Mass, you will find this up-and-down motion.

THE STRUCTURE OF THE MASS FOLLOWS THIS SAME UP-AND-DOWN MOTION,
LIKE THE ARCHES OF A CATHEDRAL:

WE GIVE TO GOD
THROUGH CHRIST

WE RECEIVE GRACES AND
BLESSINGS FROM GOD

Doxology
Prayers of Remembrance   Our Father
Prayers of Offering   Breaking of the Host
Consecration   Agnus Dei
Prayers of Offering   Communion
Prayers of Remembrance   Postcommunion
Prayer
Preface
Secret   Dismissal &
Benediction
Offertory   Last
Offertory Antiphon   Gospel

THE MASS OF THE
FAITHFUL
builds upon it.

WE OFFER
PRAYERS AND
PRAISE TO GOD

WE RECEIVE
INSTRUCTION
FROM HIM

Collects
Gloria   Epistle
Kyrie   Gradual
and Alleluia
Introit   Gospel

THE MASS OF THE
CATECHUMENS
lays the foundation.

Sermon
Prayers at
the Foot
of the Altar   Creed

WE
START
HERE

WHAT MAKES THIS MASS DIFFERENT?

For those unfamiliar with the Tridentine Mass, it helps to understand these differences.

WHY IS THE MASS SAID IN LATIN?

Most of the Mass is in Latin, but there are also elements in Greek (the *Kyrie*) and Hebrew (the words *Amen, Alleluia, Hosanna,* and *Sabaoth*). Consider: these are the three languages used for the inscription on the Cross. By using Latin, we establish continuity with a language that Christ himself would have known, and we establish unity in the liturgy—regardless of time and place. Latin is also a beautiful and well-ordered language, but what makes it most ideal for the Mass is the fact that *it is no longer a living language that is subject to changes in meaning.*

"And Pilate wrote a title also, and he put it upon the cross. And the writing was: JESUS OF NAZARETH, THE KING OF THE JEWS. This title therefore many of the Jews did read: because the place where Jesus was crucified was nigh to the city: *and it was written in Hebrew, in Greek, and in Latin.*" (John 19:19-20)

WHY DOESN'T THE PRIEST FACE THE PEOPLE?

In the Mass, the Priest serves *in persona Christi*—in the person of Christ—and in this role he is recreating the sacrifice of Calvary. He is interceding for us with God, and it is only natural that he should face the same direction we are facing: toward God, to whom our prayers are addressed. When the Priest is addressing us directly, or when he especially wishes us to join him in prayer, he will turn to face us briefly, but notice that *each time he does so, he first kisses the altar as if to excuse himself before turning his back on our Lord.*

WHY IS IT SO QUIET?
SHOULDN'T THE CONGREGATION PARTICIPATE?

From the most ancient times, man has associated silence with profound reverence. It seems fitting, then, that the most solemn parts of the Mass should be spoken silently. It is for this same reason that the server is there to make the responses on our behalf, so that we may take advantage of the silence to unite ourselves wholly with the sacrifice on the altar.

"But the Lord is in his holy temple: let all the earth keep silence before him."

(Habacuc 2:20)

WHY IS THE CALENDAR OF FEAST DAYS DIFFERENT?

Since the Tridentine Mass was supplanted by the Mass of Paul VI (now known as the Ordinary Form) in 1969, most parishes that offer the Latin Mass use the 1962 Missal, which means, by default, that they also celebrate the feasts of the Church year according to the 1962 Calendar. See page xvi for a fuller explanation.

FORMS OF CELEBRATION OF THE TRIDENTINE MASS

There are different ways of celebrating the Mass, which differ mainly in the elaborateness of the ceremonies used. If you are new to the Latin Mass, Low Mass is often the best choice, as the music of High Mass can make it difficult to discern the cues that can tell you what is happening on the altar.

Missa Solemnis SOLEMN HIGH MASS	*Missa Cantata* HIGH MASS	*Missa Privata* LOW MASS

- Celebrant is assisted by a deacon and subdeacon.
- All parts of the Mass which are said aloud are chanted.
- All sung parts of the Mass are sung by the choir.
- Incense is used.
- 6 or more candles are lit.

- Celebrant is not assisted by a deacon or subdeacon.
- Some parts of the Mass which are said aloud are chanted.
- All sung parts of the Mass are sung by the choir or a cantor.
- Incense may be used.
- 6 or more candles are lit.

- Celebrant is not assisted.
- No part of the Mass is sung, but hymns may be sung while the Priest enters and exits the Sanctuary, and during the Offertory and Communion.
- Incense is not used.
- Only two candles are lit.

> There is also a PONTIFICAL HIGH MASS, which is Solemn High Mass, celebrated by a Bishop. In this case, a seventh candle is lit to indicate the Bishop's office.

THE MUSIC OF THE TRIDENTINE MASS

One of the most noticeable differences between these forms of the Mass is their music. While there will be little or no music at a Low Mass, there are certain parts of the High Mass that *must* be sung by a cantor and/or choir. These parts are of two types: the **Ordinary** and the **Proper**. Like their names, the Ordinary parts are always the same, while the Propers change to reflect the feast being celebrated.

The Ordinary parts are:

- *Kyrie*
- *Gloria*
- *Credo* (omitted on most weekdays)
- *Sanctus* and *Benedictus*
- *Agnus Dei*

Many composers have written "Masses" for the Church. These compositions will typically include only these five parts.

The Proper parts are:

- *Asperges me* or *Vidi aquam* (sung on Sundays only)
- Introit
- Gradual
- Alleluia or Tract
- Sequence (on certain feasts)
- Offertory Antiphon
- Communion Antiphon

THE CHURCH CALENDAR

MOVABLE FEASTS

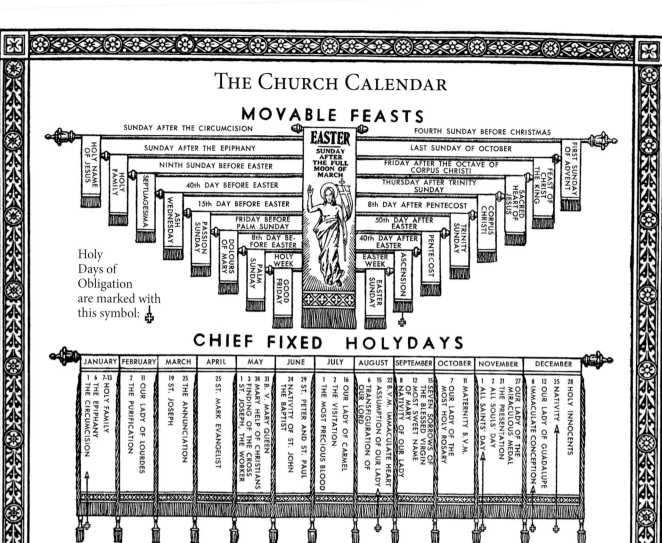

Holy Days of Obligation are marked with this symbol: ⚜

CHIEF FIXED HOLYDAYS

H ere at the center of the Church calendar, Easter is the central focus. From the earliest period in the Church, our Lord's glorious resurrection from the dead has been counted as the most important of all feasts. In fact, His rising on the first day of the week is the reason why we as Christians keep the Sabbath on Sunday, rather than on Saturday, the seventh day.

But while the celebration of Christmas is fixed on December 25, it was customary in the early Church to commemorate Christ's Resurrection two days after the Jewish Passover, a date which is set according to a lunar calendar. This meant that the feast did not always fall on a Sunday. Thus it was determined (most likely at the Council of Nicea) that Easter should be celebrated on the Sunday following the first full moon of the Spring Equinox. From this date we then calculate everything from Septuagesima in February to the Feast of the Sacred Heart in June. These feasts without a fixed date are called *movable feasts*.

Of course, not all of the Church's feasts are determined by Easter. Our commemoration of the Saints has traditionally taken place on the date of their death—their "birthday in heaven." However, the number of feasts kept and the date on which it is convenient to do so is under the authority of the Church, and thus She occasionally makes modifications to the Calendar.

Because the Tridentine Mass fell out of use in most parishes when the Mass of Paul VI was introduced in 1969, all Missals published after that point contained only the new Mass. So until such time as the Church decides to update the Tridentine Missal to reflect the calendar changes that have taken place since then, those who celebrate this Mass continue to follow the calendar as it was in the 1962 Missal (or in some cases, an even earlier Missal). That is why you may find, in the chart above, that the names and dates of some of the feasts are unfamiliar.

THE SEASONS OF THE CHURCH

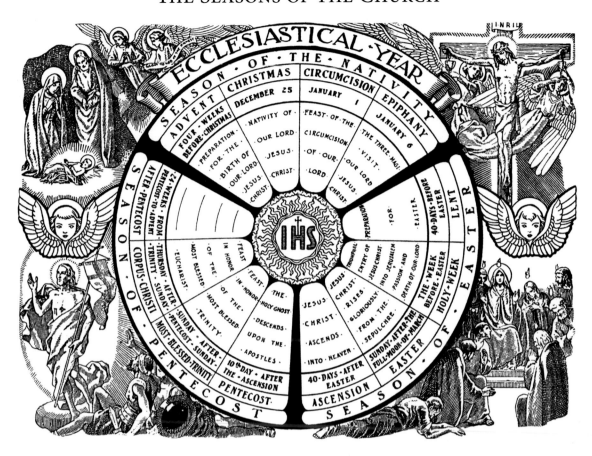

This illustration shows the three principal feasts of the Church Year: Christmas, Easter and Pentecost. Each of these three feasts has a time of preparation before and a time of commemoration following, forming the six seasons of the Ecclesiastical Year: Advent, Christmastide, Septuagesima, Lent, Paschaltide and the period from Pentecost to Advent.

The Church year begins with the first Sunday of Advent. *Advent* is a season of penitence, much like Lent, in which we prepare for Christmas. Its four weeks represent the 4000 years of waiting for the promised Messiah.

Christmastide is the period of celebration after Christmas. It includes the Circumcision, Epiphany and the Feast of the Holy Family, and ends forty days after Christmas with the feast of the Purification (also known as Candlemas). This period represents the youth and hidden life of our Lord in Nazareth.

Septuagesima (Latin for *seventieth*) is a 2½ week period of sobriety separating the joy of Christmastide from the penitence of Lent. In the early Church, many began fasting up to 70 days before Easter, in remembrance of the seventy years of the Babylonian exile. The Sundays of Septuagesima, Sexagesima and Quinquagesima represent these extra days of voluntary fasting.

Lent (or *Quadragesima—fortieth*) is a season of penitence in preparation for Easter and begins on Ash Wednesday. This forty day period, representing the public life and suffering of our Lord, actually lasts 46 days, because we do not count the six Sundays among the days of fasting and penitence.

The last two weeks of Lent are *Passion Week* and *Holy Week*, during which we follow closely the events leading to the death of our Lord.

Paschaltide is the period of rejoicing following Easter. The first forty days represent the time our Lord spent with His disciples before His Ascension into heaven. Then ten days are spent in preparation for Pentecost.

The *Period after Pentecost* is the longest of these seasons and extends from Trinity Sunday (the Sunday after Pentecost) until Advent. This period represents the time in which we look forward to the Last Judgment.

Liturgical Colors

The seasons of the Church and its special feasts are each associated with one of five colors. These colors were derived from the traditional colors used by Jewish Priests in the Temple, and each has its own symbolic meaning as shown below.

White	Red	Green	Violet	Black
Purity	*Love/Suffering*	*Hope*	*Penance*	*Sorrow*
Worn on feasts of our Lord, our Lady, and saints who were not martyrs.	Worn on feasts of the Holy Spirit, the Precious Blood, and martyrs.	Worn on all days when no other color is prescribed.	Worn in seasons of penitence, particularly Advent and Lent.	Worn on Good Friday and in Masses for the Dead.

There are a few exceptions to these colors:
- **Silver** may be used in place of White;
- **Gold** may be used in place of Red, White or Green; and
- Violet is lightened to **Rose** on *Gaudete* Sunday in Advent, and *Laetare* Sunday in Lent.

The following will all be made from the prescribed color:

- The **antependium** (the cloth which hangs down in front of the altar);
- the **tabernacle veil;**
- the **chalice veil** and **burse;** and
- all vestments not made of white linen, including the **chasuble, stole, maniple, cope, humeral veil,** and others worn by the deacon and subdeacon at Solemn High Mass (see the next page).

THE SACRED MINISTERS AT MASS

You will see many different people upon the Altar at Solemn High Mass.
Though all of them may be priests, there is a clear hierarchy, and their vestments
and other accoutrements can help tell you their role.

CELEBRANT

The **celebrant** presides at Solemn High Mass and serves *in persona Christi*, wearing the **chasuble**, a vestment which symbolizes the Yoke of Christ.

DEACON

SUBDEACON

The **dalmatic** worn by the **deacon** and the **tunicle** worn by the **subdeacon** are very similar, sometimes even the same, but if you take notice, the deacon will assist the celebrant, while the subdeacon will assist the deacon. Also, the deacon will read the Gospel, and the subdeacon will read the Epistle.

SERVERS

Various other roles, including the *Master of Ceremonies, thurifer* (or incense bearer), *acolyte* and *torchbearer* wear the *cassock* and *surplice*.

CELEBRANT OR ASSISTANT PRIEST

Before Mass starts, during the *Asperges*, the **celebrant** will wear the **cope**. Then, he will remove it and don the chasuble to begin the Mass. At Vespers or at greater Feasts, there may be four or six **assistant priests** wearing Copes.

BISHOP

You can tell if a **Bishop** is celebrant by his **mitre** and **crosier**. He wears both **dalmatic** and **chasuble**, to show the fullness of his Priestood.

THE MASTER OF CEREMONIES

You may notice that among those wearing cassock and surplice, there is one who is orchestrating the movements of all. He is the Master of Ceremonies, and it is his job to know the Mass thoroughly and ensure that all those participating perform their roles correctly and in harmony with each other. Because this role requires an intimate knowledge of the Mass, it is often best filled by a priest; however, it may also be filled by a layman.

The Priest's Vestments

When the Priest prepares for Mass, he is like a soldier of Christ donning his armor for battle.
He recites a special prayer as he puts on each of the sacred vestments.

*"Place, O Lord, on my head the **helmet of salvation,** so that I may resist the assaults of the devil."*

The **Amice** is a rectangle of fine linen. The Priest places it for a moment on his head, and then allows it to rest upon his shoulders. It was originally a covering for the head and neck and was worn like a hood.

*"**Make me white,** O Lord, and cleanse my heart; that being made white in the Blood of the Lamb I may deserve an eternal reward."*

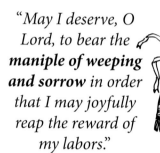

The **Alb** is a wide linen tunic reaching to the feet and covering the whole body. It symbolizes the purity of the Christian soul, having been washed in the blood of the Lamb. (Apoc. 7:14)

*"Gird me, O Lord, with the **cincture of purity,** and quench in my heart the fire of concupiscence, that the virtue of continence and chastity may abide in me."*

The **Cincture,** or girdle, is a cord of linen fastened about the waist to confine the alb. It is a symbol of chastity.

*"May I deserve, O Lord, to bear the **maniple of weeping and sorrow** in order that I may joyfully reap the reward of my labors."*

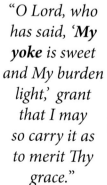

The **Maniple** is a band of silk worn on the left arm. It was originally a small towel or handkerchief worn over the arm, like a servant might carry. It is a symbol of servitude and of the cares of this world, and represents Our Lord's Passion.

*"Restore to me, O Lord, the state of **immortality** which I lost through the sin of my first parents and, although unworthy to approach Thy Sacred Mysteries, may I deserve nevertheless eternal joy."*

The **Stole** is a long band of silk of the same width and color as the maniple, but three times its length. The Priest wears it around the neck and crossed on the breast, and it represents immortality.

*"O Lord, who has said, '**My yoke** is sweet and My burden light,' grant that I may so carry it as to merit Thy grace."*

Chasuble means "little house" and it is the outer and chief vestment of the Priest. It is usually ornamented with a large cross on the back, and sometimes on the front of the garment. It symbolizes the yoke of Christ.

ADDITIONAL VESTMENTS

You may occasionally see the Priest wearing these vestments.

The *cassock* is the common garment of all clerics. It is usually black, to signify that they are dead to the world. However, the color may depend on their religious order or status in the Church hierarchy.

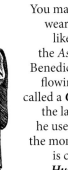

This is a **Roman Chasuble**. It is stiffer and less flowing than the **Gothic Chasuble** shown on the previous page.

You may see the Priest wearing a garment like this during the *Asperges* or at Benediction. This flowing robe is called a **Cope**, and the large scarf he uses to grip the monstrance is called the **Humeral Veil**.

WE ALSO DRESS FOR MASS

> "And the king went in to see the guests: and he saw there a man who had not on a wedding garment. And he saith to him: *Friend, how camest thou in hither not having a wedding garment? But he was silent.*"
>
> (Matthew 22:11-12)

We take great pains with our appearance for important occasions in our life, especially for events like weddings, or the visit of an important person or loved one. When Christ our King comes to us through the Sacrament of the Eucharist, will He find us ready?

We can prepare our inner wedding garment through the Sacrament of Penance, but let us also honor Him by wearing an outer wedding garment—that is, clothing that is both modest and becoming. Here are some traditional rules of thumb for how we ought to dress for Mass:

- Clothing should cover down to the knees, both while standing and while sitting;
- It should also cover at least the shoulders and the top of the arm, preferably down the elbows as well.
- Necklines should not be low-cut or otherwise revealing.
- It is customary for a man to show respect by removing his hat; therefore his head should be uncovered in the Sanctuary.
- A woman, on the other hand, covers her head in the Sanctuary as a token of modesty and purity.

A WORD ABOUT VEILS

When we think of those things which are most sacred, we find that they are veiled in mystery: the sacred vessels are kept under a veil; the tabernacle is veiled; the Ark of the Covenant was veiled. Out of respect for the dead, we cover their faces; at Life's beginning we are hidden in our mother's womb. Our Lady, that blessed vessel by which our Lord was made flesh and dwelt among us, is never seen without a veil.

God created woman to fulfill the sacred mystery of bringing new life into the world. Thus we should consider it a privilege to be veiled in the Sanctuary.

The Sacred Vessels and Linens

The vessels which will hold our Lord's Body and Blood are always made of precious metal.
Likewise, the linens and the Priest's vestments are made of fine white linen.
Linen signifies the labor and mortification necessary in purifying ourselves,
as the stems of the flax plant must be beaten, purified and bleached in order to be whitened.

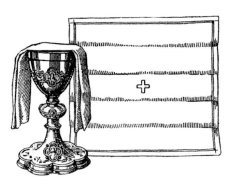

The **Chalice** is a special cup made of precious metal and lined with pure gold. Because it holds the wine that will become Jesus' blood, it is the most sacred of all the vessels.

Folded atop the Chalice is a linen cloth called the **Purificator.** The Priest will wipe his mouth and the rim of the chalice with this cloth after he consumes the Precious Blood.

The **Paten** is a plate of gold that is made especially to fit atop the chalice. The host will rest upon this paten until the Offertory.

The **Pall** is a stiffly starched square of linen which is used to cover the Chalice, to prevent dust or other matter from falling into it.

The **Chalice Veil** is a square cloth made of the same fabric as the Priest's vestments. It will cover the sacred vessels until the Offertory and after the Ablutions.

The **Corporal** is the most important of the sacred linens, for the Body and Blood of our Lord will rest upon it and any small particles will be safely enclosed within it to be properly purified later. It is a square of fine linen with a cross embroidered in the center.

The corporal is folded in three from both sides and kept inside a square folder called the **Burse,** which is placed atop the other vessels as shown.

Additional Vessels

The Chalice and Paten are the most important of all vessels,
but there are several others that are necessary at Mass or at Benediction.

The **Ciborium** is similar to the chalice, and made of the same materials, but with a lid. It is used to hold the hosts which are to be distributed amongst the faithful, or to reserve extra hosts within the tabernacle.

The **Cruets** are kept upon a special tray on a credence table to the far left (Epistle side) of the altar. They hold the water and wine used for the Consecration, the *Lavabo* and the Ablutions.

The **Aspersorium** holds holy water and the **Aspergillum** is the wand which the Priest uses for the sprinkling rite of the *Asperges* at the beginning of Mass.

A **Reliquary** is a highly ornate vessel used to display the relics of a saint. You may find these decorating the altar.

The **Thurible** or **Censer** is a special vessel for burning incense. It is swung about on a chain to disperse the aromatic smoke. Beside it is the **Incense Boat** in which the frankincense is stored.

The **Monstrance** or **Ostensorium** is similar to the reliquary, but its purpose is to display the consecrated Host. The Host is placed in a small, crescent-shaped holder called a **Luna** or **Lunette**, which is then placed inside the glass window of the Monstrance.

THE ALTAR AND ITS FURNITURE

The word **altar** comes from the Latin *altus* meaning "high thing," and the **predella** on which it sits is always raised above the floor by three steps representing the virtues of Faith, Hope and Charity.

The following things are necessary in order for an altar to be used for the Holy Sacrifice of the Mass:

1. It must be consecrated with an **altar stone** in the center, containing the relics of at least three saints.
2. The **mensa** or altar top must be covered with **three altar cloths**;
3. It must have a **crucifix**;
4. It must have **at least two candles**.

The three altar cloths are as follows:

1. First is the **cere cloth**, a waxed linen cloth which fits exactly to the top of the altar.
2. Atop this cloth is another linen cloth of the same size.
3. The topmost cloth is the same depth as the altar top, but extends in length to the predella on either side. This fine linen cloth is embroidered with five crosses: one at each corner, and one in the center, above the altar stone.

In addition to these necessities, most permanent altars will also have the following furnishings:

[a] The **tabernacle** is located in the center of the altar. In this precious home the consecrated Hosts are kept reserved under lock and key. It is usually covered with a veil, which can either be white or the same color as the vestments.

[b] There are three **altar cards.** The largest, in the center, contains the prayers for the Offertory and Canon of the Mass. There are two smaller ones: that on the Epistle side contains the prayers for the *Lavabo* and the mixing of water and wine; that on the Gospel side contains the Last Gospel.

[c] The *Missal* contains all of the prayers of the Mass, both Ordinary and Proper.

[d] A **bell** is kept at the foot of the altar to be rung by the server at the Consecration and other crucial moments in the Mass.

[e] This altar has two **candlebenches** (or **gradine**): the lower one holds the two candles that are lit for Low Mass; the upper one holds the six candles that are lit for High Mass.

[f] Some altars feature a **canopy** or **throne**. A **monstrance** may be placed here for exposition of the Blessed Sacrament during Benediction.

[g] A **sanctuary lamp** filled with pure olive oil is kept burning at all times near the altar to remind us that Christ is present in the Tabernacle.

Some additional things you may find on an altar which are not shown here:

- A cloth may hang down in front of the altar. It is called the **antependium** or **frontal** and it matches the color of the vestments.

- Flowers, statues, reliquaries and additional candles may be used to make the altar even more beautiful for our Lord.

TAKING SIDES

In the Mass, Christ is both Priest and Victim, and this is the Altar of His Sacrifice.
Most of the Mass is said at the center of the altar, where the large altar card contains the Ordinary.
However, we call the side on *His* right the Right Side, and that on *His* left, the Left Side.

His Right Side is called

THE GOSPEL SIDE

The right side is the place of honor: it is the seat Christ occupies next to His Father in Heaven. From this side we proclaim His Word in the Gospel, telling of the fulfillment of the promise of Salvation. The Missal then remains on this side throughout the Mass of the Faithful, until after Communion, when it is moved back to the Epistle Side.

"The Lord said to my Lord: Sit thou at my right hand: Until I make thy enemies thy footstool." (Psalm 109)

His Left Side is called

THE EPISTLE SIDE

The left side is where most of the Mass of the Catechumens takes place. Here we prepare for the coming of our Lord by listening to His servants in the Epistle and Psalms from the Old Testament. Then we will move to the Gospel side of the altar to hear the Word of God Himself.

The parts of the Mass which involve water (The *Lavabo*, the mixing of water and wine, and the ablutions) all take place at the far left of the altar, where an altar card with those prayers can be found.

IN THE RED

The *rubrics* govern how the Mass is said, and they can help you to understand what is happening.

You will notice as you look at any Missal that the text of the Ceremony is in black, but that there are also directions given in red. These are called **rubrics**, and they take their name from the Latin *rubrica*, the red chalk used to write the titles of Roman Law upon the monuments. Over time, this term became synonymous with the law itself, and the Church too adopted the custom of writing Her liturgical laws in red.

Rubrics, then, are rules which govern all the actions of public worship, from the time, place and manner of a given Ceremony to the actions of the Ceremony itself.

You will find these red symbols throughout this Missal. The funny-looking V stands for **Versicle** and the R stands for **Response**. Together they form a type of prayer called a **Responsory**, and they are typically taken from the Psalms. The Versicle is spoken by the leader—in most cases, the Priest—to which the congregation responds (represented by the server). See page 67 for more information about Responsories.

BODY AND SOUL: THE EUCHARISTIC FAST

> "Blessed are they that hunger and thirst after justice: for they shall have their fill."
>
> (Matthew 5:6)

As we approach the beginning of Mass, we should pause to consider how great is the Sacrament in which we are about to partake. The great gift of the Eucharist is one which we should not take lightly, lest we risk missing out on the graces that we receive by being properly disposed. We can prepare ourselves spiritually by shutting out our worries and distractions, and by beginning to focus on Him whom we shall soon see upon the Altar. You may prepare by saying some of the prayers found in the back of this book if you wish.

Meanwhile, we prepare our bodies for the Sacrament by means of the *Eucharistic Fast*. Through the discipline of denying our body, we show our humility as well as a spiritual hunger for what we are about to receive. Until 1953, this fast began at midnight the night before receiving Communion. It was reduced at that time to three hours, then to one hour in 1964. During this time, we may drink plain water but may not partake of any solid food or liquid nourishment. The sick, the elderly, and expectant or nursing mothers are exempt from this requirement.

WE PREPARE FOR MASS

The *Asperges* is recited during the sprinkling of holy water in preparation for Solemn High Mass.†
If you are attending a regular High Mass or a Low Mass, you may skip the next page.

† The Asperges was always sung before the main Mass on a Sunday.
Now that the Tridentine Mass is rarely celebrated more than once on a Sunday in a given parish, its use is less common.
If you are blessed to attend a parish where it is regularly used, the following page is for you!

Upon entering the Church we should sign ourselves with holy water. This is a sacramental which washes away our venial sins by the contrition it arouses in us, like the words of the antiphon *Asperges me*. It also reminds us that we have been delivered from the bondage of sin through the waters of Baptism.

In order to receive Communion worthily, we must be in a state of grace. The best way to be sure of this is to avail ourselves of the Sacrament of Penance regularly. While venial sins should not prevent our receiving Communion, we commit sacrilege if we knowingly receive our Lord while in a state of mortal sin.

The best way to unite ourselves with the offering of the Holy Sacrifice of the Mass is by following the prayers in the Missal. However, it is not necessary to do so. As long as we assist at Mass with reverence, attention and devotion, we are free to pray in whatever way is most helpful to us.

The Asperges and Vidi Aquam

In Solemn Masses

While the Priest sprinkles holy water before Solemn Mass,
the following Antiphon is sung:

ASPÉRGES me, Dómine, hyssópo, et mundábor:
Sprinkle me Lord, with hyssop, and I shall be cleansed:

lavábis me, et super nivem dealbábor.
wash me and above snow I shall be whitened.

Ps. 50: Miserére mei, Deus,
Be merciful to me, God,

secúndum magnam misericórdiam tuam.
according to great mercy of yours.

℣. Glória Patri et Fílio et Spirítui Sancto.
Glory to Father, and to Son, and to Spirit Holy.

℟. Sicut erat in princípio et nunc et semper,
Just as it was in beginning, and now, and always,

et in saécula saeculórum. Amen.
and unto ages of ages.

ANT: Aspérges me...(as above)

℣. Osténde nobis, Dómine, misericórdiam tuam.
Show forth to us, Lord, mercy yours.

℟. Et salutáre tuum da nobis.
And salvation yours grant to us.

℣. Dómine, exáudi oratiónem meam.
Lord, hear prayer of mine.

℟. Et clamor meus ad te véniat.
And cry of mine to thee let it come.

℣. Dóminus vobíscum.
Lord (be)with you.

℟. Et cum spíritu tuo.
And with spirit your.

ORÉMUS:
Let us pray:

Exáudi nos, Dómine sancte, Pater omnípotens, aetérne Deus,
Hear us, Lord holy, Father almighty, eternal God,

et mittere dignéris sanctum Angelum tuum de coelis,
and to send deign holy Angel your from heaven,

qui custódiat, fóveat, prótegat, vísitet atque deféndat
who (would) guard, cherish, protect, visit and defend

omnes habitántes in hoc habitáculo.
all inhabitants in this dwelling.

Per Christum Dóminum nostrum. Amen.
Through Christ Lord our.

From Easter to Pentecost inclusive, instead of
*the antiphon **Asperges me**, the following is sung, and*
***Alleluias** are added to the **Ostende Nobis** and its **Et Salutare**.*

VIDI AQUAM egrediéntem de templo a látere dextro,
I saw water flowing from temple at side right,

allelúia: et omnes ad quos pervénit aqua ista
alleluia: and all to whom it came water this

salvi facti sunt et dicent: allelúia, allelúia.
saved made were and they said: alleluia, alleluia.

Ps. 117: Confitémini Dómino, quóniam bonus:
Let us give praise to (the) Lord, because (he is) good:

quóniam in sǽculum misericórdia ejus.
because in ages (endures) mercy his.

Glória Patri...

℣. Ostende nobis... (*as above, with Allelúia.*)

The Asperges and Vidi Aquam

THOU SHALT SPRINKLE me, O Lord, with hyssop, and I shall be cleansed; Thou shalt wash me, and I shall become whiter than snow.

Ps. 50: Have mercy on me, O God, according to Thy great mercy.

℣. Glory be to the Father, and to the Son, and to the Holy Spirit.
℟. As it was in the beginning, is now, and ever shall be, world without end. Amen.

ANT: Thou shalt sprinkle...(as above)

℣. Show us, O Lord, Thy mercy.
℟. And grant us Thy salvation.
℣. O Lord, hear my prayer.
℟. And let my cry come unto Thee.
℣. The Lord be with you.
℟. And with thy spirit.

Let us pray:

Hear us, holy Lord, almighty Father, eternal God, and vouchsafe to send Thy holy Angel from heaven, to guard, cherish, protect, visit, and defend all that are assembled in this place. Through Christ our Lord. Amen.

I SAW WATER flowing from the right side of the temple, alleluia: and all they to whom that water came were saved; and they shall say: alleluia, alleluia.

Ps. 117: Praise the Lord, because He is good; because His mercy endureth forever.

Glory be to the Father...

℣. Show us... (*as above, with Alleluia.*)

1

MASS OF THE CATECHUMENS

The bell rings and we stand in reverence as the Celebrant enters the Sanctuary. After spreading the corporal upon the altar and arranging the sacred vessels, he returns to the foot of the altar and begins Mass with the Sign of the Cross.

"**I** will go in unto the Altar of God." What an excellent way to begin the Mass! Upon Mount Moriah, the Holy Mountain in Jerusalem, stood the Temple, on the ancient spot where Abraham was commanded to sacrifice his only son. Before it, the altar of holocausts burned night and day. Only here could sacrifices be offered to God. The author of this Psalm is said to have been a levite living in exile far from Jerusalem, and he sighs with longing. Yet even in his darkest hour, he places his trust in the Lord, and he clings to the hope that his prayer will soon be answered.

THE PSALMS: AN ANCIENT FORM OF PRAYER

The word *psalm* comes from the Greek *psalmoi* meaning 'music of the harp,' but the original Hebrew word for these sacred verses is *Tehillim*, or "praises." Tradition maintains that nearly all of these songs of praise, thanksgiving or lamentation were written by King David for use in the Temple services. But this official hymnal of Hebrew worship also summed up, in poetic form, the entirety of the faith of Israel. For this reason, devout Jews would pray the entire cycle of 150 psalms each week—a tradition which was continued in the **Divine Office**, the official prayer of the Catholic Church, and which later gave rise to the fifteen decades of the Rosary.

WHAT IS A LEVITE?

Jacob was given the name *Israel* by God when he wrestled with the Angel and won. His twelve sons had many children, and from them descended the **Twelve Tribes of Israel**, each named after one of these twelve sons.

The descendants of Levi were set apart from the other tribes: they could not own land, and were instead supported by **tithes**. In return, they fulfilled certain religious duties, such as singing Psalms in the Temple services, helping maintain the Temple proper, or serving as teachers or judges. Moses and Aaron were Levites; Aaron and his descendants alone served as priests.

 The *Introit* is begun as soon as the Priest enters, followed immediately by the *Kyrie*.

This is an *Antiphon*. It will be repeated again at the end of the Psalm. You will see this structure repeated in many places throughout the Mass. For more about Antiphons and their use, see pp. 18 & 67.

Because of the Joy expressed in this Psalm, it is omitted in Masses for the Dead and during Passiontide (that is, from Passion Sunday until Holy Thursday).

> We should try to detach ourselves from the world and its distractions as we approach the altar for Holy Mass.

This is a **Doxology**. We say it at the end of a Psalm before repeating the Antiphon. See page 10 to learn more about doxologies.

Now the Antiphon is repeated.

Next we are going to examine our conscience and confess our sins, so the Priest humbly asks God to assist us, using a small part, or **Versicle**, from Psalm 123.

KNEEL

The Priest, upon reaching the foot of the altar, bows and makes the sign of the cross:

IN nómine Patris, ✠ et Fílii, et Spiritus Sancti. Amen.
In name of Father, and of Son, and of Spirit Holy.

Then, with his hands joined, he begins the Antiphon:

ANT: Introíbo ad altáre Dei.
I will go in to altar of God.

The server responds:

℟ Ad Deum qui laetíficat juventútem meam.
To God Who gladdens youth my.

PSALM 42: JUDICA ME

JÚDICA ME, Deus,
Judge me, God,

et discérne causam meam de gente non sancta:
and distinguish cause my from nation not holy:

ab hómine iníquo et dolóso érue me.
from man unjust, and deceitful deliver me.

℟ Quia tu es, Deus, fortitúdo mea: quare me repulísti,
Because You are, God, strength my: why me you repulsed,

et quare tristis incédo, dum afflígit me inimícus ?
and why sad I go, while afflicts me the enemy?

℣ Emítte lucem tuam, et veritátem tuam:
Send forth light Your, and truth Your:

ipsa me deduxérunt,
they me have led,

et adduxérunt in montem sanctum tuum,
and have brought to mountain holy Your,

et in tabernácula tua.
and to tabernacle Your.

℟ Et introíbo ad altáre Dei:
And I will go in to altar of God.

ad Deum qui laetíficat juventútem meam.
To God Who gladdens youth my.

℣ Confitébor tibi in cíthara, Deus, Deus meus:
I will confess You on harp, God, God my:

quare tristis es, ánima mea, et quare contúrbas me?
why sad are you, soul my, and why you disquiet me?

℟ Spera in Deo, quóniam adhuc confitébor illi:
Hope in God, because still I will confess Him

salutáre vultus mei, et Deus meus.
salvation of face my, and God my.

℣ Glória Patri et Fílio et Spirítui Sancto.
Glory to Father, and to Son, and to Spirit Holy.

℟ Sicut erat in princípio et nunc et semper,
Just as it was in beginning, and now, and always,

et in saécula saeculórum. Amen.
and unto ages of ages.

The Priest now repeats the Antiphon:

ANT: Introíbo ad altáre Dei.
I will go in to altar of God.

℟ Ad Deum qui laetíficat juventútem meam.
To God Who gladdens youth my.

He then adds while signing himself with the sign of the cross:

℣ Adjutórium nostrum ✠ in nómine Dómini.
Help our in name of Lord.

℟ Qui fecit cælum et terram.
Who made heaven and earth.

In the name of the Father, ✠ and of the Son, and of the Holy Spirit. Amen.

ANT: I will go in unto the altar of God.

℟ Unto God who giveth joy to my youth.

PSALM 42: JUDICA ME

Judge me, O God, and distinguish my cause against an ungodly nation: deliver me from the unjust and deceitful man.

℟ For Thou, O God, art my strength: why hast Thou cast me from Thee, and why go I sorrowful while the enemy afflicteth me?

℣ O send out Thy light and Thy truth: they have led me and brought me unto Thy holy hill, even unto Thy tabernacles.

℟ Then will I go unto the altar of God, unto God, who giveth joy to my youth.

℣ I will praise thee upon the harp, O God, my God, why art thou cast down, O my soul? and why art thou disquieted within me?

℟ Hope thou in God: for yet will I praise Him, who is the health of my countenance and my God.

℣ Glory be to the Father, and to the Son, and to the Holy Spirit.

℟ As it was in the beginning, is now and ever shall be, world without end. Amen

ANT: I will go in unto the altar of God.

℟ Unto God, who giveth joy to my youth.

℣ Our help ✠ is in the name of the Lord.

℟ Who hath made heaven and earth.

WE CONFESS OUR SINFULNESS

The *Confiteor* is the traditional formula for confessing our sins,
and was recited in the confessional and in the Divine Office as well as in the Mass.
Because it is a **Sacramental**, those who recite it may obtain the forgiveness
of venial sins, provided that they are truly sorry.

"If we say that we have no sin, we deceive ourselves..."

(1 John 1:8)

Christ taught us the importance of humility and of acknowledging our sinfulness in the parable of the Pharisee and the Publican. If we are not sorry, God cannot forgive us! This necessary sorrow for our sins is called **contrition**, which comes from the Latin *conterere*, meaning 'to break.' A good way of showing our contrition is to strike our breast as if to break our stony hearts, which so often forget how He suffered for us.

WHAT IS A SACRAMENTAL?

A Sacramental is an object, prayer or action which can bring special graces—such as the remission of venial sin—to those who use them, but *only in proportion to the disposition of the user*. Several examples of Sacramentals include holy water, blessed candles, incense, rosaries, scapulars and medals like the St. Benedict or the Miraculous Medal.

The oldest of the teachings of the early Church fathers, called the **Didache** or *The Teachings of the Twelve Apostles*, stressed the importance of confessing our sins before participating in the Eucharist:

"*...But every Lord's day gather yourselves together, and break bread, and give thanksgiving after having confessed your transgressions, that your sacrifice may be pure.*"

While the Priest is saying this prayer, take a moment to examine your conscience. You may use the examination on p.88 if you wish.

Look how the Priest bows low when he recites the *Confiteor*. It is as if he were carrying the heavy load of our sins on his back, just like our Lord did in the Garden of Gethsemane.

Now that you know how powerful this prayer is in obtaining forgiveness for sins, you may want to learn it so that you can recite it along with the server.

Do you examine your conscience daily before you go to bed? We brush our hair and our teeth and clean our bodies, but if you make this a nightly habit, and say this prayer when you are done, it will help keep your soul clean and make going to confession easier.

This is the culmination of all the prayers on this page: here the Priest grants us a general absolution of our venial sins, so that we may receive our Lord with a clean "wedding garment." (Mt. 22)

Joining his hands and bowing deeply, the Priest confesses:

 ONFÍTEOR Deo omnipoténti,
I confess to God almighty,

Beátae Maríae semper Vírgini,
to blessed Mary ever virgin,

Beáto Michaéli Archángelo, Beáto Joánni Baptístae,
to blessed Michael Archangel, to blessed John the Baptist,

Sanctis Apóstolis Petro et Paulo, omnibus Sanctis,
to holy Apostles Peter and Paul, to all Saints,

et vobis, fratres,
and to you, brothers,

quia peccávi nimis cogitatióne, verbo, et ópere:
because I sinned too much in thought, word, and deed:

(he strikes his breast three times:)

mea culpa, mea culpa, mea máxima culpa.
by my fault, by my fault, by my greatest fault.

Ideo precor Beátam Maríam semper Vírginem,
Thus I beseech blessed Mary ever virgin,

Beátum Michaélem Archángelum, Beátum Joánnem Baptístam,
blessed Michael Archangel, blessed John the Baptist,

Sanctos Apóstolos Petrum et Paulum,
holy Apostles Peter and Paul,

omnes Sanctos, et vos, fratres,
all Saints, and you, brothers,

oráre pro me ad Dóminum Deum nostrum.
to pray for me to Lord God our.

The server responds:

℞ Misereátur tui omnipotens Deus, et dimíssis peccátis tuis,
May he have mercy on you almighty God, and having dismissed sins your,

perdúcat te ad vitam aetérnam. Amen.
may he lead you to life eternal.

Now the servers bow and recite:

CONFÍTEOR Deo omnipoténti, Beátae Maríae semper Vírgini,
I confess to God almighty, to blessed Mary ever virgin,

Beáto Michaéli Archángelo, Beáto Joánni Baptístae,
to blessed Michael Archangel, to blessed John the Baptist,

Sanctis Apóstolis Petro et Paulo, omnibus Sanctis, et tibi, pater,
to holy Apostles Peter and Paul, to all Saints, and to you, father,

quia peccávi nimis cogitatióne, verbo, et ópere:
because I sinned too much in thought, word, and deed:

(strike the breast three times:)

mea culpa, mea culpa, mea máxima culpa.
by my fault, my fault, my greatest fault.

Ideo precor Beátam Maríam semper Vírginem,
Thus I beseech blessed Mary ever virgin,

Beátum Michaélem Archángelum, Beátum Joánnem Baptístam,
blessed Michael Archangel, blessed John the Baptist,

Sanctos Apóstolos Petrum et Paulum,
holy Apostles Peter and Paul,

omnes Sanctos, et te, Pater,
all Saints, and you, father,

oráre pro me ad Dóminum Deum nostrum.
to pray for me to Lord God our.

Then the Priest says:

℣ Misereátur vestri omnípotens Deus,
May he have mercy on you almighty God,

et dimíssis peccátis vestris,
and having dismissed sins your,

perdúcat vos ad vitam aetérnam. ℞ Amen.
may he lead you to life eternal.

Making the sign of the cross, he pronounces the absolution:

℣ Indulgéntiam, ✠ absolutiónem,
Pardon, absolution,

et remissiónem peccatórum nostrórum,
and remission of sins our

tríbuat nobis omnípotens et miséricors Dóminus. ℞ Amen.
may he grant us almighty and merciful Lord.

I CONFESS to almighty God,
to Blessed Mary Ever Virgin,
to Blessed Michael the Archangel,
to Blessed John the Baptist,
to the Holy Apostles Peter and Paul,
to all the saints,
and to you Father,
that I have sinned exceedingly
in thought, word and deed,
(strike breast three times)
through my fault, through my fault,
through my most grievous fault.
Therefore I beseech
blessed Mary ever Virgin,
blessed Michael the archangel,
blessed John the Baptist,
the holy apostles Peter and Paul,
all the saints,
and you, Father,
to pray to the Lord our God for me.

℣. May almighty God have mercy upon you, forgive you your sins, and bring you to life everlasting.
℞. Amen.

℣. May the almighty and merciful Lord grant us pardon, ✠ absolution and remission of our sins.
℞. Amen.

THE HOLY OF HOLIES

"And it came to pass, when the priests were come out of the sanctuary, that a cloud filled the house of the Lord, And the priests could not stand to minister because of the cloud: for the glory of the Lord had filled the house of the Lord.."

(3 Kings 8:10-11)

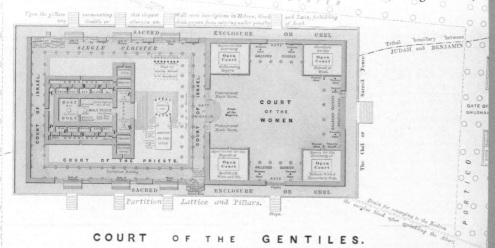

COURT OF THE GENTILES.

Upon the Temple Mount in Jerusalem were different courtyards in which the faithful gathered. Outermost was the *Court of the Gentiles,* which was open to all. Then came the *Court of the Women*, beyond which they could not pass. Men and boys were welcome in the *Court of the Israelites,* but only Priests and Levites could enter the *Court of the Priests* beyond, which enclosed the altar of the holocausts and the Temple. Even the Temple itself was divided by a veil, and while priests were permitted within the main part, called the *Holy*, <u>no one</u> could pass through the veil into the *Holy of Holies,* where the Ark of the Covenant lay, except the High Priest, and then only once a year—after specially preparing himself for six days.

The first two of these **versicles** with their **responses** come from Psalm 84, while the third comes from Psalm 101.

As the celebrant ascends the three steps and approaches the altar, he calls to mind the *Holy of Holies.*

On Good Friday, at the ninth hour when Jesus died, the veil which separated the Holy of Holies from the rest of the temple was torn in two, signifying that the new Covenant in Jesus' blood had replaced the old. Now, all that have been washed in the blood of Christ's sacrifice (through Baptism) may enter into the presence of God and themselves become a 'Holy of Holies' by receiving Him in the Eucharist.

"*I saw under the altar the souls of them that were slain for the word of God...*"

(Apocalypse 6:9)

The Priest kisses the altar in the middle—first, because it represents Jesus' body, which He sacrificed for us, but also because this is the location of the *altar stone* containing the relics of three saints, at least one of which is a martyr.

When you see these brackets, it is because this is a part of the Mass that only takes place during special Solemn Masses.

Bowing, the Priest continues:

℣. Deus, tu convérsus vivificábis nos.
God, You having turned shall enliven us.

℟. Et plebs tua laetábitur in te.
And people Your shall rejoice in You.

℣. Osténde nobis, Dómine, misericórdiam tuam.
Show to us, Lord, mercy Your.

℟. Et salutáre tuum da nobis.
And salvation Your give to us.

℣. Dómine, exáudi oratiónem meam.
Lord, hear prayer my.

℟. Et clamor meus ad te véniat.
And cry of mine to You may it come.

℣. Dóminus vobíscum
Lord (be) with you.

℟. Et cum spíritu tuo.
And with spirit your.

Extending and joining his hands, the Priest says:

ORÉMUS:
Let us pray.

THE PRIEST APPROACHES THE ALTAR

Going up to the altar, he says in a low voice:

AUFER a nobis, quaésumus, Dómine,
Take away from us, we beg, Lord,
iniquitátes nostras: ut ad Sancta sanctórum
iniquities our: that to Holy of holies
puris mereámur méntibus introíre.
(with) pure we may merit mind to enter.
Per Christum Dóminum nostrum. Amen.
Through Christ Lord our.

Placing his joined hands upon the altar, he bows and says:

ORAMUS te, Dómine,
We pray to You, Lord,
per mérita Sanctórum tuórum,
through merits of Saints Your,
(he kisses the altar)
quorum relíquiae hic sunt, et ómnium Sanctórum:
whose relics here are, and all Saints:
ut indulgére dignéris ómnia peccáta mea. Amen.
that to forgive you may deign all sins my.

[*In Solemn Masses, except Masses for the Dead, the altar is now incensed. The Priest blesses the incense, saying:*

AB ILLO ✠ benedicaris,
By him be blessed,
in cujus honore cremaberis. Amen.
in whose honor you shall be burnt.

The Priest takes the thurible from the Deacon and incenses the altar. He returns it to the Deacon, who then incenses the Priest.]

℣. Thou wilt turn, O God, and bring us to life.
℟. And thy people shall rejoice in thee.
℣. Show us, O Lord, Thy mercy.
℟. And grant us Thy salvation.
℣. O Lord, hear my prayer.
℟. And let my cry come unto Thee.
℣. The Lord be with you.
℟. And with thy spirit.

Let us pray:

THE PRIEST APPROACHES THE ALTAR

TAKE away from us our iniquities, we beseech Thee, O Lord, that with pure minds we may worthily enter into the holy of holies. Through Christ our Lord. Amen.

WE BESEECH Thee, O Lord, by the merits of Thy saints, whose relics are here, and of all the saints, that Thou wouldst vouchsafe to forgive me all my sins. Amen.

[Be blessed ✠ by Him in Whose honor thou art burnt. Amen.]

LORD, HAVE MERCY!

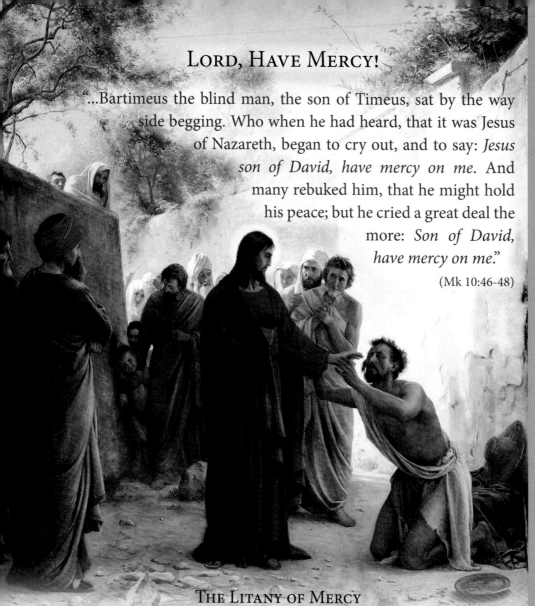

"...Bartimeus the blind man, the son of Timeus, sat by the way side begging. Who when he had heard, that it was Jesus of Nazareth, began to cry out, and to say: *Jesus son of David, have mercy on me.* And many rebuked him, that he might hold his peace; but he cried a great deal the more: *Son of David, have mercy on me.*"

(Mk 10:46-48)

THE LITANY OF MERCY

The word *litany* comes from the Greek *litaneia*, meaning supplication. This form of prayer, which originated in Jewish worship, is a series of petitions followed by a response or affirmation.

The original form of the *Kyrie* was that of a litany: a list of petitions was recited, followed each time by the response *Kyrie, eleison* or *Christe, eleison*. This litany came to be shortened during daily Masses by omitting the petitions, and over time, this shortened form took precedence.

WHAT ARE PROPERS?

Most of the Mass is the same every time, but there are parts in it that change for each feast being celebrated. These changeable parts are called **Propers**, while the rest is called the **Ordinary**. All of the Propers in this book are taken from the Mass as it is celebrated on Trinity Sunday; however, we suggest that you print out the propers for the Mass you are celebrating and bring them along. Then, when you see the box that says "See Proper of Mass for the Day," you can refer to *your* Propers. See the bottom of p.94 for suggestions on where to find Mass propers online.

DID YOU KNOW?

It is a long standing tradition to call Church documents (such as Papal Encyclicals) by their **Incipit**, or opening words. This is also the case with Mass Propers. Because the Introit is the first of the Propers, its opening word lends each Mass its name. Examples you will surely recognize include *Requiem* for Masses for the Dead, *Laetare* for the Fourth Sunday of Lent, and *Gaudete* for the Third Sunday of Advent.

The Introit is the first part of the Mass which changes each time—that is, it is **proper** to each Mass. In this way, it prepares us well for the day's particular feast.

The **Introit**, or entrance, was originally a psalm that was sung by the choir as the Priest approached the altar at the beginning of Mass. It was sung much like the *Judica Me* on p.3, with an **antiphon** before and after, as well as after each **strophe** or stanza.

At High Mass, the Introit is still sung during the entry procession; however, this chant now consists of only *part* of a psalm with an antiphon before and after.

During the Easter season, the antiphon includes an *Alleluia* as well.

DID YOU KNOW?

The *Kyrie* is the only major part of the Mass that is not in Latin: *Kyrie Eleison* is Greek. This is because its use began in the church of Antioch, which was part of the Greek-speaking world.

Look at the structure of the Kyrie: it has three groups of three. There are many places in the Mass where something is repeated three times, but this one is three times three! This is in honor of the Holy Trinity: our God who is Three in One.

First, we address God the Father, who is *Lord*. Next, we address *Christ*, the second person of the Trinity. Then the third person, the Holy Spirit, who proceeds from the Father and Son, is also addressed as *Lord*.

Each person is invoked three times to demonstrate the fact that each person of the Divine Trinity dwells within the others. This relationship is called **Perichoresis**.

The Priest stands at the right side (Epistle Side) of the altar and makes the Sign of the Cross as he begins the Inroit antiphon.

The Introit

❁ See Proper of Mass for the Day. ❁

from the proper for Trinity Sunday:

Ant: Benedícta sit sáncta Trínitas,
Blessed be Holy Trinity,

atque indivísa Unitas:
and undivided unity:

Confitébimur éi, quia fécit nobíscum
We will give glory to Him, for he has made (known) to us

misericórdiam súam.
mercy his.

Ps. Dómine Dóminus nóster:
Lord, Lord of ours:

quam admirábile est nómen túum in univérsa térra!
how wonderful is name yours in all the earth!

℣. Glória Patri et Fílio et Spirítui Sancto.
Glory to Father, and to Son, and to Spirit Holy.

Sicut erat in princípio et nunc et semper,
Just as it was in beginning, and now, and always,

et in saécula saeculórum. Amen.
and unto ages of ages.

Ant: Benedícta sit...(as above)
Blessed be...

Kyrie

Returning to the center of the Altar, the Priest alternates with the server in saying:

Kyrie, Eléison.
Lord, have mercy.

℟. Kyrie, eléison.
Lord, have mercy.

℣. Kyrie, eléison.
Lord, have mercy.

℟. Christe, eléison.
Christ, have mercy.

℣. Christe, eléison.
Christ, have mercy.

℟. Christe, eléison.
Christ, have mercy.

℣. Kyrie, eléison.
Lord, have mercy.

℟. Kyrie, eléison.
Lord, have mercy.

℣. Kyrie, eléison.
Lord, have mercy.

The Introit

❁ See Proper of Mass for the Day. ❁

from the proper for Trinity Sunday:

Ant: Blessed be the Holy Trinity, and undivided unity: we will give glory to Him; because He hath shown His mercy to us.

Ps. O Lord, our Lord, how wonderful is Thy name in all the earth!

℣. Glory be to the Father, and to the Son, and to the Holy Spirit, as it was in the beginning, is now, and ever shall be, world without end. Amen.

Ant: Blessed be...(as above)

Kyrie

℣. Lord, have mercy on us.
℟. Lord, have mercy on us.
℣. Lord, have mercy on us.

℟. Christ, have mercy on us.
℣. Christ, have mercy on us.
℟. Christ, have mercy on us.

℣. Lord, have mercy on us.
℟. Lord, have mercy on us.
℣. Lord, have mercy on us.

THE ANGELS' HYMN OF JOY

When we think of a *hymn*, we think of a song that is sung in Church. This was originally the function of the *Psalms* in Jewish worship. Most of the Psalms date back to the time of King David, and Jewish custom forbade them to be changed or added to.

Another type of song that was often used in worship was the *canticle*. These were excerpts from scripture, such as the song of Moses and the Israelites after crossing the Red Sea.

The early Christians continued to use these psalms and canticles, but they added their own songs of praise as well. The Greek word for these new songs was *hymnos*, or **Hymns**. The *Gloria in Excelsis Deo* is one example of this new sort of canticle, incorporating the angels' song of joy found in Luke's Gospel.

> "Let the word of Christ dwell in you abundantly, in all wisdom: teaching and admonishing one another in psalms, hymns, and spiritual canticles, singing in grace in your hearts to God."
>
> (Colossians 3:16)

WHAT IS A DOXOLOGY?

The Greek word *doxa* usually refers to a common belief, as used in the word *orthodox*, which means 'right belief.' But when the early Church fathers translated the Hebrew bible into Greek, they used the word *doxa* to mean 'glory.'

A *doxology*, then, is a verse praising God in the Trinity, usually beginning with the word **glory**. There are two main doxologies used in the Church: the *Gloria in Excelsis Deo*, called the **Great Doxology**, and the *Gloria Patri* (or *Glory be*), which is called the **minor doxology**.

The custom of bringing a hymn or rite to a close with this type of formula came from the Jewish synagogue, and the earliest Christians naturally emulated the style of prayer they knew. Just as each Psalm was followed by a doxology, so too the hymns written by the early Christians incorporated a doxology. See page 67 for more on the use of doxologies in antiphonal chant and responsories.

 The *Gloria* is now sung, intoned by the celebrant.

The Gloria is also called the **Great Doxology**, and it incorporates elements of our faith in the Trinity. You may also notice that it fulfills all four of the ends of worship shown on page x.

It starts by addressing God the Father...

...and now God the Son...

(Because the Gloria is a song of joy, it is not said in Masses for the Dead, nor during the seasons of penitence: Advent, Septuagesima and Lent.)

...and now the Holy Spirit.

Here's that salutation again: The Priest wants us to join with him as he offers up the next prayer.

The **Collect** is a prayer that takes its name from the Latin *colligere*, meaning 'to gather up,' and its purpose is just that: it *collects* the intentions of the feast being celebrated and presents them before our Heavenly Father.

> *"Amen, amen I say to you: if you ask the Father any thing in my name, he will give it you."*
>
> (John 16:23)

This Trinitarian formula: *"Per Dominum nostrum..."* is used in varied forms throughout the Mass. It is a little bit like the official signature on a letter. Christ told us to ask for what we need in His name, and that is just what we are doing by adding this to the end of our prayers. See p. 70 to learn more.

Standing at the center of the Altar, the Priest extends, elevates and joins his hands, slightly bowing, and says the Gloria:

GLORIA

STAND
(HIGH MASS)

GLORIA in excélsis Deo.
Glory   in   highest to God.

Et in terra pax homínibus bonae voluntátis.
And on Earth peace   to men   of good   will.

Laudámus te. Benedícimus te.
We praise You.   We bless   You.

Adorámus te. Glorificámus te.
We adore You.   We glorify   You.

Grátias ágimus tibi propter magnam glóriam tuam.
Thanks   we give to You because of   great   glory   Your.

Dómine Deus, Rex caeléstis, Deus Pater omnípotens.
Lord   God, King of Heaven, God Father   almighty.

Dómine Fili unigénite, Jesu Christe.
Lord   Son only begotten, Jesus Christ.

Dómine Deus, Agnus Dei, Fílius Patris.
Lord   God,   Lamb of God, Son of Father.

Qui tollis peccáta mundi, miserére nobis.
Who take away sins   of world,   have mercy on us.

Qui tollis peccáta mundi,
Who take away sins   of world,

súscipe deprecatiónem nostram.
receive   prayer   our.

Qui sedes ad déxteram Patris, miserére nobis.
Who   sit   at   right hand of Father, have mercy on us.

Quóniam tu solus Sanctus. Tu solus Dóminus.
Because   You alone (are) Holy.   You alone (are) Lord.

Tu solus Altíssimus, Jesu Christe.
You alone   (are) highest, Jesus Christ.

Cum Sancto Spíritu ✠ in glória Dei Patris. Amen.
With   Holy   Spirit,   in glory of God Father.

Then he kisses the altar and turning to the people says:

V. Dóminus vobíscum.
Lord   (be) with you.

℟ Et cum spíritu tuo.
And with   Spirit   your.

ORÉMUS:
Let us pray.

THE COLLECTS

❀ SEE PROPER OF MASS FOR THE DAY. ❀

Omnípotens sempitérne Deus,
Almighty   everlasting   God,

qui dedísti fámulis tuis in confessióne verae fídei,
who has given to servants of yours in   confession   of true faith,

aetérnae Trinitátis glóriam agnóscere,
of eternal   Trinity   glory   acknowledge,

et in poténtia majestátis adoráre unitátem:
and in   power   of majesty   to adore   unity:

quaésumus; ut ejúsdem fídei firmitáte,
we beseech   that in the same faith steadfastness

ab ómnibus semper muniámur advérsis.
from every   always   defend   adversity.

Per Dóminum nostrum Jesum Christum,
Through   Lord   our   Jesus   Christ,

Fílium tuum, qui tecum vivit et regnat
Son   your,   who with you lives and reigns

in unitáte Spíritus Sancti, Deus,
in unity   of Spirit Holy,   God,

per ómnia sǽcula saeculórum. ℟ Amen.
for   every   ages   of ages.

GLORIA

GLORY to God in the highest.
And on earth peace to men of good will.
We praise Thee. We bless Thee.
We adore Thee. We glorify Thee.
We give thanks to Thee for Thy great glory.
O Lord God, heavenly King, God the Father almighty.
O Lord, the only-begotten Son, Jesus Christ.
O Lord God, Lamb of God, Son of the Father.
Thou who takest away the sins of world,
have mercy upon us.
Thou who takest away the sins of the world,
receive our prayer.
Thou who sittest at the right hand of the Father,
have mercy upon us.
For Thou only art holy. Thou only art the Lord.
Thou only, O Jesus Christ, art most high.
With the Holy Spirit, ✠ in the glory of God the Father.
Amen.

V. The Lord be with you.
℟ And with thy spirit.

Let us pray:

THE COLLECTS

❀ SEE PROPER OF MASS FOR THE DAY. ❀

Almighty and everlasting God, who hast given to Thy servants grace, in the confession of the true faith to acknowledge the glory of the eternal Trinity, and in the power of Thy majesty to worship the Unity; grant that by steadfastness in the same faith we may evermore be defended from all adversities. Through our Lord Jesus Christ, Thy Son, Who liveth and reigneth with Thee in the unity of the Holy Spirit, God, world without end. ℟ Amen.

11

THE LESSON OF SCRIPTURE

Having offered our prayers and praise to God, we now receive instruction from Him through the writings of the Prophets and Apostles. (*See diagram p. xiii.*)

In their synagogue service on the Sabbath, the Jews read from the Scriptures: first from the Law, then from the Prophets. These readings were interspersed with the singing of Psalms.

Thus when the first Christians gathered on Sundays to celebrate our Lord's Resurrection, they continued this tradition; however, in addition to reading from the Law and the Prophets, they also read from the Apostles and the Evangelists.

As the readings from the New Testament came to be preferred, the psalms that were originally sung between each of the readings were combined and done at the same time.

The *Epistle* is a letter or "lesson," usually taken from the writings of St. Paul; however, it can be from the letters written by the other Apostles (Peter, John, James or Jude), or it can be a reading from the Acts of the Apostles, the book of the Apocalypse, or the Old Testament.

The *Gradual* is to be sung as soon as the Epistle is finished, followed immediately by the *Alleluia* or *Tract,* and then the *Sequence* if appropriate.

The *Gradual* gets its name from the Latin word *gradus,* meaning 'step,' because it was a psalm that was traditionally introduced *from the steps* of the ambo (or pulpit). This versicle and its antiphon are always specially selected to harmonize with the readings.

The Alleluia is a **responsory**; its versicle is intoned with two *Alleluias* in the place of an antiphon, and is completed with another *Alleluia.*

Since the Alleluia expresses praise and joy, it is omitted in Masses for the Dead and during Lent. At these times, it is replaced by a portion of a Psalm called the **Tract**, which is *not* done as a responsory.

DID YOU KNOW?

The word **(h)alleluia** comes from the Hebrew words *Hallelu,* meaning 'let us praise' and *Yah,* which is a shortened form of *Yahweh,* one of the names of God. It is the first and last word of several of the psalms, particularly numbers 113 thru 118, which are referred to as the **Hallel Psalms**. These are traditionally recited during important Jewish festivals—in particular, during the celebration of the **Passover**.

At one time, there was a **Sequence** hymn for every feast. Only five of these have been retained:

- *Victimae Paschali* is used for Easter
- *Veni Sancte Spiritus* for Pentecost
- *Lauda Sion* for the feast of Corpus Christi
- *Stabat Mater* for the Feast of the Sorrowful Mother
- *Dies Irae* in Masses for the Dead.

EPISTLE SIT

EPISTLE

❀ SEE PROPER OF MASS FOR THE DAY. ❀

Lesson from the Epistle of blessed Paul the Apostle to the Romans: O the depth of the riches of the wisdom and of the knowledge of God! How incomprehensible are His judgments, and how unsearchable His ways! For who hath known the mind of the Lord? Or who hath been His counsellor? Or who hath first given to Him, and recompense shall be made him? For of Him, and by Him, and in Him, are all things: to Him be glory for ever. Amen.

℟ Thanks be to God.

❀ SEE PROPER OF MASS FOR THE DAY. ❀

 éctio Epístolae beáti Pauli Apóstoli
Lesson   from Epistle (of) blessed Paul   Apostle

ad Romános.
to   Romans.

O altitúdo divitiárum sapiéntiae et sciéntiae Dei:
O   depth   of riches   of wisdom   and of knowledge of God:

quam incomprehensibília sunt judícia ejus,
how   incomprehensible   are   judgements of his,

et investigábiles viae ejus!
and   unsearchable   ways   of his!

Quis enim cognóvit sensum Dómini?
Who   for   has known   mind   of the Lord?

Aut quis consiliárius ejus fuit?
Or   who   counselor   his   has been?

Aut quis prior dedit illi, et retribuétur ei?
Or   who   first   gave to him and   shall be repaid   by him?

Quóniam ex ipso, et per ipsum,
Because   from   him, and   by   him,

et in ipso sunt ómnia: ipsi glória in saécula.   Amen.
and in   him   are   all things: to him   glory   in   ages.

At the end, the server answers:

℟ Deo grátias.
To God   thanks.

GRADUAL AND ALLELUIA (OR TRACT)

During Lent, when the Alleluia is not said, it is replaced by the Tract, usually a short passage from the Psalms.

GRADUAL AND ALLELUIA (OR TRACT)

❀ SEE PROPER OF MASS FOR THE DAY. ❀

Blessed art Thou, O Lord, that beholdest the depths and sittest upon the Cherubim.
V. Blessed art Thou, O Lord, in the firmament of heaven, and worthy of praise for ever. Alleluia.

Alleluia, alleluia.

V. Blessed art Thou, O Lord the God of our fathers, and worthy to be praised for ever. Alleluia.

❀ SEE PROPER OF MASS FOR THE DAY. ❀

Benedíctus es, Dómine, qui intuéris abýssos,
Blessed You are, Lord   who   beholds   the depths

et sédes super Chérubim.
and sits   above   the Cherubim

V. Benedíctus es, Dómine, in firmaménto caéli,
Blessed You are, Lord,   in   the firmament of heaven

et laudábilis in saécula.   Alleluia.
and praiseworthy in   ages

❀   ❀

Allelúia, allelúia.
Allelúia, allelúia.

V. Benedíctus es, Dómine Déus pátrum nostrórum,
Blessed You are, Lord   God   of fathers   our

et laudábilis in saécula.   Allelúia.
and praiseworthy unto   ages.

SEQUENCE
(only on certain feasts)

SEQUENCE
*On certain special Feasts, or at Requiem Masses, there will be a hymn at this point, called the **Sequence**, or "Following Out" of the Alleluia.*

THE WORD OF GOD

Like Isaiah, the Priest asks that his lips may be purified to speak God's Word worthily.

"...And one of the seraphims flew to me, and in his hand was a live coal, which he had taken with the tongs off the altar. And he touched my mouth, and said: *Behold this hath touched thy lips, and thy iniquities shall be taken away, and thy sin shall be cleansed.*"

(Isaias 6: 6-7)

No, ***domne*** is not a typo: it is a diminutive form of the word *domine* and is used here because the deacon is addressing the Priest.

At Solemn High Mass, the Deacon will read the Gospel instead of the Priest. This prayer is then modified as shown below:

> At High Mass, the Deacon prays the *Munda cor meum*. Then, taking the book from the altar, he kneels and asks for the Priest's blessing:
>
> JUBE, **domne**, benedícere.
> Decree, sir, to bless (me).
>
> Then the Priest responds:
>
> Dóminus sit in corde **tuo** et in lábiis **tuis**:
> Lord be in heart your and on lips your,
>
> ut digne et competénter annúnties
> that worthily and competently you may announce
>
> Evangélium suum:
> Gospel His:
>
> In nómine Patris, et Fílii, ✠ et Spíritus Sancti. Amen.
> In the name of Father and of Son and of Spirit Holy.
>
> After receiving this blessing, the Deacon kisses the hands of the Priest and goes to the lectern to read the Gospel.

Here we make the sign of the cross on our forehead, lips and heart, asking our Lord to keep His Word in our thoughts, words and deeds of this day and always.

"...not in bread alone doth man live, but in every word that proceedeth from the mouth of God." (Deut 8:3)

When Jesus was tempted in the wilderness, he rebuked the devil with this quote from the Old Testament book of **Deuteronomy**. It is interesting to compare the circumstances behind each use of this passage:

THE OLD	THE NEW
• The Book of Deuteronomy is a detailed account of the Law of the Old Covenant.	• The Gospels are a detailed account of the New Covenant in Jesus' Blood.
• The Israelites had just spent 40 years wandering in the desert.	• Jesus had just spent 40 days fasting and praying in the desert.
• They were preparing to cross the Jordan at Gilgal to enter the Promised Land.	• He had just been baptized by John at Gilgal and was preparing to enter His ministry.
• This passage referred to the manna with which God had fed them in the wilderness: it was not bread made as man makes bread, but came from heaven by the Will of God.	• Jesus compares himself to manna, for He is both the *Word made flesh* (John 1:14) and the *living Bread come down from heaven* (John 6:51).

Notice that the celebrant removes his maniple before giving the Homily. He will put it back on before the *Credo*. This is because he wears it specifically when he is interceding on our behalf.

14

Bowing down at the center of the Altar, the Priest prays silently:

MUNDA cor meum,
Cleanse   heart   my,

ac lábia mea, omnípotens Deus,
and lips   my,   almighty   God,

qui lábia Isaíae prophétae cálculo mundásti igníto:
Who lips of Isaiah Prophet   stone you cleaned fiery:

ita me tua grata miseratióne dignáre mundáre,
also me of Your gracious   mercy   deign   to clean,

ut sanctum Evangélium tuum digne váleam nuntiáre.
that holy   Gospel   Your worthily I may be fit to announce.

Per Christum Dóminum nostrum. Amen.
Through Christ   Lord   our.

*(While he says this prayer, the book is carried
to the Gospel side of the Altar.)*

JUBE, Dómine, benedícere.
Decree,   Lord,   to bless (me).

Dóminus sit in corde meo et in lábiis meis:
Lord   be in heart   my and on lips   my:

ut digne et competénter annúntiem
that worthily and   competently   I may announce

Evangélium suum. Amen.
Gospel   His.

Turning toward the Book with joined hands, the Priest says:

℣. Dóminus vobíscum.   **STAND**
Lord   (be) with you.

℟. Et cum spíritu tuo.
And with   Spirit   your.

THE GOSPEL

*With his thumb, the Priest makes the sign of the cross on the Gospel
to be read, then on his forehead, lips and breast, saying:*

℣. ✠ Sequentia/Initium sancti Evangelii secundum N.
Continuation Beginning of holy Gospel   according to...

℟. Glória tibi, Dómine.
Glory to You, Lord.

❀ SEE PROPER OF MASS FOR THE DAY. ❀

✠ Sequéntia sancti Evangélii secúndum Matthaéum.
Continuation of holy Gospel   according to   Matthew.

In illo témpore: Dixit Jesus discípulis suis:
At that   time: Said Jesus to disciples his:

Data est mihi omnis potéstas in caelo et in terra.
Given is to me all   power in heaven and on earth.

Eúntes ergo docéte omnes gentes, baptizántes eos
Going therefore teach all   nations,   baptizing   them

in nómine Patris, et Fílii, et Spíritus Sancti:
in the name of Father, and Son, and Spirit   Holy:

docéntes eos serváre ómnia quaecúmque
teaching them to observe all   whatsoever

mandávi vobis.
I have commanded you.

Et ecce ego vobíscum sum ómnibus diébus,
And behold I   with you   am   all   days,

usque ad consummatiónem saéculi.
even to   the consummation of ages.

At the end, the server answers:

℟. Laus tibi, Christe.
Praise to You, Christ.

Then the Priest, kissing the Book, says:

Per evangélica dicta deleántur nostra delícta.
Through the Gospel   spoken may be deleted our   sins.

The Priest now gives the Sermon or Homily.   **SIT**

Cleanse my heart and my lips, O almighty God, who didst cleanse the lips of the prophet Isaias with a burning coal: vouchsafe through Thy gracious mercy so to cleanse me that I may worthily proclaim Thy holy Gospel. Through Christ our Lord. Amen.

Pray, Lord, a blessing.

May the Lord be in my heart and on my lips, that I may meetly and fitly announce His Gospel.

℣. The Lord be with you.
℟. And with thy spirit.

THE GOSPEL

❀ SEE PROPER OF MASS FOR THE DAY. ❀

✠ Continuation of the holy Gospel according to St. Matthew: At that time Jesus said to His disciples: All power is given to Me in heaven and on earth. Going therefore, teach ye all nations, baptizing them in the name of the Father and of the Son and of the Holy Spirit, teaching them to observe all things whatsoever I have commanded you; and behold I am with you all days, even to the consummation of the world.

℟. Praise be to Thee, O Christ.

By the words of the Gospel may our sins be blotted out.

THE SYMBOL OF OUR FAITH

The Creed is recited on all Sundays and Solemnities;
it is omitted from most weekday Masses.

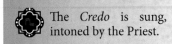

The *Credo* is sung, intoned by the Priest.

FROM APOSTLES TO SYNODS: THE DEVELOPMENT OF THE CREED

A tradition dating to the fifth century tells us that the Twelve Apostles each dictated one of the twelve articles of the Apostle's Creed, having been inspired by the Holy Spirit after Pentecost. This creed given to us by the Apostles contains all the truths of our Faith; why, then, was it made longer?

In the centuries after the death of our Lord, there were many misunderstandings about Christ's nature as both true God and true man. The Church found it necessary to discuss these issues together as a Council, so that, with the help of the Holy Spirit, the correct belief could be established, lest divisions spring up in the Body of Christ.

Once the Church Fathers had carefully considered the matter and had made a decision regarding the correct *dogma*, the erroneous belief was considered *heresy*, based on the greek word *airesis*, meaning 'sect' or 'division.' Those who continued to adhere to such *heterodox* beliefs were called *heretics*. This was a serious matter, because it meant that they were dividing themselves from the Church.

In order to fully develop each article of belief in the Apostle's Creed and eliminate confusion, the Councils of Nicaea (325 AD) and Constantinople (381 AD) expanded certain parts of the Creed.

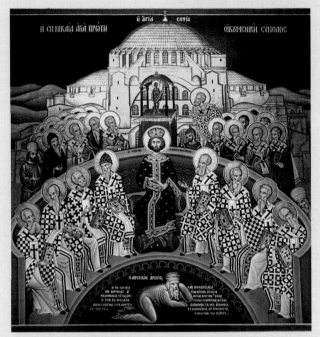

This illustration of the Council of Nicaea shows Arius in shame at the feet of the Church Fathers. It is said that during the heated debate there, Saint Nicholas, then Bishop of Myra, slapped Arius on the face.

The word *Creed* comes from the Latin *credere*, meaning 'to believe.' The Nicene Creed is the Church's statement of our belief. but if you look at its name in a Latin Missal, you will see that it is called *Symbolum Nicænum*, or the Nicene *Symbol*. Why?

In ancient Greece, a *symbolon* was a token which was used to verify the identity of an unknown person, like a messenger. Most often, it was an object that was broken in half. By matching the halves, there could be no mistake.

This was an appropriate title to give to this important division between the Mass of the Catechumens and the Mass of the Faithful. The ability to recite this creed was a good measure of a true Christian. When the Symbol was recited, the unbaptized would depart and the doors would be shut and locked for the remainder of the Mass.

Below are some of the heretical beliefs that plagued the early Church. See if you can find which parts of the Creed help to combat these errors.

- **Arianism:** Arius was an influential teacher in third century Alexandria who believed that, as God's *son*, Jesus must have been *created*, and therefore could not have existed from the beginning with God (as we read in John's Gospel). If this were true, it would make Jesus less important and powerful than God the Father. This erroneous belief led many astray, and the Council of Nicaea was convened especially to combat this popular error.

- **Gnosticism:** This form of belief takes its name from the Greek word *gnostikos*, meaning 'learned' or 'intellectual.' The gnostics sought to explain the imperfection of creation by attributing its origin to an inferior god called a **Demiurge**.

- **Marcionism:** Marcion of Sinope was a wealthy shipowner who argued that the forgiving, loving God found in the Gospels was clearly the True God, and thus the wrathful God found in the Old Testament must be an inferior and evil Demiurge. As a result, he accepted only Paul's letters and portions of the Gospel of Luke as valid scripture, rejecting the remainder of the New Testament and all of the Old Testament.

- **Docetism:** This sect, which takes its name from the Greek word *dokeo*, meaning "to seem", believed that Jesus, as God, could not have truly shared our human nature: He only *seemed to*. His eating, sleeping—even His death on the cross—they considered merely illusions for our sake.

- **Macedonian heresy:** Bishop Macedonius I of Constantinople taught that Christ was not of the same substance as the Father, but only *similar* substance. He also believed that the Holy Spirit was a creation of the Son: merely a servant of His will, like an angel, rather than being himself divine.

DID YOU KNOW?
St. Augustine once belonged to a Gnostic sect called the **Manichees**.

CREED   STAND

CREDO in unum Deum,
I believe   in   one   God,

Patrem omnipoténtem, factórem caeli et terrae,
Father   almighty,   maker of heaven and earth,

visibílium ómnium, et invisibílium.
visible things   all,   and invisible things.

Et in unum Dóminum Jesum Christum,
And in one   Lord   Jesus   Christ,

Fílium Dei unigénitum.
Son   of God only begotten.

Et ex Patre natum ante ómnia saécula.
And from Father born   before   all   ages.

Deum de Deo, lumen de lúmine,
God from God, light from light,

Deum verum de Deo vero.
God   true from God true.

Génitum, non factum, consubstantiálem Patri:
Begotten,   not   made,   of the same substance with Father:

per quem ómnia facta sunt.
through Whom all things made were.

Qui propter nos hómines et propter nostram salútem
Who for the sake of us   men,   and for the sake of our   salvation

descéndit de caelis.
he descended from Heaven.

(here all genuflect:)

Et incarnátus est de Spíritu Sancto
And   he was made flesh   by   Spirit   Holy

ex María Vírgine: et homo factus est.
of   Mary   Virgin: and man   he was made.

Crucifíxus étiam pro nobis:
He was crucified also   for   us

sub Póntio Piláto passus, et sepúltus est.
under Pontius Pilate suffered, and buried was.

Et resurréxit tértia die, secúndum Scriptúras.
And he rose again (on) third day, according to   Scriptures.

Et ascéndit in caelum, sedet ad déxteram Patris.
And he ascended into Heaven, He sits at   right hand   of Father.

Et íterum ventúrus est cum glória
And again   he will come   with   glory

judicáre vivos et mórtuos: cujus regni non erit finis.
to judge living and dead: (of) Whose reign not will be end.

Et in Spíritum Sanctum, Dóminum et vivificántem.
And in   Spirit   Holy,   Lord,   and   life-giver,

Qui ex Patre Filióque procédit.
Who from Father and Son   proceeds.

Qui cum Patre et Fílio
Who with Father and Son

simul adorátur, et conglorificátur.
likewise is adored   and is glorified with:

Qui locútus est per Prophétas.
Who   has spoken through Prophets.

Et unam, sanctam, cathólicam
And One,   Holy,   Catholic,

et apostólicam Ecclésiam.
and Apostolic   Church.

Confíteor unum baptísma in remissiónem peccatórum.
I confess   one   baptism in   remission   of sins.

Et exspécto resurrectiónem mortuórum.
And I expect   the resurrection   of the dead.

(here all make the sign of the cross:)

Et vitam ✠ ventúri saéculi. Amen.
And life   of coming   age.

I BELIEVE in one God
The Father almighty, maker of heaven and earth,
and of all things visible and invisible.
And in one Lord Jesus Christ,
the only-begotten Son of God;
Born of the Father before all ages.
God of God, light of light, true God of true God;
Begotten, not made;
being of one substance with the Father;
through whom all things were made.
Who for us men, and for our salvation,
came down from heaven.
AND WAS MADE FLESH BY THE HOLY SPIRIT
OF THE VIRGIN MARY: AND WAS MADE MAN.
He was crucified also for us,
suffered under Pontius Pilate, and was buried.
And the third day He rose again
according to the Scriptures.
And ascended into heaven.
He sitteth at the right hand of the Father.
And He shall come again with glory
to judge both the living and the dead;
of whose kingdom there shall be no end.
And I believe in the Holy Spirit,
the Lord and giver of life.
Who proceedeth from the Father and the Son.
Who together with the Father and the Son
is adored and glorified.
Who spake by the Prophets.
And in one, holy, catholic and apostolic Church.
I confess one baptism for the remission of sins.
And I look for the resurrection of the dead.
And the life ✠ of the world to come. Amen.

THE MASS OF THE FAITHFUL

We have now crossed the "bridge" (*see diagram p. xiii*) from the Mass of Preparation to the Mass of Fulfillment. As if arriving for the first time in the Promised Land, the Priest greets the altar with a kiss, then he salutes us with *Dominus Vobiscum.*

As we prepare to celebrate the sacred mystery of the Eucharist, we now offer our bread and wine to God for His blessing, but we should also add our own gifts. In the days of the early Christians, the members of the church would form a long line, bringing their gifts of food, wine, gold and precious jewels to the altar. Today it is customary to offer the gift of money for the support of the Church and her Priests, but more importantly, we should *offer ourselves to God,* lifting up our hearts to Him along with the host on the Paten, as many of the saints did.

 The *Offertory Antiphon* is now sung.

In the early Church, a psalm was sung while the offerings of bread and wine were brought to the altar by the faithful. The Offertory Antiphon is a vestige of that Psalm.

DID YOU KNOW?

The Offertory is one of the most important ceremonies of the Mass. In order to fulfill our obligation to attend Mass on Sundays and Holy days, we must be present by this point.

WHAT IS AN ANTIPHON?

The Greek word *antiphonon* means 'sounding against,' and describes the elaborate way that psalms were sung in the synagogue at the time of Christ: two groups of men would alternate in singing each **strophe** or stanza.

Each psalm was preceded by a brief verse from that psalm, or from scripture, which served as a sort of theme. As each strophe of the Psalm was completed, this *antiphon* would be repeated.

The early Church continued this practice, but over time, the psalms were truncated, and sometimes the antiphon alone is used, as here in the Offertory. See p. 67 for more about antiphons.

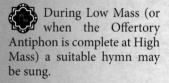 During Low Mass (or when the Offertory Antiphon is complete at High Mass) a suitable hymn may be sung.

Here the Priest mentions 3 main categories of sin:

1. *Peccatis:* when we break God's commandments, we hurt God, who loves us.

2. *Offensionibus:* when we do things that cause scandal to others, we are hurting them.

3. *Negligentiis:* when we fail to do the things we should as followers of Christ, we hurt ourselves.

The Host is now resting upon the Corporal. This sacred square of fine linen helps to ensure that even the tiniest particle of our Lord's precious Body is not lost.

18

The Priest kisses the altar, turns toward the people and says:

℣. Dóminus vobíscum.
    Lord   (be) with you.

℟. Et cum spíritu tuo.
   And with   Spirit   your.

ORÉMUS:
Let us pray:

SIT

OFFERTORY ANTIPHON

❁   SEE PROPER OF MASS FOR THE DAY.   ❁

Benedíctus sit Déus Páter, unigenitúsque Déi Fílius,
Blessed   be   God the Father, and the only-begotten God's Son,

Sánctus quoque Spíritus:
Holy   and also   Spirit

quia fécit nobíscum misericórdiam súam.
for He has shown to us   mercy   His.

OFFERTORY

The Priest now removes the veil and pall from the chalice,
and lifting the paten with the Host on it,
he offers it to God, saying:

USCIPE, sancte Pater omnípotens,
Receive,   holy Father   all powerful

aetérne Deus,
eternal   God,

hanc immaculátam hóstiam,
this   stainless   victim,

quam ego indígnus fámulus tuus óffero tibi,
which I   unworthy   servant   your   offer to You

Deo meo vivo et vero,
God my living and true,

pro innumerabílibus peccátis,
for   countless   sins,

et offensiónibus, et negligéntiis meis,
and offenses   and negligences my,

et pro ómnibus circumstántibus,
and for   all   those standing around

sed et pro ómnibus fidélibus christiánis
but also for   all   faithful   Christians

vivis atque defúnctis: ut mihi, et illis
living and   dead   that for me and these

profíciat ad salútem in vitam aetérnam. Amen.
may it profit to salvation into life   eternal.

The Priest makes the sign of the cross with the paten,
then he allows the Host to slip off the paten
onto the Corporal.

℣. The Lord be with you.
℟. And with thy spirit.

Let us pray:

OFFERTORY ANTIPHON

❁   SEE PROPER OF MASS FOR THE DAY.   ❁

Blessed be God the Father, and the only-begotten Son of God, and also the Holy Spirit; because He hath shown His mercy to us.

OFFERTORY

Receive, O holy Father, almighty and eternal God, this spotless host, which I, Thy unworthy servant, offer unto Thee, my living and True God, for mine own countless sins, offenses and negligences, and for all here present; as also for all faithful Christians living and dead, that it may avail both for my own and their salvation unto life eternal. Amen.

GOD AND CREATION ARE JOINED

The wine now being poured into the Chalice represents Jesus' divine nature, while the drop of water that is mixed with it represents his human nature— and with it ourselves. Just as the two are mingled in the chalice and can no longer be separated, by joining our sacrifice to the one being offered on the altar, we hope to become one with Christ through the Eucharist.

This blessing of the water calls to mind Christ's human nature and our hope that, by partaking of it, we may share in His divine nature. Therefore, in Masses for the Dead, this blessing of the water is omitted, because the one for whom the Mass is offered is no longer among the Church Militant here on Earth.

DID JESUS MIX WATER WITH WINE AT THE LAST SUPPER?

Yes! The vine and its fruit were a symbol of the Israelite people (think "*I am the vine...*"), and the drinking of the four cups of blessed wine during the Passover meal reaffirmed the status of each partaker as one of God's chosen people. For this reason, *the wine could not be omitted or substituted*. Thus, to avoid drunkenness, it was common to mix water with the wine.

> **DID YOU KNOW?**
> If no water is available for this mingling, Mass cannot be said!

Now that the chalice contains the blessed mixture of wine and water, the Priest will keep it covered with the *pall*, in order to ensure that nothing will fall in.

"And the Word was made flesh, and dwelt among us..."
(John 1:14)

When Jesus was conceived in Mary's womb, it was *by the will* of God the Father, and it was *accomplished by* the Holy Spirit. Through this, we see that when one person of the Trinity acts, it is in harmony with the other two. In the same way, it is the unity of God's will with the working of the Holy Spirit that will cause the bread and wine we now offer to become the Body and Blood of our Lord.

"And Mary said to the angel: How shall this be done, because I know not man? And the angel answering, said to her: The Holy Ghost shall come upon thee, and the power of the most High shall overshadow thee."
(Luke 1:34)

This was the prayer of Sidrach, Misach, and Abdenago when they were cast into the fiery furnace (Daniel 3:39-40).
Psalm 50 also tells us:
"*A sacrifice to God is an afflicted spirit: a contrite and humbled heart, O God, thou wilt not despise.*"
This serves to remind us that *we have not deserved Jesus' sacrifice for us.*

The prayers we have offered thus far have been directed to God the Father, through His Son. Now we ask the Holy Spirit to be present and bless the sacrifice on our altar.

20

*The Priest now pours wine and water into the chalice,
blessing the water before it is mixed, saying:*

EUS, qui humánae substántiae dignitátem
God, Who of human substance dignity

mirabíliter condidísti,
marvelously did create,

et mirabílius reformásti:
and more marvelously reformed:

da nobis per hujus aquae et vini mystérium,
give to us through this (of) water and wine mystery,

ejus divinitátis esse consórtes,
His divinity to be sharers

qui humanitátis nostrae fíeri dignátus est párticeps,
Who of humanity our to become he deigned partaker,

Jesus Christus, Fílius tuus, Dóminus noster:
Jesus Christ Son Your Lord our:

Qui tecum vivit et regnat
Who with You lives and reigns

in unitáte Spiritus Sancti, Deus,
in unity of Spirit Holy, God,

per ómnia saécula saeculórum. Amen.
for all ages of ages.

Now offering up the chalice, the Priest says:

FFERIMUS tibi, Dómine, cálicem salutáris,
We offer to You, Lord, the chalice of salvation

tuam deprecántes cleméntiam:
Your begging for mercy:

ut in conspéctu divínae majestátis tuae,
that in sight of divine majesty Your,

pro nostra, et totíus mundi salúte
for our and whole world's salvation

cum odóre suavitátis ascéndat. Amen.
with odor of sweetness may it ascend.

*Then making the Sign of the Cross with the chalice,
and placing it on the Corporal, he covers it with the Pall.*

*Bowing down, with hands joined upon the altar,
the Priest says:*

N spíritu humilitátis, et in ánimo contríto
In a spirit of humility, and in soul contrite

suscipiámur a te, Dómine: et sic fiat
may we be received to You, Lord: and so may be made

sacrifícium nostrum in conspéctu tuo hódie,
sacrifice our in sight Your today,

ut pláceat tibi, Dómine Deus.
that it may please you, Lord God.

*Standing erect, he extends and then joins his hands,
lifting his eyes toward Heaven.*
*Then making the Sign of the Cross over Host and Chalice,
he invokes the Holy Spirit:*

ENI, sanctificátor omnípotens aetérne Deus:
Come, Sanctifier almighty eternal God:

et bénedic ✠ hoc sacrifícium
and bless this sacrifice,

tuo sancto nómini praeparátum.
to Your holy name prepared.

O GOD, who in a wonderful manner didst create and enoble human nature, and still more wonderfully hast renewed it; grant that, by the mystery of this water and wine, we may be made partakers of His divinity who vouchsafed to become partaker of our humanity, Jesus Christ Thy Son, our Lord: who liveth and reigneth with Thee in the unity of the Holy Spirit, One God, world without end. Amen.

W E OFFER unto Thee, O Lord, the chalice of salvation, beseeching Thy clemency, that it may ascend in the sight of Thy divine majesty with a sweet savour, for our own salvation and for that of the whole world. Amen.

I N the spirit of humility and with a contrite heart receive us, O Lord, and grant that the sacrifice which we offer this day in Thy sight, may be pleasing unto Thee, O Lord God.

C OME, O Sanctifier, almighty and eternal God, and bless ✠ this sacrifice prepared for Thy holy name.

AN ODOUR OF SWEETNESS

Just as Mary Magdalene anointed Jesus' feet with costly ointment,
we "cloud in fragrance" our offering and all those participating in it.
During Solemn High Mass, the offerings and all those present are incensed.
If you are attending a Low Mass or a *Missa Cantata*, you may skip this page.

The word ***Incense*** comes from the Latin *incendere*, which means 'to burn.' Frankincense is an aromatic resin derived from the sap of the *Boswellia* plant and its use is very ancient. Because it had to be imported from distant lands, it was a very costly sacrifice and a fitting gift for the King of Kings.

Incense was burned twice daily on a special altar in the Temple in Jerusalem, and once a year, on the Day of Atonement, coals from this altar were taken in a censer, along with two handfuls of incense, into the Holy of Holies, where it was burned in a solemn ceremony before the mercy seat of the Ark of the Covenant, where the *Shekinah*, or presence of the Lord, was said to dwell.

We invoke the intercession of Saint Michael, prince of the Heavenly Host.

This portion of Psalm 140 is especially appropriate here:
"Let my prayer be directed as incense in thy sight..."

"And another angel came, and stood before the altar, having a golden censer; and there was given to him much incense, that he should offer of the prayers of all saints upon the golden altar, which is before the throne of God. And the smoke of the incense of the prayers of the saints ascended up before God from the hand of the angel."

(Apocalypse 8:3-4)

When the congregation is incensed, we stand and bow our heads.

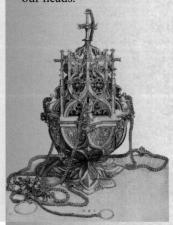

INCENSING

At Solemn Masses, the offerings of bread and wine
are incensed, also the altar and all those present.
The Celebrant blesses the incense, saying:

PER intercessiónem beáti Michaélis Archángeli,
Through intercession of blessed Michael Archangel,

stantis a dextris altáris incénsi,
standing on right hand of altar of incense,

et ómnium electórum suórum,
and (of) all elect his,

incénsum istud dignétur Dóminus
incense such may he deign Lord

benedícere ✠ et in odórem suavitátis accípere.
to bless and in odor of sweetness to accept.

Per Christum Dóminum nostrum. Amen.
Through Christ Lord our.

Receiving the thurible, he incenses the bread and wine:

INCENSUM istud a te benedíctum,
Incense such by you blessed,

ascéndat ad te, Dómine:
may it ascend to you, Lord:

et descéndat super nos misericórdia tua.
and may it descend over us mercy your.

Incensing the altar, he prays the words of Psalm 140:

DIRIGATUR, Dómine, orátio mea,
May it be directed, Lord, prayer my,

sicut incénsum in conspéctu tuo:
just as incense in sight your:

elevátio mánuum meárum
lifting of hands my

sacrifícium vespertínum.
(as) sacrifice evening.

Pone, Dómine, custódiam ori meo,
Set, Lord, a watch (for) mouth my,

et óstium circumstántiae lábiis meis:
and a door round about lips my:

Ut non declínet cor meum in verbo malítiae,
That not may it incline heart my in word of evil,

ad excusándas excusatiónes in peccátis.
to be excused (by) excuses in sins.

Passing the thurible to the Deacon, he says:

ACCENDAT in nobis Dóminus ignem sui amóris,
May he enkindle in us Lord the fire (of) his love,

et flammam aetérnae caritátis. Amen.
and the flame (of) eternal charity.

Then the Celebrant, the clergy, **STAND**
and the congregation are incensed.

INCENSING

THROUGH the intercession of blessed Michael the Archangel standing at the right hand of the altar of incense, and of all His elect, may the Lord vouchsafe to bless ✠ this incense, and to receive it in the odour of sweetness. Through Christ Our Lord. Amen.

MAY THIS INCENSE which Thou hast blessed, O Lord, ascend to Thee, and may Thy mercy descend upon us.

LET MY PRAYER, O Lord, be directed as incense in Thy sight; the lifting up of my hands as an evening sacrifice.

Set a watch, O Lord, before my mouth, and a door round about my lips: That my heart may not incline to evil words, and seek excuses in sins.

MAY THE LORD kindle within us the fire of His love, and the flame of everlasting charity. Amen.

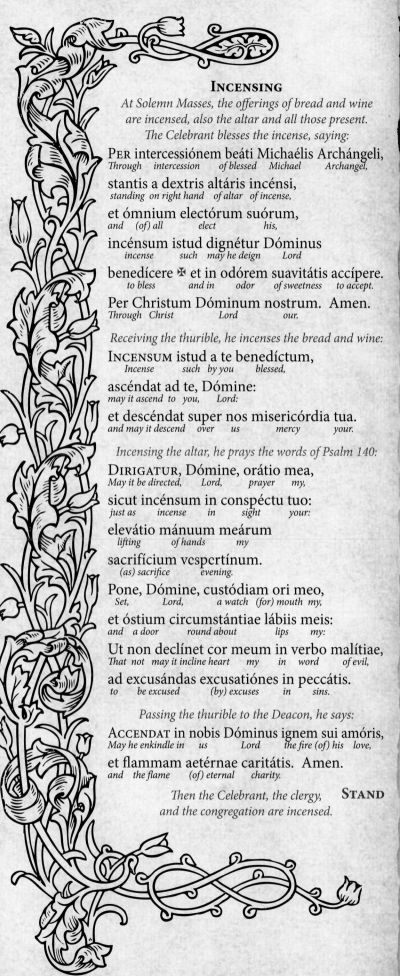

WHITER THAN SNOW

Just as the Priest prayed that his lips should be purified
before speaking the words of the Gospel, so he now purifies his hands
to prepare them to touch what will soon become the Body of Christ.

WHY ALL THIS WASHING?

Once a year, on the Day of Atonement, the High Priest was permitted to enter the Holy of Holies, to burn incense and to sprinkle the altar with the blood of the sacrifices. To prepare for this honor, he spent six days in the temple precinct, purifying himself and memorizing every detail of the ceremony so that he would make no mistakes. The night before, he kept a vigil, fasting and reading from the Psalms. Then, on the Day of Atonement, he washed his entire body five times, and his hands and feet ten times.

We also are preparing to enter the presence of our God, but we have already been washed in the water of our Baptism. In the *Confiteor*, we cleansed our hearts as we prayed that our sins would be washed away. We renewed the Faith we received at Baptism in the Creed. Now that we are drawing near to the heart of the Mass, this symbolic washing calls upon the Holy Spirit to purify us further, so that our bodies may become a fitting vessel for the Body of our Lord.

WHAT IS AN OBLATION?

The word *oblation* comes from the Latin *oblatio*, which means 'offering.'
It refers to something that is surrendered to God.

"Wash me yet more from my iniquity, and cleanse me from my sin. For I know my iniquity, and my sin is always before me." (Psalm 50:4-5)

Hands which are to touch the most sacred Body of Our Lord can never be sufficiently pure, so as the Priest washes his hands with water in this symbolic cleansing, he recites Psalm 25, praying that he may remain pure through God's help.

DID YOU KNOW?

In the early church, the members would bring many offerings of bread, wine and other earthly goods to the altar. After receiving all of these, the washing of the hands at this point was somewhat necessary!

As with all the other places in the Mass where the doxology occurs, it is omitted here in Masses for the Dead and during Passiontide.

We offer our *oblation* to the holy Trinity, calling to mind that it was not only Christ's suffering and death that brought about our salvation: it was made complete by his rising from the dead and ascending in glory.

Here the word *istorum*, meaning 'of these,' refers to those saints whose relics are enclosed in the altar stone.

Look back at the *Confiteor* on page 5. Do you notice some similarities between that prayer and this?

The Priest now washes his fingers:

AVABO inter innocéntes manus meas:
I will wash among innocents hands my:

et circúmdabo altáre tuum, Dómine:
and I will go around altar Your, Lord:

Ut áudiam vocem laudis,
that I may hear the voice of praise,

et enárrem univérsa mirabília tua.
and I may tell all marvelous works Your.

Dómine, diléxi decórem domus tuae,
Lord, I have loved beauty of house Your,

et locum habitatiónis glóriae tuae.
and place of habitation of glory Your.

Ne perdas cum ímpiis, Deus, ánimam meam,
Do not destroy with the wicked, God, soul my,

et cum viris sánguinum vitam meam:
and with men of blood life my:

In quorum mánibus iniquitátes sunt:
In whose hands iniquities are:

déxtera eórum repléta est munéribus.
right hand their filled is (with) gifts.

Ego autem in innocéntia mea ingréssus sum:
I however in innocence my I have walked:

rédime me, et miserére mei.
redeem me, and have mercy on me.

Pes meus stetit in dirécto:
Foot my stood in the straight way:

in ecclésiis benedícam te, Dómine.
in churches I will bless You, Lord.

Glória Patri et Fílio et Spirítui Sancto.
Glory to Father, and to Son, and to Spirit Holy.

Sicut erat in princípio et nunc et semper,
Just as it was in beginning, and now, and always,

et in saécula saeculórum. Amen.
and unto ages of ages.

Bowing before the center of the altar
and placing his joined hands upon it, the Priest prays:

USCIPE, sancta Trínitas, hanc oblatiónem
Receive, holy Trinity, this oblation,

quam tibi offérimus
which to You we offer

ob memóriam passiónis, resurrectiónis et ascensiónis
for the memory of passion, resurrection, and ascension

Jesu Christi Dómini nostri:
of Jesus Christ Lord our:

et in honórem beátae Maríae semper Vírginis,
and in honor of Blessed Mary always Virgin,

et beáti Joánnis Baptístae,
and of Blessed John the Baptist

et sanctórum Apostolórum Petri et Pauli,
and of holy Apostles Peter and Paul

et istórum, et ómnium Sanctórum:
and of these, and of all Saints:

ut illis profíciat ad honórem,
that for them it may profit to honor

nobis autem ad salútem:
for us and also to salvation:

et illi pro nobis intercédere dignéntur in caelis,
and these for us to intercede may they deign in Heaven

quorum memóriam ágimus in terris.
whose memory we celebrate on Earth.

Per eúmdem Christum Dóminum nostrum. Amen.
Through the same Christ Lord our.

I WILL WASH my hands among the innocent: and will compass Thy altar, O Lord. That I may hear the voice of Thy praise, and tell of all Thy wondrous works. I have loved, O Lord, the beauty of Thy house, and the place where Thy glory dwelleth. Take not away my soul, O God, with the wicked, nor my life with men of blood. In whose hands are iniquities: their right hand is filled with gifts. But as for me, I have walked in my innocence: redeem me, and have mercy on me. My foot hath stood in the direct way: in the churches I will bless Thee, O Lord. Glory be to the Father, and to the Son, and to the Holy Spirit. As it was in the beginning, is now, and ever shall be, world without end. Amen.

RECEIVE, O Holy Trinity, this oblation which we make to Thee in remembrance of the Passion, Resurrection and Ascension of our Lord Jesus Christ, and in honour of blessed Mary ever Virgin, of blessed John the Baptist, the holy Apostles Peter and Paul, of these (*the martyrs whose relics are contained in the altar stone*) and of all the saints, that it may avail to their honour and our salvation: and that they may vouchsafe to intercede for us in heaven, whose memory we now keep on earth. Through the same Christ our Lord. Amen.

My Sacrifice and Yours

The Priest is about to recreate Christ's sacrifice on the altar for us, in the silence of reverence. It will be as if he were the High Priest passing through the veil into the Holy of Holies.

"...pray that my sacrifice *and yours* may be acceptable..."

In the Mass, Christ offers the perfect sacrifice for us, but He asks us to join our own sacrifices with His as well. When we "take up our cross and follow Him," uniting ourselves with the host upon the altar, then we shall be consecrated with Him, and our sufferings will become like the rungs of a ladder reaching up to Heaven. Martyrs like St. Julia, pictured here, gave the ultimate sacrifice for our Lord, but our own little daily sacrifices please Him too.

Up to now, when the Priest wanted us to unite our prayers with his, he has greeted us with "*Dominus Vobiscum*", followed by *Oremus*. Now, before he begins the Canon, he turns to us one last time and invites us to join our prayers and sacrifices with his in a more formal and solemn way.

The server responds for us during the Mass, but it is a good practice for us to recite the responses in our hearts too, because we gain the fruits of the Mass in proportion to our participation in it.

Why the *Secret*?

Though this prayer gets its name from the fact that it is spoken inaudibly, there is nothing "secret" about it: it is a prayer of petition, asking for the acceptance of our offerings for the sake of our salvation. It is a **proper** prayer, so it often makes reference to the feast being celebrated.

Here's that Trinitarian formula mentioned on p.10. It can vary depending on whom a given prayer is addressed to. If you have a Missal, see if you can find all the different versions. They are listed on p.70.

The Secret prayer is the last of the propers to occur until after our Communion. The Priest will soon be taking our Lord's Sacred Body in his consecrated hands, and will want to use the Missal as little as possible, to prevent any Sacred Particles from being left behind on its pages.

Did you know?

The Latin phrase *saecula saeculorum* doesn't seem to make sense when translated. But it is based on the way that the Hebrew language would apply a superlative, for example "King of Kings" or "Holy of Holies." In this case, "ages of ages" means "forever and ever."

...Now consider this: if Hebrew superlatives are formed by doubling a word, think what it means when a word is tripled...such as in the *Sanctus*.

Here, with the Secret prayer, ends the Offertory portion of the Mass.

The Priest kisses the altar, and turning toward the people, he extends his hands and says aloud:

RATE, FRATRES:
Pray,   brothers:

ut meam ac vestrum sacrifícium
that   my   and   your   sacrifice

acceptábile fiat apud Deum Patrem omnipoténtem.
acceptable   may be before   God   Father   almighty.

The server responds:

℟ Suscípiat Dóminus sacrifícium de mánibus tuis,
May He receive   the Lord   sacrifice   from   hands   your,

ad laudem, et glóriam nóminis sui,
for   praise   and   glory   of name   His,

ad utilitátem quoque nostram,
for   benefit   also   our,

totiúsque Ecclésiae suae sanctae.
and of the whole   Church   His   holy.

In a low voice, the Priest answers:

℣. Amen.

Then, with hands extended, he silently recites the Secret prayer.

SECRET

> ❀ SEE PROPER OF MASS FOR THE DAY. ❀
>
> Sanctífica, quaésumus, Dómine Deus noster,
> *Sanctify,   we beseech,   Lord   God   our,*
>
> per tui sancti nóminis invocatiónem,
> *by   your   holy   name   the invocation,*
>
> hujus oblatiónis hóstiam:
> *of this   oblation   victim:*
>
> et per eam nosmetípsos
> *and by   them   ourselves*
>
> tibi pérfice munus aetérnum.
> *to you establish   offering   eternal.*
>
> Per Dóminum nostrum Jesum Christum,
> *Through   Lord   our   Jesus   Christ,*
>
> Fílium tuum, qui tecum vivit et regnat
> *Son   your,   who with you   lives   and reigns*
>
> in unitáte Spíritus Sancti, Deus...
> *in   unity   of Spirit   Holy,   God...*

When he has finished the prayer(s), he speaks the closing aloud:

℣. ...Per ómnia sǽcula saeculórum.   **STAND**
...for   all   ages   of ages.

℟ Amen.

He then follows immediately with the Responsory for the Preface.

Brethren, pray that my sacrifice and yours may be acceptable to God the Father almighty.

℟ May the Lord receive the sacrifice at thy hands, to the praise and glory of His name, to our own benefit, and to that of all His holy Church.

℣. Amen.

SECRET

> ❀ SEE PROPER OF MASS FOR THE DAY. ❀
>
> Sanctify, we beseech Thee, O Lord our God, by the invocation of Thy holy name, the victim of this oblation, and by its means make us an eternal oblation to Thee. Through our Lord Jesus Christ, Thy Son, Who liveth and reigneth with Thee in the unity of the Holy Spirit, God...

℣. ...world without end.
℟ Amen.

HEAVEN ON EARTH

As we prepare to enter the heart of the Mass, where our Lord will come to us,
it is as though we too were being lifted up into heaven amidst the chorus of angels.

The *Sanctus* is a hymn called the **Tersanctus**, from the Latin words *Ter* and *Sanctus*, meaning 'Thrice Holy.' The first part of this hymn is the praise of the angels that both Isaiah and St. John heard during their visions of heaven. The second half is the acclamation of the people when Jesus entered Jerusalem.

"...I looked, and behold a door was opened in heaven, and the first voice...said: Come up hither...And immediately I was in the spirit: and behold there was a throne set in heaven, and upon the throne one sitting...And they rested not day and night, saying: *Holy, holy, holy, Lord God Almighty, who was, and who is, and who is to come.*"

(Apocalypse 4:1-2,8)

"I saw the Lord sitting upon a throne high and elevated:...Upon it stood the seraphims:...And they cried one to another, and said: *Holy, holy, holy, the Lord God of hosts, all the earth is full of his glory.*"

(Isaias 6:1-3)

DID YOU KNOW?

Hosanna is Aramaic Hebrew and its literal meaning is "Save me! I pray!" but it has traditionally been used as a liturgical formula for praise.

"...And the multitudes that went before and that followed, cried, saying: Hosanna to the son of David: *Blessed is he that cometh in the name of the Lord: Hosanna in the highest.*"

(Matthew 21:9)

Though he does not turn to the people, the Priest once more salutes us with *Dominus vobiscum*, alerting us that something important is about to happen.

The set of responsories you see here is found in the very earliest known liturgies of the Church, and is believed to have been instituted by the Apostles themselves.

The Preface is a hymn prayer based on those used during the ceremonies of the Jewish Passover.

At one time, each Mass had its own proper preface, but now there are only 15 which are used on special feasts.

The reason the preface is not marked here as one of the propers is because this one is the **Preface of the Most Holy Trinity,** and it is used at most Sunday Masses.

DID YOU KNOW?

The melody used to intone the Preface is the same one used by the ancient Greeks when proclaiming the deeds of a hero during a feast in his honor.

Notice that, as the Preface comes to a close, it now brings to mind the angels, whose song of heavenly praise follows.

The *Sanctus* is now sung.

As musical settings of the Mass became longer and more complex, many times the *Sanctus* had to be split in two parts so that the music would end in time for the Consecration. After the elevation of the Chalice, the music could then resume with the *Benedictus*.

℣. Dóminus vobíscum.
Lord (be) with you.

℟. Et cum spíritu tuo.
And with spirit your.

℣. Sursum corda.
Upwards hearts.

℟. Habémus ad Dóminum.
We hold (them) to the Lord.

℣. Grátias agámus Dómino Deo nostro.
Thanks let us give to Lord God our.

℟. Dignum et justum est.
Fitting and just it is.

The Priest extends his hands and keeps them in this position until the end of the Preface:

PREFACE

ERE dignum et justum est,
Truly fitting and just it is,

aequum et salutáre,
right and salutary,

nos tibi semper et ubíque grátias ágere:
we to You always and everywhere thanks to give:

Dómine sancte, Pater omnípotens, aetérne Deus:
Lord Holy, Father almighty, eternal God:

Qui cum unigénito Fílio tuo, et Spíritu Sancto,
Who with only begotten Son Your, and Spirit Holy,

unus es Deus, unus es Dóminus:
one You are God, one You are Lord:

non in uníus singularitáte persónae,
not in one single person,

sed in uníus Trinitáte substántiae.
but in one Trinity of substance,

Quod enim de tua glória, revelánte te, crédimus,
What truly of Your glory, from revelation from You, we believe,

hoc de Fílio tuo, hoc de Spíritu Sancto,
this about Son Your, this about Spirit Holy,

sine differéntia discretiónis sentímus.
without difference of separation we perceive.

Ut in confessióne verae sempiternaéque Deitátis,
That in confession of true and of eternal Deity,

et in persónis propríetas, et in esséntia únitas,
and in persons distinct, and in essence unity,

et in majestáte adorétur aequálitas.
and in majesty may be adored (in) equality.

Quam laudant Angeli atque Archángeli,
Whom they praise Angels and Archangels,

Chérubim quoque ac Séraphim:
Cherubim also and Seraphim:

qui non cessant clamáre quotídie, una voce dicéntes:
who do not cease to cry out every day, one voice saying:

He joins his hands and bows his head, saying:

ANCTUS, SANCTUS, SANCTUS,   **KNEEL**
Holy, Holy, Holy,

Dóminus Deus Sábaoth.
Lord God of Hosts.

Pleni sunt caeli et terra glória tua.
Filled are Heaven and Earth (of) glory Your.

Hosánna in excélsis.
Hosanna in highest.

Benedíctus qui venit in nómine Dómini.
Blessed who comes in name of the Lord.

Hosánna in excélsis.
Hosanna in highest.

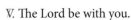

℣. The Lord be with you.
℟. And with thy spirit.
℣. Lift up your hearts.
℟. We lift them up to the Lord.
℣. Let us give thanks to the Lord our God.
℟. It is meet and right.

PREFACE

IT IS TRULY meet and just, right and availing unto salvation that we should at all times and in all places give thanks unto Thee, O holy Lord, Father almighty and everlasting God. Who with Thine only-begotten Son and the Holy Spirit art one God, one Lord; not in the oneness of a single person, but in the Trinity of one substance. For that which we believe from Thy revelation concerning Thy glory, that same we believe also of Thy Son, and of the Holy Spirit, without difference or separation. So that in confessing the true and everlasting Godhead, we shall adore distinction in persons, oneness in being, and equality in majesty. Which the angels and archangels, the cherubim also and the seraphim do praise nor cease to cry out as with one voice:

HOLY, HOLY, HOLY,
Lord God of hosts.
Heaven and earth are full of Thy glory.
Hosanna in the highest.
Blessed is He that cometh in the name of the Lord.
Hosanna in the highest.

THE CANON OF THE MASS

"And Moses, entering into the midst of the cloud,
went up into the mountain..." (Exodus 24:18)

Like Moses on Sinai, the Priest will "enter the cloud" as he begins the Canon, speaking all the following prayers silently until the *Pater Noster*.

CANON = RULE

This is the unchangeable heart of the Mass.

The formula of prayers that make up this part of the Mass must be followed in all Masses. With the exception of a few additions, it is of Apostolic origin, and has not been significantly modified since Gregory the Great (540-604 AD).

In many early Missals, the T in *Te Igitur* was lavishly decorated, and over time it came to include the figure of Christ on the Cross. These designs became larger and larger until they eventually filled the facing page. This tradition still continues today: you would have a hard time finding a Missal without a crucifixion scene on this page.

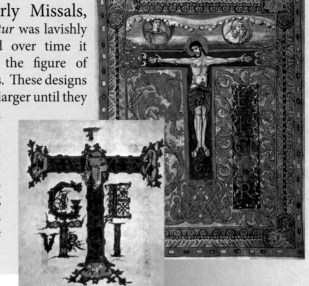

The structure of the Canon is symmetrical as shown in this diagram:

First, there are three prayers of Remembrance, followed by two Offertory Prayers.

After these, the Consecration of both species takes place.

This is then followed by three Offertory prayers and two more prayers of Remembrance.

It is worth noting that the very first word of the Canon, *Te,* refers to God. This is not the case in the English translation.

The *Te Igitur* is the first of the prayers of Remembrance. In it, we call to mind the whole Church Militant, beginning with the Pope and our Bishop. It was once customary to mention the King as well, but this practice was discontinued by Pius V during the Counter-Reformation, as the faith of many leaders no longer permitted this.

WHAT DOES IT MEAN TO *ASSIST* AT MASS?

You may sometimes hear the phrase "assist at Mass" used in place of "attend Mass." This is because it is crucial that we not merely be present, but that we should add our faith and devotion so that we may fully partake of the fruits of the Mass.

	OFFERTORY PRAYERS	CONSECRATION OF THE HOST	CONSECRATION OF THE WINE

2

1

3

PRAYERS OF REMEMBRANCE

OFFERTORY PRAYERS

OFFERTORY PRAYERS

PRAYERS OF REMEMBRANCE

*Hanc Igitur
Quam Oblationem*

*Unde et Memores
Supra quae Propitio
Supplices te Rogamus*

*Te Igitur
Memento
Communicantes*

*Memento
Nobis quoque Peccatoribus*

CANON

The Priest extends, raises and joins his hands,
lifting his eyes toward heaven.
Then deeply bowing, he says in a low voice:

E ÍGITUR, clementíssime Pater,
You therefore, most merciful Father,

per Jesum Christum Fílium tuum
through Jesus Christ Son Your

Dóminum nostrum,
Lord our,

súpplices rogámus, ac pétimus,
humbly beseeching we request, and we ask,

(he kisses the altar and joins his hands)

uti accépta hábeas, et benedícas,
that accepted you may hold, and may bless

(he signs the oblation three times with the sign of the cross)

haec ✠ dona, haec ✠ múnera,
these gifts, these offerings,

haec ✠ sancta sacrifíca illibáta.
these holy sacrifices unspotted,

(then extending his hands, he proceeds:)

In primis, quae tibi offérimus
in the first place, which to You we offer

pro Ecclésia tua sancta cathólica:
for Church Your holy catholic:

quam pacificáre, custodíre, adunáre,
which to pacify, to guard, to unite,

et régere dignéris toto orbe terrárum:
and to guide may You deign in entire world of earth,

una cum fámulo tuo Papa nostro N.,
one with servant Your Pope our...,

et Antístite nostro N.,
and Bishop our...,

et ómnibus orthodóxis atque cathólicae
and all orthodox, and of Catholic

et apostólicae fídei cultóribus.
and of Apostolic faith worshippers.

WE THEREFORE humbly pray and beseech Thee, O most merciful Father, through Jesus Christ Thy Son, our Lord, that Thou wouldst vouchsafe to receive and bless these ✠ gifts, these ✠ offerings, these ✠ holy and unblemished sacrifices.

Which in the first place, we offer up to Thee for Thy holy Catholic Church, that it may please Thee to grant her peace, to protect, unite and govern her throughout the world, together with Thy servant N. our Pope, N. our Bishop, and all true believers and professors of the Catholic and Apostolic Faith.

31

THE DIPTYCHS

We now remember the living: that is, the *Church Militant*. Near the end of the Canon, the other Diptych will be read in memory of the dead: the *Church Suffering*.

These prayers, and those like them which come at the end of the Canon, are called the *Diptychs*, the Greek word for the folding tablets which contained the names to be included in the Priest's prayers at this point.

Over the years, as the number of persons to be included became burdensome, this practice was discontinued. At that time, the lists were shortened and codified into the prayers we find here.

It is customary for the Priest to offer each Mass for a specific person or intention. However, we can and should also offer up our assistance at each Mass for some intention, as the Council of Trent tells us, "...*no other work can be performed by the faithful so holy and Divine as this tremendous Mystery* [of the Mass]." Here, then, let us unite our own intentions with those of the Priest.

In 1962, Pope John XXIII modified the phrase shown in brackets here, adding the name of St. Joseph to the *Communicantes* prayer. This is the only alteration made to the Canon of the Mass since the seventh century.

The *Communicantes* is yet another prayer, like the Preface, which may be replaced by a proper prayer on certain feasts—in this case, during the Octaves of Christmas, Easter and Pentecost and on the feasts of Epiphany and the Ascension.

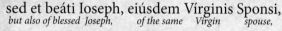

[sed et beáti Ioseph, eiúsdem Vírginis Sponsi,
but also of blessed Joseph, of the same Virgin spouse,

et beatórum Apostolórum ac Mártyrum tuórum,
also of blessed Apostles and Martyrs Your,]

"Precious in the sight of the Lord is the death of his saints."

(Psalm 115)

In the Holy Mass, we experience a showering of graces as the merits of Christ are applied to our souls.

The saints mentioned here are worth noting: First the Apostles are named. The rest are all martyrs representing various stations in life: **Linus, Cletus and Clement** were Popes who were ordained by Peter; **Xystus and Cornelius** were also early Popes. **Cyprian** was a bishop and **Laurence** a deacon. The rest were laymen.

Why this special focus on the martyrs?

The Canon is of very early origin in the Church, and at that time, the most profound reverence was reserved for the martyrs, because they had offered up the ultimate sacrifice for their faith.

The three prayers we have just said in commemoration of the Church (including the *Te Igitur* on p.31) are grouped together and terminated as one in Christ's name.

COMMEMORATION OF THE LIVING

EMENTO, Dómine,
Remember,   Lord,

famulórum famularúmque tuárum N. et N.
male servants   and female servants   Your,

(the Priest joins his hands and calls to mind those for whom he intends to pray; then extending his hands, he proceeds:)

et ómnium circumstántium,
and   all   standing around,

quorum tibi fides cogníta est,
whose   to You faith   known   is,

et nota devótio, pro quibus tibi offérimus:
and known devotion,   for   whom   to You we offer:

vel qui tibi ófferunt hoc sacrifícium laudis,
or   who to You they offer   this   sacrifice   of praise,

pro se, suísque ómnibus:
for themselves, and their everything:

pro redemptióne animárum suárum,
for   redemption   of souls   their,

pro spe salútis, et incolumitátis suae:
for   hope of salvation and   safety   their:

tibíque reddunt vota sua
and to You they render prayers their

aetérno Deo, vivo et vero.
eternal   God   living and true.

OMMUNICANTES, et memóriam venerántes,
In communion with,   and   the memory   venerating,

in primis gloriósae semper Vírginis Maríae,
in the first place of glorious   ever   Virgin   Mary,

Genitrícis Dei et Dómini nostri Jesu Christi:
Mother of God and   Lord   our   Jesus   Christ:

[sed et beatórum Apostolórum
but also of blessed   Apostles

ac Mártyrum tuórum,
and   Martyrs   Your,]

Petri et Pauli, Andréae, Jacóbi,
Peter and Paul,   Andrew,   James (the Greater),

Joánnis, Thomae, Jacóbi,
John,   Thomas,   James (the Less),

Philíppi, Bartholomaéi, Matthaéi,
Phillip,   Bartholomew,   Matthew,

Simónis et Thaddaéi,
Simon,   and   Thaddeus:

Lini, Cleti, Cleméntis, Xysti, Cornélii,
Linus, Cletus,   Clement,   Sixtus,   Cornelius,

Cypriáni, Lauréntii, Chrysógoni,
Cyprian,   Laurence,   Chrysogonus,

Joánnis et Pauli, Cosmae et Damiáni,
John   and Paul,   Cosmas and Damian:

et ómnium Sanctórum tuórum;
and   of all   Saints   Your;

quorum méritis precibúsque concédas,
(by) whose   merits   and prayers   may You grant,

ut in ómnibus protectiónis tuae
that in   all things   of protection   Your

muniámur auxílio.
may we be defended by aid.

(he joins his hands:)

Per eúmdem Christum Dóminum nostrum. Amen.
Through the same   Christ   Lord   our.

BE MINDFUL, O Lord, of Thy servants and handmaids N. and N. (the Priest calls to mind the living he wants to pray for) and of all here present, whose faith and devotion are known to Thee, for whom we offer, or who offer up to Thee this sacrifice of praise for themselves and all those dear to them, for the redemption of their souls, the hope of their safety and salvation; who now pay their vows to Thee, the eternal, living and true God.

IN COMMUNION WITH, and venerating the memory in the first place of the glorious ever Virgin Mary, Mother of our God and Lord Jesus Christ; also of Thy blessed Apostles and Martyrs, Peter and Paul, Andrew, James, John, Thomas, James, Philip, Bartholomew, Matthew, Simon and Thaddeus, Linus, Cletus, Clement, Sixtus, Cornelius, Cyprian, Laurence, Chrysogonus, John and Paul, Cosmas and Damian, and of all Thy saints; by whose merits and prayers grant that we may be defended in all things by the help of Thy protection. Through the same Christ our Lord. Amen.

Tiie Sacrifice of the Old Law and the New

As we prepare this perfect sacrifice, we ask that our sins may be taken away.

"And putting both hands upon his head, let him confess all the iniquities of the children of Israel, and all their offences and sins: and praying that they may light on his head..." (Leviticus 16:21)

The bell alerts us that something important is happening. Look at the Priest's hands. He is stretching them out over the bread and wine in the same way that the High Priest of the Old Law would do over the sin offerings: with hands together, palms down, thumbs forming a cross. By this act of consecration, the Priest asked that God might accept the blood of this victim in the place of the blood of sinners.

Jesus' death on the cross fulfilled the Old Law and replaced it with the New Covenant in His Blood. In the garden at Gethsemane, our Lord suffered greatly as he took upon Himself the weight of all our sins.

Did you know?

According to Jewish tradition, all ceremonial offerings were first *lifted up*—that is, they were first raised up and offered to God, then lowered and "waved" to the north, south, east and west, making a cross. This was true of all offerings, from the sacrificial animals offered in the temple to the bread and wine Jesus shared with his disciples during His Last Supper. Thus, when we bless our offerings with the sign of the cross, we are continuing this same tradition while also imposing the sign of our Lord's Passion.

Did you know?

The "upper room" where Jesus and his disciples celebrated the last supper was part of a synagogue led by Joseph of Arimathea and Nicodemus, and was one of a group of buildings built by King Herod over the location of the tombs of David, Solomon and Melchisedech. We know from the Gospels that the disciples continued to meet there after the death of our Lord, and there He appeared to them on Easter Sunday. It was only natural to celebrate Mass here, where the very first Eucharist had taken place. Thus it became the very first Christian church and it still survives today.

This prayer contains a four-fold petition:
1. That God may accept our offering.
2. That He may grant us peace in our times.
3. That He may save us from eternal damnation.
4. That He may grant us life everlasting.

One last time, the Priest blesses the offerings, making the Sign of the Cross three times over both, then once over each species separately.

This fivefold blessing represents Jesus' five wounds.

By this sign of Christ's Passion, we beg of God our Father to deem them worthy of becoming the Body and Blood of his beloved Son.

JESUS OUR KING IS NOW ABOUT TO COME TO US.
LET US PREPARE TO WELCOME HIM.

Spreading his hands over the oblation, the Priest says:

ＨANC ÍGITUR oblatiónem servitútis nostrae,
This therefore oblation of service our,

sed et cunctae famíliae tuae,
but also of whole family Your,

quaésumus, Dómine, ut placátus accípias:
we beseech, Lord, that graciously you may accept:

diésque nostros in tua pace dispónas,
and days our in Your peace you may dispose,

atque ab aetérna damnatióne nos éripi,
and from eternal damnation us to be rescued,

et in electórum tuórum júbeas grege numerári.
and in the elect of Your you may decree flock to be numbered.

(he joins his hands:)

Per Christum Dóminum nostrum. Amen.
Through Christ Lord our.

QUAM oblatiónem tu, Deus,
Which oblation You God,

in ómnibus, quaésumus,
in all things, we beseech,

(the Priest makes the sign of the cross over the offerings three times:)

✠ ✠ ✠

benedíctam, adscríptam , ratam, rationabilem,
blessed, approved, ratified, rational,

acceptabilémque fácere dignéris:
and acceptable to make may You deign:

(he signs the host and then the chalice:)

✠ ✠

ut nobis Corpus, et Sanguis fiat
that for us the Body, and Blood it may become

dilectíssimi Fílii tui Dómini nostri Jesu Christi.
of most beloved Son Your Lord our Jesus Christ.

THIS oblation, therefore, of our service and that of Thy whole family, we beseech Thee, O Lord, graciously to accept, and to order our days in Thy peace and bid us to be delivered from eternal damnation and numbered among the flock of Thy elect. Through Christ our Lord. Amen.

WHICH oblation do Thou, O God, vouchsafe in all things to bless ✠ , approve ✠ , ratify ✠ , make worthy and acceptable: that it may become for us the Body ✠ and Blood ✠ of Thy most beloved Son our Lord Jesus Christ.

THE CONSECRATION OF THE HOST

"...thou didst feed thy people with the food of angels, and gavest them bread from heaven prepared without labour; having in it all that is delicious, and the sweetness of every taste." (Wisdom 16:20)

"I AM THE LIVING BREAD which came down from heaven. If any man eat of this bread, he shall live for ever; and the bread that I will give, is my flesh, for the life of the world.

If Jesus had meant that we should eat his body and drink his blood only *figuratively*, wouldn't he have explained that to his disciples, instead of letting them walk away? Many miracles have proven the truth of this teaching: the piece of bread you see in the Priest's hands now *is truly the Body of our Lord.*

...Amen, amen I say unto you: Except you eat the flesh of the Son of man, and drink his blood, you shall not have life in you. He that eateth my flesh, and drinketh my blood, hath everlasting life: and I will raise him up in the last day.

Many therefore of his disciples, hearing it, said: This saying is hard, and who can hear it?...After this many of his disciples went back; and walked no more with him."

(John 6:51-52, 54-55, 61, 67)

DID YOU KNOW?
During the ordination of a Priest, his fingers and thumbs are specially consecrated with holy oil, that they may be fit to touch Christ's body. The Council of Trent affirmed this tradition, handed down by the Apostles: only a Priest may take in his hands the Most Holy Eucharist.

Like a fanfare of trumpets announcing the arrival of an earthly king, when you hear these bells ring, you know that our Heavenly King has come to us.

Look reverently upon the Sacred Host as the Priest raises it up for all to see and say with Thomas the Apostle,

"My Lord and My God!"

When we do this, not only do we show our Lord how much we adore Him, but we can also gain an indulgence.

From this moment, each time the Priest touches the Sacred Host, he will genuflect both before and after.

UI prídie quam paterétur,
Who the day before that he suffered,

(he takes the host:)

accépit panem in sanctas,
He took bread in holy

ac venerábiles manus suas:
and venerable hands His,

(he raises his eyes to heaven:)

et elevátis óculis in caelum
and (with) lifted up eyes into heaven

ad te Deum Patrem suum omnipoténtem,
to You God father his almighty,

(bowing his head:)

tibi grátias agens,
to You thanks giving,

(he signs the host with the sign of the cross:)

bene ✠ díxit, fregit, dedítque discípulis suis, dicens:
blessed, broke, and gave to disciples His, saying:

Accípite, et manducáte ex hoc omnes.
Take, and eat from this all of you.

*(holding the host in both hands, he bows low,
pronouncing the words of consecration over the host:)*

Hoc Est Enim Corpus Meum.
This Is For Body My

*The Priest genuflects to adore the Sacred Host,
which is now truly Christ's Body.
Then he elevates the Host so that all may adore.
Placing it on the corporal, he again genuflects.*

Who the day before He suffered took bread into His holy and venerable hands, and with His eyes lifted up to heaven, unto Thee, God, His almighty Father, giving thanks to Thee, He blessed ✠, broke and gave it to His disciples, saying:

Take and eat ye all of this,

For This Is My Body.

THE CONSECRATION OF THE WINE

"Because the life of the flesh is in the blood: and I have given it to you, that you may make atonement with it upon the altar for your souls, and the blood may be for an expiation of the soul." (Leviticus 17:11)

The Old Covenant...

...has been fulfilled in the New:

"...and they offered holocausts, and sacrificed pacific victims of calves to the Lord. Then Moses took half of the blood, and put it into bowls: and the rest he poured upon the altar. And taking the book of the covenant, he read it in the hearing of the people: and they said: All things that the Lord hath spoken we will do, we will be obedient. And he took the blood and sprinkled it upon the people, and he said: *This is the blood of the covenant which the Lord hath made with you concerning all these words.*"

(Exodus 24:5-8)

"...But this man offering one sacrifice for sins, for ever sitteth on the right hand of God...*Having therefore, brethren, a confidence in the entering into the holies by the blood of Christ;* A new and living way which he hath dedicated for us through the veil, that is to say, his flesh, And a high priest over the house of God: Let us draw near with a true heart in fulness of faith, having our hearts sprinkled from an evil conscience, and our bodies washed with clean water."

(Hebrews 10:12, 19-22)

"The chalice of benediction, which we bless, is it not the communion of the blood of Christ? And the bread, which we break, is it not the partaking of the body of the Lord?" (1 Cor 10:16)

When the Priest takes the chalice in his hands, you may notice that his thumb and forefingers remain pressed together.

His fingers have touched the Body of our Lord.

He will not separate them again, except to hold a consecrated Host, until after Communion, when he will carefully purify them with wine and water. Only then, after every trace of our Lord's Body has been consumed or carefully collected within the Sacred Linens, will he separate his fingers.

Christ poured out His precious blood for us in love, though we have not deserved it. Look upon the chalice as the Priest raises it up for all to see and strike your breast like the humble publican, saying with him:

"Lord, have mercy on me, a sinner!"

"...In remembrance of Me..." By means of this simple phrase, our Lord conferred upon His Apostles the power, as well as the duty, to repeat this miraculous Mystery, thereby instituting the Sacraments of the Eucharist and of the Priesthood in the New Law.

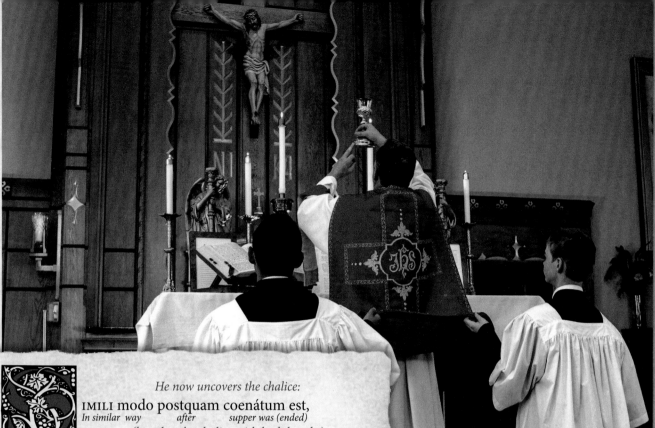

He now uncovers the chalice:

SIMILI modo postquam coenátum est,
In similar way   after   supper was (ended)

(he takes the chalice with both hands:)

accípiens et hunc praeclárum Cálicem
taking   also this   splendid   Chalice

in sanctas ac venerábiles manus suas:
in   holy   and   venerable   hands   His,

(he bows his head:)

item tibi grátias agens,
likewise to You thanks   giving,

(he makes the sign of the cross over the chalice:)

bene✠díxit, dedítque discípulis suis, dicens:
He blessed,   and gave   to disciples His, saying:

Accípite, et bíbite ex eo omnes.
Take,   and drink from it all of you.

(raising the chalice slightly, he pronounces the words of Consecration:)

HIC EST ENIM CALIX SANGUINIS MEI,
This   Is   For   Chalice   Of Blood   My,

NOVI ET ÆTERNI TESTAMENTI:
Of New   and   Eternal   Testament:

MYSTERIUM FIDEI:
Mystery   of Faith:

QUI PRO VOBIS ET PRO MULTIS
Which   For   You   and   For   Many

EFFUNDETUR IN REMISSIONEM
Will Be Shed   in   Remission

PECCATORUM.
of Sins.

(he replaces the chalice on the corporal)

Haec quotiescúmque fecéritis, in mei memóriam faciétis.
These   as often as   you shall do, in   my   memory   you will do.

Now he genuflects to adore the Precious Blood.
He then elevates the chalice so that all may adore.
Replacing it again on the corporal, he genuflects once more.

In like manner, after He had supped, taking also this excellent chalice into His holy and venerable hands, and giving thanks to Thee, He blessed ✠ and gave it to His disciples, saying: Take and drink ye all of this,

FOR THIS IS THE CHALICE
OF MY BLOOD,
OF THE NEW
AND ETERNAL TESTAMENT:
THE MYSTERY OF FAITH:
WHICH SHALL BE SHED
FOR YOU AND FOR MANY
UNTO THE REMISSION
OF SINS.

As often as you shall do these things, ye shall do them in remembrance of Me.

A Pleasing Sacrifice

These three offertory prayers sum up the three most important ends of the Mass:

{ As an *oblation* or offering for sin } { In remembrance of Christ's sacrifice for us. } { To receive Christ in the Eucharist. }

We know from Scripture that the sacrifices of Abel, Abraham and Melchisedech were pleasing to God. These three sacrifices were *types* of the sacrifice we are about to offer:

ABEL

Offered an unblemished lamb as an oblation for sin

ABRAHAM

Offered his only son in obedience to God

MELCHISEDECH

Offered bread and wine as a blessing upon Abraham

"And it came to pass after many days, that Cain offered, of the fruits of the earth, gifts to the Lord. Abel also offered of the firstlings of his flock, and of their fat: **and the Lord had respect to Abel, and to his offerings.** But to Cain and his offerings he had no respect: and Cain was exceedingly angry, and his countenance fell."

(Gen 4:3-5)

"By my own self have I sworn, saith the Lord: *because thou hast done this thing, and hast not spared thy only begotten son for my sake: I will bless thee,* and I will multiply thy seed as the stars of heaven, and as the sand that is by the sea shore: thy seed shall possess the gates of their enemies. And in thy seed shall all the nations of the earth be blessed, because thou hast obeyed my voice."

(Gen 22:16-18)

"But Melchisedech the king of Salem, *bringing forth bread and wine, for he was the priest of the most high God, Blessed him,* and said: Blessed be Abram by the most high God, who created heaven and earth. And blessed be the most high God, by whose protection the enemies are in thy hands. And he gave him the tithes of all."

(Gen 14:18-20)

Long before the printing press had ushered in an era of literacy among the common people, the Church taught her flock through the murals and mosaics of its cathedral walls. This mosaic from the Basilica of San Vitale in Ravenna, Italy dates to the 6th century AD. We can see that it illustrates the sacrifices offered by Abel, Melchisedech and Abraham, mentioned in the prayer on this page.

In longer settings of the Mass requiring a splitting of the *Sanctus*, the *Benedictus* is now sung.

Did you notice that, in the prayer that came immediately before the consecration, the Priest blessed the offerings with the sign of the cross five times just like this?

WHAT IS A TYPE?

A *type* (or figure) is a person, thing or action which exists in its own right but is intended by God as a prefiguration of a future person, thing or action.

During the Offertory, we laid our gifts upon the altar. Now we pray that they may be carried into God's presence by the hands of His holy angel.

The three prayers on this page are as one, summed up here with one of the "signatures" mentioned on pp. 10, 26 and 32.

With his hands held apart, he then proceeds:

NDE ET MÉMORES, Dómine, nos servi tui,
Wherefore also mindful, Lord, we servants Your,

sed et plebs tua sancta,
but also people Your holy,

ejúsdem Christi Fílii tui Dómini nostri
of the same Christ Son Your Lord our,

tam beátae Passiónis,
so blessed the passion,

nec non et ab ínferis Resurrectiónis,
and also from lower regions Resurrection,

sed et in caelos gloriósae Ascensiónis:
but also into heaven glorious Ascension:

offérimus praeclárae majestáti tuae
we offer to splendid majesty Your

(he makes the sign of the cross thrice over both species:)

de tuis donis, ac datis, hóstiam ✠ puram,
of Your gifts and presents, victim pure,

hóstiam ✠ sanctam, hóstiam ✠ immaculátam,
victim holy, victim immaculate,

(then he signs separately first the Host, then the chalice:)

Panem ✠ sanctum vitae aetérnae
Bread holy of life eternal,

et Cálicem ✠ salútis perpétuae.
and Chalice of salvation perpetual.

Extending his hands, he proceeds:

UPRA QUAE PROPÍTIO ac seréno vultu
Upon which gracious and serene face

respícere dignéris, et accépta habére,
to look upon may You deign: and accepted to have,

sicúti accépta habére dignátus es
just as accepted to have you deigned

múnera púeri tui justi Abel,
offerings of servant Your just Abel,

et sacrifícium Patriárchae nostri Abrahae:
and sacrifice of Patriarch our Abraham:

et quod tibi óbtulit
and which to You he offered

summus sacérdos tuus Meschísedech,
most high Priest Your Melchisedech,

sanctum sacrifícium, immaculátam hóstiam.
holy sacrifice, immaculate victim.

Bowing low, with his hands joined upon the altar, the Priest says:

UPPLICES TE ROGÁMUS, omnípotens Deus:
Humbly begging You we beseech, almighty God:

jube haec perférri per manus sancti Angeli tui
decree these to be brought by hands of holy Angel Your

in sublíme altáre tuum,
to exalted altar Your,

in conspéctu divínae majestátis tuae:
in presence of divine majesty Your;

(he kisses the altar:)

ut quotquot ex hac altáris participatióne
that however many from this altar participation

sacrosánctum Fílii tui,
most sacred of Son Your

(he joins his hands, then signs first the Host, then the Chalice:)

Corpus ✠ et Sánguinem ✠ sumpsérimus,
Body and Blood we shall have received,

(he signs himself with the sign of the cross:)

omni benedictióne caelésti et grátia repleámur.
every blessing heavenly and grace may we be filled.

Per eúmdem Christum Dóminum nostrum. Amen.
Through same Christ Lord our.

WHEREFORE, O Lord, we Thy servants, and likewise Thy holy people, calling to mind the blessed Passion of the same Christ Thy Son our Lord, and also His Resurrection from hell and also His glorious Ascension into heaven, offer unto Thy most excellent Majesty, of Thy gifts and presents, a pure ✠ Victim, a holy ✠ Victim, a spotless ✠ Victim, the holy ✠ Bread of eternal life, and the Chalice ✠ of everlasting salvation.

UPON which vouchsafe to look with a propitious and serene countenance, and to accept them as Thou wert pleased to accept the gifts of Thy just servant Abel, and the sacrifice of our Patriarch Abraham, and that which Thy high priest Melchisedech offered to Thee, a holy sacrifice, a spotless Victim.

WE most humbly beseech Thee, almighty God, command these things to be carried up by the hands of Thy holy angel to Thine altar on high, in the sight of Thy divine majesty, that as many of us who, by participation at this altar, shall receive the most sacred Body ✠ and Blood ✠ of Thy Son may be filled with every heavenly blessing and grace. Through the same Christ or Lord. Amen.

THE SECOND DIPTYCH

Continuing the symmetrical structure of the Canon,
we once more commemorate the members of Christ's Mystical Body.

"So we being many, are one body in Christ,
and every one members one of another." (Romans 12:5)

"It is therefore a holy and wholesome thought to pray for the dead,
that they may be loosed from sins." (2 Mach. 12:46)

THE COMMUNION OF SAINTS

The Church is the Mystical Body of Christ and, like the Trinity, it is one Body, but with three aspects, each of which help one another through prayer and good works:

1. The Church Triumphant: This is what we call the angels and the saints in Heaven who have already gained the crown of victory.

2. The Church Militant: The faithful here on earth must constantly struggle against the enemies of their souls.

3. The Church Suffering: The souls of the faithful departed must serve out the temporal punishment for their sins in Purgatory before they may enter Heaven.

In the Mass, the living and the dead are united as the Mystical Body of Christ.

"...*refreshment, light and peace...*"
This line reminds us that those suffering in purgatory have none of these things.

This is the **only place** in the Canon where the Priest speaks aloud. If you've lost your place, just listen for the Priest to say this phrase.

At first glance, this prayer may seem to contain a meaningless list of names, but they represent the many states of life of the members of the Church Triumphant. In the order listed, here are those named:

- **John** the Baptist was a *prophet* and precursor of the Messiah.
- **Stephen**, a *deacon*, was the first Martyr.
- **Matthias** was the *Apostle* who took the place of Judas.
- **Barnabas**, a *Levite*, was a disciple and companion of St. Paul.
- **Ignatius** of Antioch was a *Bishop* Martyr.
- **Alexander** was a *Pope* Martyr.
- **Marcellinus** was a *Priest* Martyr.
- **Peter** was an *exorcist* (a minor cleric) who was martyred with Marcellinus.
- **Felicity** and **Perpetua** were *married* women and *mothers*.
- **Agatha, Lucy, Agnes** and **Cecilia** were all *virgin* martyrs.
- **Anastasia** was a *widow* and martyr.

This brief doxology reminds us that it is through the merits of Christ that we receive every blessing.

At one time, bread, wine, fruits and vegetables were brought to Mass by the faithful and placed near the altar. This prayer was initially intended, then, to confer a blessing upon these fruits of the earth.

COMMEMORATION OF THE DEAD

EMENTO étiam, Dómine,
Remember   also,   Lord,

famulórum, famularumque tuárum N. et N.
male servants   and female servants   Your,

qui nos praecessérunt cum signo fídei
who us   they went before   with the sign of faith,

et dórmiunt in somno pacis.
and they sleep in   sleep   of peace.

The Priest joins his hands and calls to mind the dead for whom
he intends to pray; then extending his hands, he proceeds:

Ipsis, Dómine, et ómnibus in Christo quiescéntibus,
To these, Lord,   and   to all   in   Christ   resting,

locum refrigérii, lucis et pacis,
place   of refreshment, light and peace,

ut indúlgeas, deprecámur.
that may You grant,   we beseech.

(he joins his hands and bows his head:)

Per eúmdem Christum Dóminum nostrum. Amen.
Through same   Christ   Lord   our.

Now he strikes his breast
and speaks the next three words audibly:

OBIS QUOQUE PECCATÓRIBUS
To us   likewise   sinners

fámulis tuis,
servants Yours

de multitúdine miseratiónum tuárum sperántibus,
from the multitude   of mercies   Your   hoping,

partem áliquam, et societátem donáre dignéris,
part   some,   and   society   to grant may You deign,

cum tuis sanctis Apóstolis, et Martyribus:
with Your   holy   Apostles   and   Martyrs:

cum Joánne, Stéphano, Matthía, Bárnaba,
with   John,   Stephen,   Matthias,   Barnabas,

Ignátio, Alexándro, Marcellíno, Petro,
Ignatius,   Alexander,   Marcellinus,   Peter,

Felicitáte, Perpétua, Agatha, Lúcia,
Felicity,   Perpetua,   Agatha,   Lucy,

Agnéte, Caecília, Anastásia,
Agnes,   Cecilia,   Anastasia,

et ómnibus Sanctis tuis:
and with all   Saints   Your:

intra quorum nos consórtium,
among   whose   us   company,

non aestimátor mériti,
not   to be esteemed   deserved,

sed véniae, quaésumus, largítor admítte.
but of pardon,   we beseech,   of your bounty   grant.

Per Christum Dóminum nostrum. Amen.
Through   Christ   Lord   our.

The Priest joins his hands and makes the sign of the cross
three times over the Host and chalice:

ER QUEM HAEC ÓMNIA,
By Whom   these   all,

Dómine, semper bona creas,
Lord,   always good things you create,

sanctíficas ✠, vivíficas ✠, benedícis ✠,
You sanctify,   You give life to,   You bless,

et praestas nobis.
and you give   to us.

BE MINDFUL also, O Lord, of Thy servants and handmaids N. and N. who are gone before us with the sign of faith and repose in the sleep of peace. To these, O Lord, and to all that rest in Christ, grant, we beseech Thee, a place of refreshment, light and peace. Through the same Christ our Lord. Amen.

AND TO US SINNERS ALSO, Thy servants, hoping in the multitude of Thy mercies, vouchsafe to grant some part and fellowship with Thy holy apostles and martyrs: with John, Stephen, Matthias, Barnabas, Ignatius, Alexander, Marcellinus, Peter, Felicitas, Perpetua, Agatha, Lucy, Agnes, Cecilia, Anastasia, and with all Thy saints, into whose company admit us, we beseech Thee, not considering our merits but pardoning our offenses. Through Christ our Lord.

THROUGH WHOM, O Lord, Thou dost always create, sanctify ✠, quicken ✠, bless ✠, and bestow upon us all these Thy gifts.

GIVE US THIS DAY OUR DAILY BREAD

Now that the sacrificial part of the Mass is complete (*see diagram p. xiii*),
we seek to apply the fruits of this perfect sacrifice to our souls.

Perfect prayer always gives to God first, then asks to receive, and the *Our Father*, coming from our Lord himself, sets the paradigm for this perfection. Saint Thomas Aquinas and Saint Augustine both pointed out that all prayer should be modeled on this perfect example, which even teaches us those things for which we should ask, and the order in which we should ask them.

This doxology is the solemn crowning of the Canon and in some ways it mirrors the *Sanctus* which immediately preceded the Canon. It was during that song of praise that the Priest entered the "Holy of Holies" and with this hymn of praise he once again emerges.

Because this symbolism was essential in the ancient liturgy of the Mass, it was only at this point that the consecrated species were first shown to the congregation for their adoration.

This part of the doxology is spoken aloud so that we may respond "amen" in affirmation of what has until now taken place in silence.

Take special note of the line, "forgive us our trespasses *as we forgive those who trespass against us.*" Jesus told us, "with what judgment you judge, you shall be judged" (Mt 7:2) so we must be sure to *forgive others* if we wish for God to *forgive us*.

> Now that Jesus is here with us, this is an ideal chance to ask Him for the grace to forgive some old injury.
>
> "Leave there thy offering before the altar, and go first to be reconciled to thy brother: and then coming thou shalt offer thy gift."
>
> (Matthew 5:24)

PATER NOSTER.

Our Father, who art in heaven,

Hallowed be thy name.

Thy Kingdom come,

Thy will be done on earth as it is in heaven.

Give us this day our daily bread,

And forgive us our trespasses as we forgive those who trespass against us.

And lead us not into temptation

But deliver us from evil. Amen.

This illustration sums up the seven precepts of the *Our Father* prayer. The first three concern God, while the other four concern us.

It is through these last four—that is, through the grace of the Eucharist, the forgiveness of sins, the resisting of temptation and the deliverance from the penalty of sin—that we are best able to accomplish the first three, and thus to give glory to God by doing His will.

THE MINOR ELEVATION

Now he uncovers the chalice and genuflects.
Taking the Host in his right hand and the chalice in his left,
he makes the sign of the cross three times over the chalice, saying:

PER ✠ IPSUM, ET CUM ✠ IPSO, ET IN ✠ IPSO,
Through   Him,   and with   Him,   and in   Him,

(he signs twice between himself and the chalice:)

EST TIBI DEO PATRI ✠ OMNIPOTÉNTI,
is   to You God Father   almighty,

IN UNITÁTE SPÍRITUS ✠ SANCTI,
in   the unity   of Spirit   Holy,

(he elevates them slightly:)

OMNIS HONOR, ET GLÓRIA,
all   honor,   and   glory.

He replaces the host, covers the chalice,
then genuflects, saying aloud:

℣. PER ÓMNIA SAÉCULA SAECULÓRUM.
For   all   ages   of ages.

℟. Amen.

STAND
(HIGH MASS)

Still speaking aloud, the Priest joins his hands and says:

ORÉMUS:
Let us Pray:

Praecéptis salutáribus móniti,
By the precepts of salvation advised,

et divína institutióne formáti, audémus dícere:
and by divine institution guided, we dare to say:

(he extends his hands:)

OUR FATHER

ATER NOSTER, qui es in caelis:
Father   our,   Who are in Heaven,
Sanctificétur nomen tuum:
may it be sanctified   name   Your:

Advéniat regnum tuum:
May it come   reign   Your:

Fiat volúntas tua, sicut in caelo, et in terra.
be done   will   Your just as in heaven, and in earth.

Panem nostrum quotidiánum da nobis hódie:
Bread   our   daily   give to us   today:

Et dimítte nobis débita nostra,
And dismiss for us debts our,

sicut et nos dimíttimus debitóribus nostris.
just as we dismiss (them) of debtors our.

Et ne nos indúcas in tentatiónem.
And not us may You lead into   trial.

℟. Sed líbera nos a malo.
But   free   us from evil.

In a low voice, the Priest answers:

℣. Amen.

T HROUGH ✠ Him, and with ✠ Him, and in ✠ Him,
be unto Thee, O God the Father ✠ almighty, in the
unity of the Holy ✠ Spirit, all honour and glory, ℣. world
without end.
℟. Amen.

Let us Pray:
Taught by Thy saving precepts and guided by the divine
institution, we make bold to say:

O UR FATHER who art in heaven, hallowed be Thy
name; Thy kingdom come; Thy will be done on
earth as it is in heaven. Give us this day our daily bread;
and forgive us our trespasses, as we forgive them that
trespass against us. And lead us not into temptation.

℟. But deliver us from evil.
℣. Amen.

The Breaking of Bread

We continue to enlarge what was said in the *Pater Noster*:
We wish to be freed from all our sins so that we may be at peace with God,
with our neighbor, and with ourselves.

"Now when it was late that same day, the first of the week, and the doors were shut, where the disciples were gathered together, for fear of the Jews, Jesus came and stood in the midst, and said to them: Peace be to you." (John 20:19)

In this, our Lord's very first greeting to his disciples upon his Resurrection, he wishes them peace. We also hope to partake of this fruit of the Sacrament.

The blessing and breaking of unleavened bread is a central feature of the Jewish Passover ceremony. As Christ celebrated this feast with his disciples, He broke the bread—signifying the separation of His Body and Soul at the moment of His death—thereby bringing to fulfillment what had been a *type,* with the institution of the Eucharist. Consequently, the early Christians came to refer to the celebration of the Eucharist as "the Breaking of Bread."

As the Priest breaks the Sacred Host at Mass, we also recall two important moments in the Gospel of Luke: the feeding of the five thousand, and the Supper at Emmaus, in which Jesus' disciples recognized their Lord in the breaking of the bread. These *figures* of the Eucharist serve to remind us that Jesus is "the true bread from heaven" (John 6:32), come to fulfill the new covenant in his blood.

"And taking the five loaves and the two fishes, he looked up to heaven, and blessed them; and he broke, and distributed to his disciples, to set before the multitude. And they did all eat, and were filled." (Luke 9:16-17)

Listen closely to see if you can hear the Host being broken!

"And it came to pass, whilst he was at table with them, he took bread, and blessed, and brake, and gave to them. And their eyes were opened, and they knew him: and he vanished out of their sight."

(Luke 24:30-31)

Why do we place a particle of the Host in the Chalice?

This mingling of the bread and wine in the chalice symbolizes the miraculous reunion of Jesus' body and blood at his Resurrection.

At one time, it was common to reserve the particle broken from the host for the next day's Mass. This reserved piece was called the *Sancta.*

These particles could also be shared with other churches, in which case they were referred to as the *Fermentum,* the Latin word for 'leaven.' These shared particles signified the unity of each and every celebration of the Mass in the one Sacrifice of the Cross.

 The *Agnus Dei* is now sung.

IBERA nos, quaésumus, Dómine,
Free   us,   we beseech,   Lord,

ab ómnibus malis,
from   all   evils,

praetéritis, praeséntibus et futúris:
past,   present,   and future:

et intercedénte beáta et gloriósa semper Vírgine
and by intercession of blessed and   glorious   ever   Virgin

Dei Genitríce María,
of God the Mother   Mary,

cum beátis Apóstolis tuis Petro et Paulo,
with   blessed   Apostles Your Peter and Paul,

atque Andréa, et ómnibus Sanctis,
and   Andrew,   and all   Saints,

(he signs himself with the paten:)

da propítius pacem in diébus nostris:
give graciously   peace in   days   our:

(he kisses the paten:)

ut ope misericórdiae tuae adjúti,
that by wealth of mercy   Your   helped,

et a peccáto simus semper líberi,
both from sin   we may be always   free,

et ab omni perturbatióne secúri.
and from all   disturbance   secure.

He places the host on the paten, uncovers the chalice and genuflects. Then holding the Host over the chalice, he breaks it in half, saying:

Per eúmdem Dóminum nostrum
Through same   Lord   our

Jesum Christum, Fílium tuum,
Jesus   Christ,   Son   your.

Placing the right half on the paten, he breaks a particle from the remaining half:

qui tecum vivit et regnat
Who with you   lives and reigns

in unitáte Spiritus Sancti Deus,
in the unity of Spirit Holy   God.

He places the the left half on the paten and holds the particle over the chalice, saying aloud:

℣. per ómnia saécula saeculórum. ℟. Amen.
for   all   ages   of ages.

He now makes the sign of the cross three times over the chalice with the particle:

℣. Pax ✠ Dómini sit ✠ semper ✠ vobíscum.
Peace   of the Lord be   always   with you.

℟. Et cum spíritu tuo.
And with   spirit your.

KNEEL

Finally, he places the particle in the chalice, saying silently:

AEC commíxtio, et consecrátio
This   mingling,   and consecration

Córporis et Sánguinis
of Body   and of Blood

Dómini nostri Jesu Christi,
of Lord   our   Jesus   Christ,

fiat accipiéntibus nobis in vitam aetérnam. Amen.
may be made receiving   for us into life   eternal.

He then covers the chalice and genuflects.

Deliver us, we beseech Thee, O Lord, from all evils, past, present and to come, and by the intercession of the blessed and glorious ever Virgin Mary, Mother of God, together with Thy blessed apostles Peter and Paul, and Andrew, and all the saints, mercifully grant peace in our days: that through the bounteous help of Thy mercy we may be always free from sin and secure from all disturbance.

Through the same Jesus Christ Thy Son our Lord, who liveth and reigneth with Thee in the unity of the Holy Spirit, one God,...
℣. ...world without end.
℟. Amen.

℣. The peace ✠ of the Lord be ✠ always ✠ with you.
℟. And with thy spirit.

May this mingling and consecration of the Body and Blood of our Lord Jesus Christ be to us who receive it effectual to life everlasting. Amen.

THE SACRIFICIAL LAMB

Up to now, the prayers of the Mass have been addressed
to God the Father or to the Trinity. Now the Priest addresses Christ himself,
the Sacrificial Lamb Who lies on the altar before him.

The blood of the Passover Lamb saved the Israelites from the Angel of Death, who was to pass throughout the land of Egypt, striking down all the firstborn.

Now in the New Covenant, the blood of the Lamb—that is, Christ—saves us from the death of sin, giving us the grace which is the food of our souls.

"The Lamb that was slain is worthy to receive power, and divinity, and wisdom, and strength, and honour, and glory, and benediction."

(Apocalypse 5:12)

The Priest strikes his breast each time he repeats this prayer, and so should we.

In Masses for the dead, the phrase "*miserere nobis*" is replaced with "*Dona eis requiem*" and the phrase "*Dona Nobis Pacem*" is replaced with "*Dona eis sempiternam requiem.*" Then the prayer which follows is omitted.

In the *Agnus Dei*, we are asking our Lord to forgive us for three kinds of sins: those of thought, of word, and of deed.

Having prayed for the fruit of peace, in Solemn Masses the Priest begins by kissing the altar close to where the Host lies. Thus when he offers this same kiss of peace to the Deacon, he is offering the peace that comes from our Lord himself, through the sacrifice of the Eucharist.

"With desire I have desired to eat this pasch with you, before I suffer."

(Luke 22:15)

Consider the anticipation with which our Lord had looked forward to this moment! This Passover meal would mark the birth of the Mass and of the Priesthood—those means by which the merits of His sacrifice the next day could be applied to our souls. Thousands of years of waiting were about to end, and a new covenant was about to begin.

Note the beginning of this prayer. It reminds us that all three Persons of the Trinity participated equally in the death and resurrection of our Lord.

In this prayer, the Priest asks our Lord for three specific gifts from the partaking of His Body:
1. That we may be freed from our sins.
2. That we may always follow His commandments.
3. That He will never permit us to be separated from Him.

LAMB OF GOD

The Priest bows and strikes his breast each time as he says:

AGNUS DEI, qui tollis peccáta mundi:
Lamb   of God, who takes away   sins   of world:

miserére nobis.
have mercy   on us.

Agnus Dei, qui tollis peccáta mundi:
Lamb of God, who takes away sins   of world:

miserére nobis.
have mercy   on us.

Agnus Dei, qui tollis peccáta mundi:
Lamb of God, who takes away sins   of world:

dona nobis pacem.
grant   to us   peace.

Bowing and placing his joined hands upon the altar,
he prays silently:

OMINE Jesu Christe,
Lord   Jesus   Christ,

qui dixísti Apóstolis tuis:
who   said   to Apostles Your:

Pacem relinquo vobis, pacem meam do vobis;
Peace I leave behind for you,   peace   My   I give to you:

ne respícias peccáta mea, sed fidem Ecclésiae tuae:
that not may You note sins   my,   but faith   of Church   Your:

eámque secúndum voluntátem tuam pacificáre
and to her   according   to will   Your   to grant peace

et coadunáre dignéris: Qui vivis et regnas Deus
and   to unite   may You deign Who lives and reigns   God

per ómnia saécula saeculórum.   Amen.
for   all   ages   of ages.

⎡ *At Solemn High Mass, the Priest now kisses the altar,*
⎢ *then gives the Kiss of Peace to the deacon, saying:*

℣. Pax Tecum.
peace with you.

℟. Et cum spiritu tuo.
And with   spirit   your. ⎤

OMINE Jesu Christe,
Lord   Jesus   Christ,

Fili Dei vivi,
Son of God living,

qui ex voluntáte Patris, cooperánte Spíritu Sancto,
who out of the will   of Father, in cooperation   of Spirit   Holy,

per mortem tuam mundum vivificásti:
through death   Your   the world   You brought to life:

líbera me per hoc sacrosánctum
free   me through this   most holy

Corpus et Sánguinem tuum
Body   and   Blood   Your

ab ómnibus iniquitátibus meis, et univérsis malis:
from all   iniquities   my,   and   every   evil:

et fac me tuis semper inhaerére mandátis,
and make me Your   always   to adhere to commandments,

et a te numquam separári permíttas:
and from You never   to be separated may You permit:

Qui cum eódem Deo Patre et Spíritu Sancto
Who with the same God the Father and Spirit   Holy

vivis et regnas, Deus, in saécula saeculórum.   Amen.
lives and reigns, God, for ages   of ages.

L AMB OF GOD, who takest away the sins of the world, have mercy on us.
Lamb of God, who takest away the sins of the world, have mercy on us.
Lamb of God, who takest away the sins of the world, grant us peace.

O LORD Jesus Christ, who saidst to Thy Apostles, Peace I leave with you, My peace I give unto you; look not upon my sins, but upon the faith of Thy Church; and vouchsafe to grant her peace and unity according to Thy will: O God who livest and reignest world without end. Amen.

O LORD Jesus Christ, Son of the Living God, who according to the will of the Father, through the cooperation of the Holy Spirit, hast by Thy death given life to the world: deliver me by this Thy most holy Body and Blood from all my transgressions and from all evils; make me always adhere to Thy commandments and never suffer me to be separated from Thee; who with the same God the Father and the Holy Spirit livest and reignest God, for ever and ever. Amen.

LORD, MAKE US WORTHY!

We pray that it may not be said of us: "The marriage indeed is ready; but they that were invited were not worthy." (Matthew 22:8)

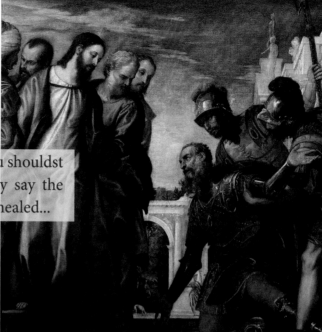

"And when he had entered into Capharnaum, there came to him a centurion, beseeching him, and saying, Lord, my servant lieth at home sick of the palsy, and is grievously tormented. And Jesus saith to him: I will come and heal him. And the centurion making answer, said:

Lord, I am not worthy that thou shouldst enter under my roof: but only say the word, and my servant shall be healed...

And Jesus hearing this, marvelled; and said to them that followed him: Amen I say to you, I have not found so great faith in Israel...Go, and as thou hast believed, so be it done to thee. And the servant was healed at the same hour."
(Matthew 8:5-8, 10, 13)

Here we take a moment to recall St. Paul's admonition:
"*For as often as you shall eat this bread, and drink the chalice, you shall shew the death of the Lord, until he come. Therefore whosoever shall eat this bread, or drink the chalice of the Lord unworthily, shall be guilty of the body and of the blood of the Lord.*"
(I Corinthians 11: 26-27)

This phrase is from Psalm 115.

Only the first line of this phrase is spoken aloud by the Priest.

"Behold, I stand at the gate, and knock. If any man shall hear my voice, and open to me the door, I will come in to him, and will sup with him, and he with me."
(Apocalypse 3:20)

If you look carefully at this picture, you will notice that there is no handle on the door. It can only be opened from the inside. This is the door of your heart, and our Lord stands and knocks, waiting for you to open the door so that He may enter His new home.

Is your heart ready to receive the King?

The greatest beauty of the Mass is that our Lord comes to us even though He knows we can never be worthy. A mere word from Him can heal us, but we must do our part: we must open the door. Like the centurion, we strike our breast in humility, acknowledging our weakness and inviting His help.

The first three lines of this prayer are taken from Psalm 115, and the last two are from Psalm 17.

✠ If the faithful are to receive communion, the server would now recite the *Confiteor* (p.5) once more on their behalf. However, in the 1962 revision of the Missal, this practice was discontinued. Whether or not your parish follows this practice, you may wish to take a moment to ask our Lord's help in preparing your heart to receive Him.

PERCEPTIO Corpóris tui, Dómine Jesu Christe,
Partaking of Body Your, Lord Jesus Christ,

quod ego indígnus súmere praésumo,
which I unworthy to take presume,

non mihi provéniat in judícium
not to me may it come forth in judgment

et condemnatiónem:
and condemnation:

sed pro tua pietáte prosit mihi
but for Your goodness may it profit me

ad tutaméntum mentis et córporis,
to protection of mind and body,

et ad medélam percipiéndam:
and to remedy to be gained:

Qui vivis et regnas cum Deo Patre
Who lives and reigns with God the Father

in unitáte Spíritus Sancti Deus,
in the unity of Spirit Holy God,

per ómnia saécula saeculórum. Amen.
for all ages of ages.

The Priest genuflects before the Blessed Sacrament and says:

Panem caeléstem accípiam, et nomen Dómini invocábo.
The bread of Heaven I will take, and name of the Lord I will invoke.

Then, bowing slightly,
he takes both parts of the Host with the paten beneath.
Striking his breast each time, he repeats three times:

DOMINE, NON SUM DIGNUS,
Lord, not I am worthy,

ut intres sub tectum meum:
that you enter under roof my:

sed tantum dic verbo et sanábitur ánima mea.
but only say the word and will be healed soul my.

He makes the sign of the cross with the Host over the paten:

CORPUS Dómini nostri Jesu Christi
Body of Lord our Jesus Christ

custódiat ánimam meam
may it preserve soul my

in vitam aetérnam. Amen.
unto life eternal.

Then, bowing down, he reverently consumes both parts of the Host,
joins his hands, and remains a short time in prayer.

Now he uncovers the chalice, genuflects,
and gathers with the paten whatever particles may remain
on the corporal, placing them in the chalice, saying:

QUID retríbuam Dómino
What shall I repay the Lord

pro ómnibus quae retríbuit mihi?
for all which he rendered to me?

Cálicem salutáris accípiam, et nomen Dómini invocábo.
Chalice of salvation I will take and name of Lord I will invoke.

Laudans invocábo Dóminum,
Praising I will invoke Lord,

et ab inimícis meis salvus ero.
and from enemies my saved I will be.

Making the sign of the cross with the chalice, he says:

SANGUIS Dómini nostri Jesu Christi
Blood of Lord our Jesus Christ

custódiat ánimam meam
may it preserve soul my

in vitam aetérnam. Amen.
in life eternal.

Holding the paten under the chalice with his left hand, he takes the
chalice with his right and reverently consumes the Precious Blood.

LET NOT the partaking of Thy Body, O Lord Jesus Christ, which I, though unworthy, presume to receive, turn to my judgment and condemnation: but through Thy goodness may it be unto me a safeguard and a healing remedy both of soul and body; who livest and reignest with God the Father in the unity of the Holy Spirit, God, world without end. Amen.

I will take the bread of heaven, and call upon the name of the Lord.

LORD, I am not worthy that Thou shouldst enter under my roof; say but the word and my soul shall be healed.

MAY the body of our Lord Jesus Christ preserve my soul to life everlasting. Amen

WHAT shall I render to the Lord for all the things He hath rendered to me? I will take the chalice of salvation, and I will call upon the name of the Lord. Praising, I will call upon the Lord, and I shall be saved from my enemies.

MAY the Blood of our Lord Jesus Christ preserve my soul to life everlasting. Amen.

BEHOLD THE LAMB OF GOD!

As the Priest shows us the Sacred Host, he uses the words of John the Baptist.

In preparation for the Passover feast, the Jews would form bands of 10-20 men with whom they would celebrate the Passover meal. They would then select a spotless lamb from among the yearlings, carefully wash and anoint it, and keep it separate for three days before it was sacrificed. During this time, it was called the "*Lamb of God.*"

When John cried out upon seeing Jesus, there would have been no mistake as to his meaning: this was the Messiah who had come to deliver them.

DID YOU KNOW?
If you look at the illustration of the Lamb here, you may notice something hanging down from the book on which He is seated. These are the seven seals mentioned in the Apocalypse: "Thou art worthy, O Lord, to take the book, and to open the seals thereof; because thou wast slain, and hast redeemed us to God, in thy blood..." (Apoc. 5:9)

"...John saw Jesus coming to him, and he saith: *Behold the Lamb of God:* behold him who taketh away the sin of the world."

(John 1:29)

We receive the Body of our Lord and King while kneeling at the altar rail. When the Priest displays the Host to you (see p.53), you need not respond "amen." Simply tilt your head back slightly and extend your tongue, then allow the Host to soften before swallowing.

Those faithful who cannot receive the Eucharist should recite an act of Spiritual Communion, that they too may partake of the graces of the Sacrament, at least in part.

Though we are brimming with excitement at receiving our Lord, we remind ourselves once more of our sinful nature. It is now our turn to strike our breast and declare our unworthiness like the Centurion. This is a fitting disposition for receiving Him: one of humble confidence in his love and mercy.

SPIRITUAL COMMUNION

My Jesus, I believe that Thou art present in the Blessed Sacrament. I love Thee above all things and I desire Thee in my soul. Since I cannot now receive Thee sacramentally, come at least spiritually into my heart. As though thou wert already there, I embrace Thee and unite myself wholly to Thee; permit not that I should ever be separated from Thee.

At High Mass, the *Communion Antiphon* is now sung, and may be followed by a suitable hymn. At Low Mass, a hymn may now be sung.

The Priest takes a Sacred Host from the ciborium.
Elevating it slightly, he turns to the people, saying:

ECCE AGNUS DEI:
Behold   the Lamb   of God,

ecce qui tollit peccáta mundi.
behold who takes away   sins   of world

The people respond three times, striking the breast each time:

DOMINE, NON SUM DIGNUS,
Lord,   not I am   worthy,

ut intres sub tectum meum:
that you enter under   roof   my:

sed tantum dic verbo et sanábitur ánima mea.
but   only   say the word and will be healed   soul   my.

COMMUNION

Descending the steps, the Priest goes to the Altar rail
and administers Holy Communion, saying to each:

Corpus Dómini nostri Jesu Christi
Body   of Lord   our   Jesus   Christ

custódiat ánimam tuam
may it preserve   soul   your

in vitam aetérnam. Amen.
in   life   eternal.

BEHOLD the Lamb of God, behold Him who taketh away the sins of the world.

LORD, I am not worthy that Thou shouldst enter under my roof: say but the word and my soul shall be healed.
Lord, I am not worthy that Thou shouldst enter under my roof: say but the word and my soul shall be healed.
Lord, I am not worthy that Thou shouldst enter under my roof: say but the word and my soul shall be healed.

MAY the Body of our Lord Jesus Christ preserve thy soul to life everlasting. Amen.

Thanksgiving

The King of Kings has come to be with us for a time.
While the Priest purifies the sacred vessels, we should make the most of His visit.
What will you ask Him? What would you like to tell Him?
If you are unsure of what to say, you may use the prayers at the back of this book.

In the age of Kings, courtiers would go to great lengths and pay hefty bribes to have a few moments alone with the king, so they could present their petitions to him in private.

How fortunate we are that the King has come to us! We should make the best use of the time we have with Him to lay our petitions before Him, and to thank Him for the many graces He has brought to our souls in the Eucharist. Cover your eyes so that you won't be distracted and imagine yourself seated with Jesus, just like in this picture. Tell Him how glad you are that He has come and ask for His help with any troubles you may have.

Once Communion has been distributed to the faithful, all of the crumbs—visible or not—are carefully gathered into the chalice, then the Priest purifies it with wine only.

Next, after purifying his fingers with wine and water, he separates them for the first time since the consecration.

When you receive Holy Communion, think of this: In the Eucharist, Jesus comes to be with us just as He did on that first Christmas. So in a way, every Mass is like Christmas Day!

"Therefore, if you be risen with Christ, seek the things that are above; where Christ is sitting at the right hand of God: Mind the things that are above, not the things that are upon the earth."

(Colossians 3:1-2)

Did you know?

The Priest must always drink from the same side when purifying the chalice to ensure that no trace of the sacred Blood is left on the rim. For this purpose, the chalice has a small cross engraved on its foot to mark this side.

ABLUTIONS

After Communion has been distributed,
the Priest replaces the Ciborium in the Tabernacle.
Then he purfies the chalice with wine, saying:

UOD ore súmpsimus, Dómine,
What by mouth we have received, Lord,

pura mente capiámus:
with pure mind may we possess:

et de múnere temporáli
and from gift temporal

fiat nobis remédium sempitérnum.
be it for us remedy eternal.

He takes the chalice and holds over it his fingers,
which until now have only been separated
to hold the Sacred Host, and the server pours
wine and water over them, while the Priest prays:

ORPUS tuum, Dómine,
Body Your, Lord,

quod sumpsi,
which I have received,

et Sanguis quem potávi,
and Blood which I have drunk,

adhaéreat viscéribus meis: et praesta,
may it adhere to insides my: and provide

ut in me non remáneat scélerum mácula,
that in me not may remain of sin stain,

quem pura et sancta
whom pure and holy

refecérunt sacraménta:
they have refreshed sacraments:

Qui vivis et regnas
Who lives and reigns

in saécula saeculórum. Amen.
unto ages of ages.

He dries his fingers and drinks the mixture,
then wipes his mouth and the chalice
with the purificator.

He then folds the corporal carefully
and places it back in the burse,
reassembling all the Sacred vessels
and linens under the veil,
as they were at the beginning of Mass,
in the center of the altar.

Meanwhile, the server has moved the Missal
from the Gospel side of the altar
and replaced it on the Epistle side.

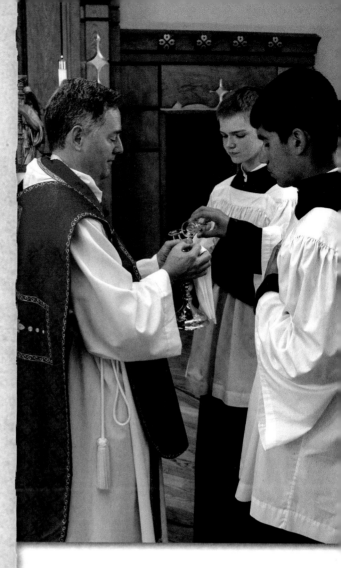

GRANT, O Lord, that what we have taken with our mouth, we may receive with a pure mind: and that from a temporal gift it may become for us an eternal remedy.

MAY Thy Body, O Lord, which I have received, and Thy Blood which I have drunk, cleave to my inmost parts, and grant that no stain of sin may remain in me, whom these pure and holy sacraments have refreshed. Who livest and reignest world without end. Amen.

ABIDE IN ME, AND I IN YOU

Christ remained with His disciples for 40 days before ascending into heaven, after which He sent them the Holy Spirit. Christ now remains with us for a time, and His Holy Spirit will abide in our hearts.

"If you love me, keep my commandments. And I will ask the Father, and He shall give you another Paraclete, that he may abide with you for ever. The spirit of truth, whom the world cannot receive, because it seeth him not, nor knoweth him: but you shall know him; because *he shall abide with you,* and shall be in you. I will not leave you orphans, I will come to you."

(John 14:15-18)

"And when Moses lifted up his hands, Israel overcame: but if he let them down a little, Amalec overcame." (Exodus 17:11)

Y ou may notice that the Priest's hands are lifted up as he prays the Postcommunion prayer. This is called the *Orans* position, after the Latin word for *praying,* and he uses this gesture *whenever he is interceding on our behalf.*

The origin of this gesture is found in the book of Exodus, when Moses lifted up his hands in prayer so that the Israelites might prevail in battle over the Amalekites.

This gesture is also a figure of Christ spreading his arms on the cross. Early Christian art often depicts Mary and other saints in this manner, to show their intercession for us.

Notice that the Communion Antiphon is the first of the propers to occur since before the beginning of the Canon. See the note at the bottom of p. 26 for an explanation of the wisdom in this.

The Communion Antiphon, like the Offertory Antiphon, is but a vestige of the Psalm or Canticle that was once sung during the distribution of Communion. See p. 67 for more about antiphons.

> The Priest greets us once more: "The Lord be with you." How especially meaningful this greeting is, now that we hold our Lord within the tabernacle of our hearts!

The Postcommunion prayer, as the name implies, is our prayer asking that God may grant us in abundance the fruits of the Sacrament we have just received. Each of us has spent some time privately welcoming our Lord since receiving Him, but this is our collective prayer of thanksgiving for the gift of Jesus' Body and Blood, on behalf of the whole Church.

Sometimes there is more than one Postcommunion prayer, depending on the feast being celebrated.

The Priest will now silently read the Communion Antiphon:

COMMUNION ANTIPHON

❀ SEE PROPER OF MASS FOR THE DAY. ❀

Benedícimus Déum caéli,
We bless   the God of heaven,

et coram ómnibus vivéntibus confitébimur éi:
and before   all   the living   we shall praise him:

quia fécit nobíscum misericórdiam súam.
for he has shown to us   mercy   his.

The Priest kisses the altar, then turns to the people, saying:

℣. Dóminus vobíscum.   **STAND**
Lord   (be) with you.

℞ Et cum spíritu tuo.
And with   spirit   your.

ORÉMUS:
Let us pray:

POST COMMUNION

❀ SEE PROPER OF MASS FOR THE DAY. ❀

Profíciat nobis ad salútem córporis et ánimae,
May it profit for us to salvation of body and of soul,

Dómine Deus noster,
Lord   God   our,

hujus sacraménti suscéptio:
of this   sacrament   reception:

et sempitérnae sanctae Trinitátis,
and   of eternal   holy   Trinity,

ejusdémque indivíduae unitátis conféssio.
and of the same   indivisible   unity   confession.

Per Dóminum nostrum Jesum Christum,
Through Lord   our   Jesus   Christ,

Fílium tuum, qui tecum vivit et regnat
Son   your, who with you lives and reigns

in unitáte Spíritus Sancti, Deus...
in the unity   of Spirit   Holy,   God...

When he has finished the prayer(s),
he speaks the closing in a clear voice:

℣. ...Per ómnia sǽcula saeculórum.
...for   every   ages   of ages.

℞ Amen.

COMMUNION ANTIPHON

❀ SEE PROPER OF MASS FOR THE DAY. ❀

We bless the God of heaven, and before all the living we will praise Him: because He has shown His mercy to us.

℣. The Lord be with you.
℞ And with thy spirit.

Let us Pray:

POST COMMUNION

❀ SEE PROPER OF MASS FOR THE DAY. ❀

May the reception of this sacrament, O Lord our God, and the confession of the holy and eternal Trinity and of its undivided unity, profit us to the salvation of body and soul. Through our Lord Jesus Christ, Thy Son, Who liveth and reigneth with Thee in the unity of the Holy Spirit, God...

℣. ...world without end.
℞ Amen.

Sent Forth into the World

"You are the light of the world...So let your light shine before men, that they may see your good works, and glorify your Father who is in heaven." (Matthew 5: 14-16)

If we have been dismissed, why don't we leave right away?

Up until the twelfth century, this was actually where the Mass ended—in fact, the prayer which follows the dismissal, *Placeat Tibi*, used to be known as the "Prayer after Mass" because it was said privately by the Priest after Mass.

But we must not leave and forget that we are now carrying the light of Christ inside us. Therefore we will receive one more final blessing and instruction to remind us of our commission as Catholics to bring this light to the world.

"And he led them out as far as Bethania: and lifting up his hands, he blessed them. And it came to pass, whilst he blessed them, he departed from them, and was carried up to heaven." (Luke 24:50-51)

Did you know?

Ite, Missa est was a formal pronouncement used by the Romans to dismiss public assemblies. Later, when the Holy Sacrifice celebrated in remembrance of Christ's last supper came to be called the *Missa*, this dismissal came to have a double meaning.

Why don't we say *Ite, Missa est* during Lent and Advent, or in Masses for the Dead? Because it is a dismissal—a joyful one—but during these seasons of penitence, it is good to remain a while in prayer or meditation.

We have become living monstrances, carrying the light of Christ inside us. Before we bring this light to the world, we kneel to receive one last blessing, as the knights of old would receive their shields before being sent into battle.

Because Requiem Masses are for the dead, not for the living, this Benediction is not said, and is replaced instead with a prayer for the Dead, known as the *Lux Aeterna*.

The Dismissal

The Priest kisses the altar, turns to the people and says:

℣. Dóminus vobíscum.
Lord   (be) with you.

℟. Et cum spíritu tuo.
And with   spirit   your.

℣. Ite, missa est.
Go,   the dismissal it is.

℟. Deo grátias.
To God thanks.

> *Or in Masses where the Gloria is not said:*
>
> ℣. Benedicámus Dómino.
> *Let us bless   the Lord.*
>
> ℟. Deo grátias.
> *To God thanks.*
>
> *Or in Masses for the Dead:*
>
> ℣. Requiéscant in pace.
> *May they rest   in peace,*
>
> ℟. Amen.

Bowing before the altar, and placing his joined hands upon it,
the Priest silently prays:

 LACEAT tibi, sancta Trínitas,   **Kneel**
Be it pleasing to You, holy   Trinity,

obséquium servitútis meae:
the performance of homage   my:

et praesta; ut sacrifícium,
and grant;   that the sacrifice

quod óculis tuae Majestátis indígnus óbtuli,
which in the eyes of Your majesty   unworthy I have offered,

tibi sit acceptábile,
to You be it acceptable,

mihíque, et ómnibus, pro quibus illud óbtuli,
both for me, and for all   for   whom   that   I offered,

sit, te miseránte, propitiábile.
be it, by Your mercy,   propitious.

Per Christum Dóminum nostrum. Amen.
Through Christ   Lord   our.

Benediction

The Priest kisses the altar, extends, raises, then joins his hands,
bowing to the cross, and says:

Benedicat vos omnípotens Deus,
May He bless you   almighty   God,

> *(now turning toward the people, he continues,*
> *blessing them with the sign of the cross:)*

Pater et Filíus ✠, et Spíritus Sanctus.
Father, and Son,   and Spirit   Holy.

℟. Amen.

Then he goes to the Gospel side of the altar for the Last Gospel.

Last Gospel   **Stand**

℣. Dóminus vobíscum.
Lord   (be) with you.

℟. Et cum spíritu tuo.
And with   spirit   your.

> *Making the sign of the cross first upon the altar,*
> *then on his forehead, lips and breast, he says:*

℣. ✠ Inítium sancti Evangélii secúndum Joánnem.
Beginning of holy Gospel   according to   John.

℟. Glória tibi, Dómine.
Glory to You, Lord.

℣. The Lord be with you.
℟. And with thy spirit.

℣. Go, you are dismissed.
℟. Thanks be to God.

> ℣. Let us bless the Lord.
> ℟. Thanks be to God.
>
> ℣. May they rest in peace,
> ℟. Amen.

MAY the homage of my bounden duty be pleasing to Thee, O holy Trinity; and grant that the sacrifice which I, though unworthy, have offered in the sight of Thy majesty may be acceptable to Thee, and through Thy mercy be a propitiation for me and for all those for whom I have offered it. Through Christ our Lord. Amen.

May almighty God bless you, the Father, ✠ the Son and the Holy Spirit,
℟. Amen.

℣. The Lord be with you.
℟. And with thy spirit.

℣. The beginning of the holy Gospel according to John.
℟. Glory be to Thee, O Lord.

AND DWELT AMONG US

At the beginning of Mass, we prayed: *"Send forth, O Lord, Thy Light and Thy Truth!"* How fitting, then, that it should end with the words: *"...and we saw His glory, the glory as of the only-begotten of the Father, full of grace and truth."*

WE'VE BEEN DISMISSED, BLESSED, AND SENT FORTH... WHY ARE WE READING THIS GOSPEL NOW?

This custom originated in the Middle Ages. The faithful would sometimes ask the Priest to read a Gospel over them as a form of blessing, because the Gospel is the Word of God himself. The beginning of John's Gospel was a natural favorite, being a poetic summation of our creation and salvation, all brought about by God's immense love for us. It reminds us once more that the "true light which enlighteneth every man" is now living inside us.

Over time, it became customary for the Priest to begin reciting it at the altar at the end of Mass, and to continue from memory as he processed out of the Sanctuary. This eventually extended to reading the entire Gospel at the altar, and in 1570, Pope Pius V officially added it as part of the Mass.

"*...He came unto his own, and his own received him not.*"

Once St. Philip Neri observed a man leaving the church immediately after communion. He quickly sent two altar boys with lighted candles to accompany him. When asked why he had done this, he explained that when carrying the Blessed Sacrament outside the church, it is always accompanied with this much honor at the very least.

HIGH MASS OR SOLEMN HIGH MASS IS NOW ENDED.
LOW MASS CONTINUES WITH PRAYERS AT THE FOOT OF THE ALTAR.

"After Mass, one should not omit to make thanksgiving... The time that follows Mass is a time for amassing treasures of grace."
—St. Alphonsus Liguori

There is no greater worship, praise or thanksgiving we can offer to God than the sacrifice of His own beloved Son that is offered at every Mass. Whenever we are blessed to have assisted in this perfect worship of the Mass, we should not leave without offering our own prayers of thanksgiving for this immense gift.

A pious practice instituted by St. Gertrude is to say the following at this point:
"I thank and bless Thee, O good Jesus, that for love of me Thou didst deign to be made man."

At High Mass, a hymn may now be sung.

IN PRINCÍPIO erat Verbum,
In the beginning was the Word,

et Verbum erat apud Deum,
and the Word was with God,

et Deus erat Verbum.
and God was the Word.

Hoc erat in princípio apud Deum.
The same was in the beginning with God.

Omnia per ipsum facta sunt:
All things through Him made were:

et sine ipso factum est nihil, quod factum est:
and without Him made was nothing, that made was:

in ipso vita erat, et vita erat lux hóminum:
in Him life was, and life was light of men:

et lux in ténebris lucet,
and light in darkness shines,

et ténebrae eam non comprehendérunt.
and darkness it not comprehended.

Fuit homo missus a Deo,
There was man sent from God,

cui nomen erat Joánnes.
whose name was John.

Hic venit in testimónium,
This one came in testimony,

ut testimónium perhibéret de lúmine,
that testimony he might give of light,

ut omnes créderent per illum. Non erat ille lux,
that all might believe through him. Not was he light,

sed ut testimónium perhibéret de lúmine.
but that testimony he might give of light.

Erat lux vera, quae illúminat
This was light true, which illuminates

omnem hóminem veniéntem in hunc mundum.
all men coming into this world.

In mundo erat, et mundus per ipsum factus est,
In the world He was, and the world through Him made was,

et mundus eum non cognóvit.
and the world Him not it knew.

In própria venit, et sui eum non recepérunt.
Into his own He came and his Him not they received.

Quotquot autem recepérunt eum,
However many also received Him,

dedit eis potestátem fílios Dei fíeri,
He gave to them power sons of God to become,

his, qui credunt in nómine ejus:
those, who believe in name His:

qui non ex sanguínibus,
who not from blood,

neque ex voluntáte carnis,
neither from the will of flesh,

neque ex voluntáte viri, sed ex Deo nati sunt.
nor from the will of men, but from God born they were.

(here all genuflect:)

ET VERBUM CARO FACTUM EST,
And the Word flesh made was,

et habitávit in nobis:
and dwelt among us:

et vídimus glóriam ejus,
and we saw glory His,

glóriam quasi Unigéniti a Patre,
glory as it were only-begotten from the Father,

plenum grátiae et veritátis.
full of grace and truth.

℞ Deo gratias.
To God thanks.

In the beginning was the Word,
and the Word was with God,
and the Word was God.
The same was in the beginning with God.
All things were made by Him,
and without Him was made nothing that was made.
In Him was life, and the life was the light of men:
and the light shineth in darkness,
and the darkness did not comprehend it.
There was a man sent from God,
whose name was John.
This man came for a witness,
to bear witness of the light,
that all men through Him might believe.
He was not the light, but was to bear witness of the light.
That was the true light, which enlighteneth
every man that cometh into this world.
He was in the world, and the world was made by Him,
and the world knew Him not.
He came unto His own, and His own received Him not.
But as many as received Him,
to them gave He power to become the sons of God:
to them that believe in His name:
who were born, not of blood, nor of the will of the flesh,
nor of the will of man, but of God.
AND THE WORD WAS MADE FLESH, and dwelt among us:
and we saw His glory,
the glory as of the only-begotten of the Father,
full of grace and truth.
℞ Thanks be to God.

SPECIAL PETITIONS OF THE CHURCH

These prayers, said only after Low Mass, collect our prayers in a special way toward the intentions of our Holy Mother Church.

At various times throughout history, the Church has endured persecution. During these periods of trial, the Church has added special prayers of petition at the end of Mass.

The first of these was instituted by **Pius IX** during the occupation of Rome by the Italian Army as part of its campaign for unification. He feared that the loss of his temporal power would lead to a loss of freedom of worship for Catholics, as it had during the French Revolution. Therefore he asked that one *Our Father* and one *Hail Mary* be said after Mass for an end to the occupation and the restoration of the Papal States.

His successor, **Leo XIII**, added to these prayers during further persecutions brought about by the secular humanism that was sweeping Europe. In 1884 he added the *Salve Regina*, asking for the help of the '*woman whose foot shall crush the serpent's head*' from Genesis 3:15. Then in 1886 he added the prayer to St. Michael, whose task was to cast Satan and his angels into hell (Apoc.12:9).

The final invocation to the Sacred Heart was added by **Pius X** in 1904, and later **Pius XI** added the prayer for the '*conversion of sinners and for the liberty and exaltation of holy mother Church*.' He asked that these prayers be said for the intention of the conversion of the '*godless communists*' of Russia, who strove to stamp out all faith in that country. We still pray these prayers for this same intention.

LOW MASS IS NOW ENDED.

Please remember that as long as the sanctuary lamp remains lit, our Lord is present in the tabernacle, and we should maintain due reverence.
Wait until you have left the sanctuary to visit with your fellow Massgoers.

DID YOU KNOW?

In response to growing unbelief and heterodoxy in the nineteenth century, Pope Pius IX issued the encyclical *Quanta Cura* in 1864, which contained a *Syllabus of Errors*—ideas which had taken hold due to the secular humanism of the age, but which were contrary to the teaching of the Church. Some of these erroneous beliefs still hold sway today, even among Catholics. Check out this *Syllabus* sometime and see where you stand!

"All ye works of the Lord, bless the Lord: praise and exalt him above all for ever."

(Daniel 3:57)

When he has completed these prayers, the Priest ascends to the altar once more to retrieve the sacred vessels. Genuflecting at the foot of the altar, he recites the *Canticle of the Three Young Men* from the Book of Daniel (also known as the *Trium Puerorum* or the *Benedicite*) as he returns to the sacristy. ***We stand out of respect for him as he leaves the church.***

 At Low Mass, a hymn may now be sung.

PRAYERS AFTER LOW MASS

After Low Mass, the Priest, kneeling at the altar steps, says with the people the prayers which follow:

These prayers after Low Mass are typically recited in the vernacular. We have provided the Latin for those who are interested and for those parishes that prefer it.

Ave Maria, grátia plena, Dóminus tecum;
benedícta tu in muliéribus,
et benedíctus fructus ventris tui, Jesus.
Sancta María, Mater Dei, ora pro nobis peccatóribus,
nunc et in hora mortis nostrae. Amen.
(*repeat three times*)

Salve Regína, Mater misericórdiae;
vita, dulcédo et spes nostra, salve.
Ad te clamámus, éxsules fílii Evae.
Ad te suspirámus geméntes et flentes
in hac lacrimárum valle.
Eia ergo, advocáta nostra,
illos tuos misericórdes óculos ad nos convérte.
Et Jesum, benedíctum fructum ventris tui,
nobis, post hoc exsílium, osténde.
O clemens, o pia, o dulcis Virgo María

℣. Ora pro nobis, sancta Dei Génitrix.
℟. Ut digni efficiámur promissiónibus Christi.

ORÉMUS:

Deus, refúgium nostrum et virtus,
pópulum ad te clamántem propítius réspice;
et intercedénte gloriósa et immaculáta
Virgine Dei Genitríce María,
cum beáto Joseph, ejus Sponso,
ac beátis Apóstolis tuis Petro et Paulo,
et ómnibus Sanctis,
quas pro conversióne peccatórum,
pro libertáte et exaltatióne sanctae Matris Ecclésiae,
preces effúndimus, miséricors et benígnus exáudi.
Per eúmdem Christum Dóminum nostrum.
℟. Amen.

Sancte Míchael Archángele, defénde nos in proélio;
contra nequítiam et insídias diáboli esto praesídium. Imperet illi Deus, súpplices deprecámur:
tuque, Princeps milítiae caeléstis,
Sátanam aliósque spíritus malígnos,
qui ad perditiónem animárum
pervagántur in mundo,
divína virtúte in inférnum detrúde. Amen.

℣. Cor Jesu sacratissimum,
℟. Miserere nobis.
(*repeat three times*)

Hail Mary, full of grace, the Lord is with thee. Blessed art thou amongst women, and blessed is the fruit of thy womb, Jesus. Holy Mary, Mother of God, pray for us sinners, now, and at the hour of our death. Amen.
(*repeat three times*)

Hail, holy Queen, Mother of mercy, our life, our sweetness, and our hope!
To thee do we cry, poor banished children of Eve.
To thee do we send up our sighs, mourning and weeping in this valley of tears.
Turn then, most gracious Advocate, thine eyes of mercy towards us,
And after this our exile show unto us the blessed fruit of thy womb, Jesus.
O clement, O loving, O sweet Virgin Mary.

℣. Pray for us, O holy Mother of God.
℟. That we may be made worthy of the promises of Christ.

LET US PRAY:

O God, our refuge and our strength, look down with favor upon Thy people who cry to Thee; and through the intercession of the glorious and immaculate Virgin Mary, Mother of God, of her spouse, blessed Joseph, of Thy holy apostles, Peter and Paul, and all the saints, mercifully and graciously hear the prayers which we pour forth to Thee for the conversion of sinners and for the liberty and exaltation of holy mother Church.
Through the same Christ our Lord.
℟. Amen.

St. Michael, the archangel, defend us in battle. Be our protection against the wickedness and snares of the devil. May God rebuke him, we humbly pray. And do thou, O prince of the heavenly host, by the divine power thrust into hell Satan and all the other evil spirits who wander through the world seeking the ruin of souls. Amen.

℣. Most Sacred Heart of Jesus.
℟. Have mercy on us!
(*repeat three times*)

A COMMON ANCESTOR: THE DIVINE OFFICE

In order to understand the elements of the Mass in the context of their history and meaning, it is helpful to examine its close cousin, the Divine Office. Because both forms of prayer originated in the practice of the Jewish Synagogue, the two have many similarities and one can help us understand the other better.

The custom of praying at specific times of the day is said to have begun with Abraham, and was developed into the ceremonies of the Temple and Synagogue by Moses and the Prophets. Devout Jews would meet in the synagogues, in groups of at least ten men called *batlanim*, to chant aloud the Psalms and readings from the Law and the Prophets, and to receive instruction from their leader, the Rabbi. Jesus and His Apostles followed this practice, as we know from scripture:

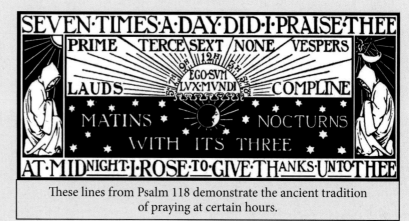

SEVEN·TIMES·A·DAY·DID·I·PRAISE·THEE
PRIME TERCE SEXT NONE VESPERS
EGO·SVM
LAUDS LVX·MVNDI COMPLINE
MATINS NOCTURNS
WITH ITS THREE
AT·MIDNIGHT·I·ROSE·TO·GIVE·THANKS·UNTO·THEE

These lines from Psalm 118 demonstrate the ancient tradition of praying at certain hours.

"And they entered into Capharnaum, and forthwith upon the sabbath days going into the synagogue, he taught them."
(Mk 1:21)

"Peter went up to the higher parts of the house to pray, about **the sixth hour.**"
(Acts 10:9)

"Now Peter and John went up into the temple at the **ninth hour of prayer.**"
(Acts 3:1)

After Christ's death, the Apostles continued to follow the custom of praying in the Synagogue; however, as the infant Church came under persecution from other Jews, it became necessary to form their own gatherings. These **synaxes** convened on Saturday evening and would include the traditional psalm prayers and readings but would then culminate in the celebration of the Eucharist at dawn on Sunday, in remembrance of Christ's resurrection at first light on Sunday. We have a description of one of these synaxes in the Acts of the Apostles:

"And on the first day of the week, when we were assembled to break bread, Paul discoursed with them, being to depart on the morrow: and he continued his speech until midnight... Then going up, and breaking bread and tasting, and having talked a long time to them, until daylight, so he departed."
(Acts 20:7, 11)

As Christian congregations grew, these all-night gatherings became impractical and thus the synaxis was broken up into two separate liturgies: the Mass of the Catechumens (when combined with the Eucharist) and an early Divine Office consisting of Vespers (prayed at sundown), Vigils (prayed during the night) and Matins (prayed at dawn).

64

THE CANONICAL HOURS

By the third century, Christian writings frequently mention the custom of daily prayer,
but it was the growth of Monasticism that helped refine its structure and practices.
By the end of the sixth century, the Divine Office as we know it had been fully established.

The writings of Tertullian (160-220 AD) confirm that the ancient custom of praying at certain hours had continued in the Christian community:

"As regards the time, there should be no lax observation of certain hours—I mean of those common hours which have long marked the divisions of the day, **the third, the sixth, and the ninth,** *and which we may observe in Scripture to be more solemn than the rest"*

("De Oratione," xxiii, xxv, in P.L., I, 1191-3).

The hours of prayer were counted as shown by the Roman numerals in this diagram: sunup was counted as the first hour of the day and sunset the twelfth. And just as each hour shown here corresponds to an episode in Christ's Passion, likewise each hour of prayer has its own specific theme and relative importance, lending an order to our time as we pass each day.

MATINS

Matins is considered the most important of the hours, as its solemn nocturnal prayers formed the bulk of the Synaxis Vigils. It is composed of three nocturns, corresponding to the watches of the night, and it is recited prior to dawn, often immediately followed by Lauds.

LAUDS

Lauds derives its name from the word *laudate*, meaning *praise*: an oft-repeated word in its selection of Psalms, and this hour's theme. Recited at dawn, it formed the very end of the Synaxis Vigils. It celebrates the coming of light into the world, and devotes our first thoughts of the day to God.

The four "Little Hours" below are all nearly identical in length, structure, and their use of portions of Psalm 118.

PRIME

This first hour was one of the last to be added. It forms a bridge between Lauds at dawn and the beginning of the day's work. Thus its theme is the consecration of that work to God.

TERCE

The third hour saw our Lord condemned by Pilate. It was also at this hour that the Holy Spirit descended upon the Apostles, and thus it features the Third Person of the Trinity.

SEXT

The sixth hour, noon, is one of culmination. At this hour Adam and Eve ate of the forbidden fruit, the three angels visited Abraham, and Christ was nailed to the Cross.

NONE

The ninth hour was the closing of the work day, and is held to be the hour at which Adam and Eve were cast out of Paradise, as well as the hour when Christ died on the cross.

VESPERS

Vespers are recited "at the lighting of the lamps;" hence it was originally called *Lucernalia*, the Office of Lights. It once formed the beginning of the Synaxis Vigils. As Lauds consecrates the beginning of day, so Vespers consecrates its ending, and both hours have a similar structure and solemnity.

COMPLINE

Compline derives its name from the Latin *completorium*, forming as it does the completion of the hours and of the day. Its theme is one of committing ourselves to God's care as we go to our rest. It includes an examination of conscience and the praying of the *Confiteor*.

THE STRUCTURE OF THE DIVINE OFFICE

The basic elements that make up both the Mass and the Divine Office
can be classified into one of the following forms:

PSALMS
AND
CANTICLES

HYMNS
❊
ANTIPHONS

LESSONS
FROM
SCRIPTURE

PRAYERS
❊
RESPONSORIES

The word *officium* means duty, and the recitation of this Official Prayer of the Church is indeed the duty of all priests and most religious throughout the world. The roots of this ancient liturgy lie within the Psalms of David, which were the preferred method of divine praise for roughly a millenium before Christ's birth. In the Synagogues, devout Jews would gather to chant the entire cycle of 150 Psalms each week, along with readings from the Law and the Prophets. The structure and methods they used were carried on by the Apostles and eventually gave birth to the Liturgy of the Divine Office. The main parts of this Liturgy are as follows:

PSALMS AND CANTICLES

These songs of praise form the backbone and the most ancient element of the Divine Office. They are arranged into a weeklong schedule called a **Psalter** so that over the course of the week, all 150 of the Psalms and all 10 Scriptural Canticles are recited.

LESSONS FROM SCRIPTURE

The Lessons found in the Divine Office are taken from the Old Testament, the Acts of the Saints, and the writings of the Church Fathers. The custom of interspersing these lessons with the praise of the Psalms has its origins in the ancient practices of the Synagogue.

HYMNS

Hymns are songs of praise that imitate the Psalms. There is a proper hymn for each of the hours, as well as for most major feasts.

PRAYERS

Prayers may use poetic language like Psalms or Hymns, but they are intended as direct invocations of petition, praise or thanksgiving.

ANTIPHONS

Usually derived from the Psalms or from Scripture, Antiphons involve not merely a *type* of prayer or praise, but rather a *method*.

RESPONSORIES

This method of prayer involves two persons or groups, one responding to the other. See the next page for more about responsories.

A COMMON METHOD OF PRAYER

Some of the elements that make up both the Mass and the Divine Office
are distinguished not by their *content* but the *method* by which they are prayed.

The **Antiphon** and the **Responsory** are a common feature in the Mass and the Divine Office. Both describe a specific *method* of prayer in which two persons or groups alternate in singing or chanting. A study of each of these methods as found in the Divine Office can help shed some light on their use in the Mass.

Antiphonal singing was the traditional way of chanting the Psalms in the Synagogue. The simplest way to explain how Antiphonal psalmody works in the Divine Office is by looking at the following diagram:

> **ANTIPHON**
> ⇩
> **PSALM OR PART OF A PSALM (OR A CANTICLE)**
> ⇩
> **DOXOLOGY**
> ⇩
> **ANTIPHON**

Shown here, an **Antiphon** is a brief verse that serves as a sort of theme. It is typically derived from a Psalm or from Scripture. When a Psalm is sung antiphonally, the antiphon acts as a sort of bookend, being intoned at the beginning and repeated at the end. Then each line or verse of the Psalm to be sung is divided into two parts: the first is intoned by a cantor or by the first choir, and the second choir (or the congregation) answers. A **Doxology** (usually the *Glory be*—see page 10) then serves to bring the Psalm to a suitable close before the Antiphon is repeated once more.

At one time, all of the Psalms used in the Mass were sung antiphonally in this manner. There are a few places in the Mass where this form is preserved, most notably in the *Asperges Me* on page 1, and the *Judica Me* on page 3. However, in many places this form has been truncated, as in the *Introit*, where only a fragment of the original Psalm is recited along with its doxology and antiphons, or in the Offertory and Communion Antiphons, where no psalm is recited at all—only the Antiphon itself.

Responsories are a type of prayer that can be composed from a psalm, canticle or other sacred text; what sets them apart is how they are sung. The Priest or cantor will **intone a versicle** (or verse) and the choir or congregation will **respond with a refrain.** You can see these pairings, also called **preces**, throughout the Mass, denoted by the red ℣. and ℟. These can be as simple as the salutation:

℣. Dóminus vobíscum
    Lord   (be) with you.

℟. Et cum spíritu tuo.
    And with   spirit   your.

Or they can be like this responsory from Prime:

℣. Christe fili Dei vivi, miserere nobis.
    Christ   son of God living,   have mercy   on us.

℟. Christe fili Dei vivi, miserere nobis.
    Christ   son of God living,   have mercy   on us.

℣. Qui sedes ad dexteram Patris.
    Who   sits   at   the right   of the Father.

℟. Miserere nobis.
    Have mercy   on us.

℣. Gloria Patri, et Filio, et Spiritui Sancto.
    Glory to Father, and to Son, and to Spirit   Holy.

℟. Christe fili Dei vivi, miserere nobis.
    Christ   son of God living,   have mercy   on us.

THE CATHOLIC BIBLE

The Scriptures used in the Latin Mass differ from other English Bibles not only in translation,
but in the naming and numbering of chapters and verses, especially in the Book of Psalms.
This timeline is designed to help explain why.

The Tanakh
(c. 13th-3rd century BC)

The Hebrew *Tanakh* is roughly equivalent to what we know as the Old Testament. The name itself is an acronym descriptive of its contents: the *Torah* (books of Moses) the *Nevi'im* (books of the prophets) and the *Ketuvim* (psalms and chronicles).

The Septuagint or LXX
(3rd-2nd century BC)

Ptolemy II of Egypt commissioned 72 of the finest Jewish scholars (six from each of the twelve tribes of Israel) to translate the Ancient Hebrew *Tanakh* into Greek for inclusion in the library at Alexandria. Their work became known as the *versio septuaginta interpretum*—that is, "translation of the seventy interpreters" or **Septuagint** for short. Because it is the first, and thus oldest, translation—predating Christianity by nearly two centuries—it is commonly held to be the most reliable and authoritative of ancient texts.

The Hexapla *(circa 231-260 AD)*

A work of immense scholarship by Origen, the Hexapla sought to create a critically amended version of the Septuagint by comparing it against other Greek translations of the Old Testament, as well as the original Hebrew, in six side-by-side columns. ***St. Jerome used Origen's text heavily in the creation of the Vulgate;*** however, the original manuscript disappeared at the beginning of the 7th century, and only fragments of copies survive today.

The Vetus Itala or "Old Latin"
(Prior to 382 AD)

The Vetus Itala was the most well-known complete translation of the Bible in Latin prior to the third century, but it was only one among many. Variations among these versions compelled Pope Damasus I in 382 AD to commission St. Jerome to create an official Latin translation of the Gospels.

Jerome and the Latin Vulgate *(382-405 AD)*

After being commissioned by Pope Damasus I to revise the Latin Gospels, St. Jerome came to realize the need for a standard Latin version of the whole Bible. Over the next several decades, he compared Hebrew texts with the Septuagint, as well as the Hexapla of Origen, to faithfully translate nearly all of the Old Testament into Latin. Though it took several centuries to supplant the *Vetus Itala*, Jerome's work was eventually acknowledged to be far superior and in time became known as the "Vulgate," indicating its common use.

The Masoretic Text *(prior to 1525)*

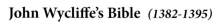

The Masoretes were Jewish scribes and scholars whose job was to preserve and copy faithfully the ancient Hebrew scriptures. They tended to view the Septuagint with suspicion due to its use by Christians, despite its age and careful preparation by Jewish scholars. As a result, ***other manuscripts were often preferred in the compilations of the Masoretes, which sometimes differed from the much older Septuagint,*** particularly in the numbering of the Psalms and the canon of books included. For their base text, the translators of the King James Version used a Masoretic text produced in Venice in 1524-25.

John Wycliffe's Bible *(1382-1395)*

Violent anti-clerical sentiment in 14th century England led John Wycliffe to reject the authority of the Church and rely exclusively on the teachings of the Bible. He and his followers, called Lollards, translated the Vulgate into English and preached throughout the countryside. He was declared a heretic in 1415 and the English bishops suppressed his Bible, requiring any new translations to be first approved by ecclesiastical authority.

Martin Luther's Bible *(1522-1534)*

Martin Luther's rejection of Church teaching led him to accept Scripture alone as a source of divine revelation. Therefore he sought to create a Bible for the common man, using vernacular German. Seeking to avoid the Catholic Vulgate and having no access to original manuscripts, Luther consulted recently printed copies of the Septuagint and the Hebrew Masoretic Text. Though his bible was unprecedented in its popularity and influence, ***it is universally noted that his translation contained significant bias based on his beliefs.***

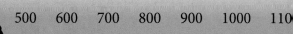

1000 500 250 100 BC | AD 100 200 300 400 500 600 700 800 900 1000 110

William Tyndale's Bible *(1525-1536)*

Inspired by Luther's German Bible, Tyndale sought the permission of the Bishop of London to create an English translation, but it was denied. Undaunted, he fled to the continent, where he printed a version of the New Testament and parts of the Old Testament. *These translations were condemned in England, particularly by St. Thomas More, who pointed out that many terms had been mistranslated in favor of anti-clerical views.* In addition, his work included many of the heterodox commentaries from Luther's Bible. Condemned as a heretic, Tyndale was put to death, but his translation nevertheless laid the groundwork for subsequent English Bibles.

The Great Bible *(1538)*

Just two years after Tyndale's death, King Henry VIII's first authorized English translation was published under the supervision of Thomas Cromwell. As a staunch supporter of Tyndale, Myles Coverdale produced this volume by amending Tyndale's Bible, using the Vulgate and Luther's German editions.

The Geneva Bible *(1560)*

Many Protestants fled to Geneva during the reign of the Catholic Queen Mary, where they created the very first "Study Bible" with copious notes that were stridently Puritanical. Due to advances in printing, it was mass produced at a reasonable cost and thus became very popular. In fact, John Knox's involvement with its production led the Scots to require every household of sufficient means to own a copy.

The Bishop's Bible *(1568)*

The English Bishops under Elizabeth I were dissatisfied with the Great Bible, due to its translation from the Vulgate, yet the Geneva Bible was far too Calvinistic. They collaborated to create their own version, but its size and cost were prohibitive, leaving most people to continue in using the much more compact and affordable Geneva edition.

The Clementine Revision of the Vulgate *(1560-1592)*

Pope Paul III convened the Council of Trent in 1545 to combat the errors of the Protestant Reformation. *It was here that St. Jerome's Vulgate was declared to be the authoritative version of the Bible.* At the same time, the Church Fathers saw the importance of creating a standardized version of the Vulgate, as it had suffered from the errors of copyists over its many centuries of life. *Many years were spent in carefully tracking down the oldest possible codices and comparing them with contemporary Masoretic texts in order to carefully reconstruct the text as St. Jerome wrote it.* This revision of the Vulgate was issued in its final form in 1592, during the reign of Clement VIII.

The Rheims New Testament *(1582)* and the Douay Old Testament *(1609-10)*

Dismayed by the proliferation of Protestant Bibles and their biased translations, the English Catholic Church in exile sought to provide a translation that was safe for the faithful to use. *Not trusting the purity of modern Greek and Hebrew manuscripts, they relied solely on the Clementine reconstruction of Jerome's Vulgate, since it had been carefully translated from ancient originals that no longer existed.* Countless notes were also included to clarify the Church's traditional interpretation of difficult passages. The focus on accuracy led the translators to be slavish to the Latin, resulting in a text that was at times almost unreadable. *A notable feature of the Douay-Rheims is that even the Latinate names found in the Vulgate (i.e. Noe, Isaias and Esdras) were retained, rather than Anglicizing them.*

The King James Version *(1604-1611)*

By 1604, the various English translations of the Bible were still failing to meet the needs of the Church of England, so James I proposed a new version. Using the Bishop's Bible as their framework, the 54 translators compared its text against numerous other versions (including both the erroneous Tyndale and the Catholic Douay-Rheims). They then checked their work against currently available Greek and Masoretic texts. *Where these modern versions departed from the Vulgate (which was based on much more ancient manuscripts), the non-Catholic version was preferred, sometimes resulting in significant changes, including the canon of books.* While the final product is considered a pinnacle of literary achievement, sadly, it was still plagued by incorrect doctrine. Even so, this Authorized Version became the standard upon which most English Bibles have since then been based.

Challoner's Revision of the Douay-Rheims *(1749-52)*

The awkwardness of the translation found in the Douay-Rheims Bible had not endeared it to English ears, and its scarcity ensured that many Catholics were still reading Protestant Bibles. Bishop Richard Challoner set out to remedy this by revising the original text and bringing its language more in line with the King James Version. He also removed many of the extensive notes so that it could be printed as a compact, one-volume edition. *Challoner's version is the Catholic Church's officially approved English Bible.* Though this version is not as easy to read as more modern, less literal translations, *we can rest assured that it is free from any doctrinal errors.*

DIFFERENCES FOUND IN THE DOUAY-RHEIMS BIBLE

Most Catholics are accustomed to the Anglicized names and standardized numbering used in today's Bibles. The Douay-Rheims, however, uses the Latinized names from the Vulgate and the numbering of the Septuagint. Here are some of the differences you may expect to find:

This book of the Bible...	...is known as:
Joshua	Josue
1 Samuel	1 Kings
2 Samuel	2 Kings
1 Kings	3 Kings
2 Kings	4 Kings
1 Chronicles	1 Paralipomenon
2 Chronicles	2 Paralipomenon
Ezra	1 Esdras
Nehemiah	2 Esdras
Tobit	Tobias
Song of Songs	Canticle of Canticles
Sirach	Ecclesiasticus
Isaiah	Isaias
Jeremiah	Jeremias
Ezekiel	Ezechiel
Hosea	Osee
Obadiah	Abdias
Jonah	Jonas
Micah	Micheas
Habakkuk	Habacuc
Zephaniah	Sophonias
Haggai	Aggeus
Zachariah	Zacharias
Malachi	Malachias
Maccabees	Machabees
Revelation	Apocalypse

Besides these variations in the names of the books of the Douay-Rheims Bible, you will notice that these common names are also different:

Noah	→	**Noe**
Shem	→	**Sem**
Ham	→	**Cham**
Eli	→	**Heli**
Elijah	→	**Elias**
Elisha	→	**Eliseus**
Shadrach	→	**Sidrach**
Meschach	→	**Misach**
Abednego	→	**Abdenago**

The numbering of the Psalms in the Douay-Rheims comes from the Septuagint, while most modern Bibles take their numbering from the King James Version, a system based on that found in the 16th century Masoretic text. The differences in the two numbering schemes are as follows:

Modern Bibles:	Douay-Rheims Bible:
1-8	same
9 & 10	combined as Psalm 9
11-113	10-112
114-115	combined as Psalm 113
116	divided into Psalms 114 and 115
117-146	116-145
147	divided into Psalms 146 and 147
148-150	same

TRINITARIAN FORMULAE

The prayers used in the Mass and the Divine Office have endings intended to present our petitions in Christ's name. These formulae are nearly identical, but have slight variations that depend upon whom the prayer is addressed to. The most common version is listed first below, and its translation can be found at the bottom of p.11. These are the main variations, with their differences highlighted in bold letters:

When addressed to God the Father:	...and Christ is mentioned at the beginning:	...and Christ is mentioned at the end:	...and the Holy Ghost is mentioned:	When addressed to God the Son:	Simpler version used for less solemn prayers:
Per Dominum nostrum Jesum Christum, Filium tuum: Qui tecum vivit et regnat in unitate Spiritus Sancti Deus: per omnia saecula saeculorum.	Per **eumdem** (the same) Dominum nostrum Jesum Christum, Filium tuum: Qui tecum vivit et regnat in unitate Spiritus Sancti Deus: per omnia saecula saeculorum.	(here we drop the beginning and go straight to...) Qui tecum vivit et regnat in unitate Spiritus Sancti Deus: per omnia saecula saeculorum.	Per Dominum nostrum Jesum Christum, Filium tuum: Qui tecum vivit et regnat in unitate **eiusdem** (the same) Spiritus Sancti Deus: per omnia saecula saeculorum.	Qui **vivis et regnas** (this is the second person form of these verbs) **cum Deo Patre** (with God the Father) in unitate Spiritus Sancti Deus: per omnia saecula saeculorum.	Per Christum Dominum nostrum.

GLOSSARY AND SELECTIVE INDEX

Many of the concepts covered in this book are explained in greater detail here.
In some cases, however, you may wish to refer to the page on which they are discussed.

ablutions　from the Latin word *ablutio*, meaning 'washed away,' an ablution is a ritual cleansing with water. In the context of the Mass, it refers to the cleansing of the Priest's fingers and the chalice with wine and water after Communion. Baptism is also conferred by means of ablution. *See pp. 54-55.*

absolution　from the Latin word *absolvere*, meaning 'to release from,' absolution is the act by which a Priest releases a penitent from sin.

abstinence　from the Latin word *abstinere*, meaning 'to keep away from,' to abstain is to refrain from partaking in something. In the context of our faith, it typically refers to our avoidance of eating flesh meat and sometimes eggs, milk, butter and cheese. Our obligation to abstinence may seem like a small matter, but it is one of the Commandments of the Church, intended as a way of offering to God reparation for sin. Thus to disregard this obligation is a grievous sin.

acolyte　from the Greek word *akólouthos*, meaning attendant, the acolyte is the highest of the four minor orders. Among the duties of the acolyte are the lighting of the candles on the altar, carrying them in procession, preparing wine and water for the Mass, and assisting the sacred ministers at the Mass. As the minor orders were largely suppressed in 1972 by Pope Paul VI, today altar boys or servers typically perform the duties of the acolyte. *See entry for Holy Orders.*

adoration　from the Latin *ad + orare*, meaning 'to pray to' or 'to worship.' To adore God is to offer Him the highest honor, devotion, homage and love. Adoration is one of the four ends of sacrifice.

Advent　from the Latin word *adventus*, which means 'coming near,' Advent is the season of the Church in which we await the coming of Christ into the world. This season begins with the Sunday nearest to the feast of St. Andrew (November 30) and spans four Sundays, ending on Christmas Eve.

Agnus Dei　Latin phrase meaning 'Lamb of God.' This formula, based on the declaration of John the Baptist, is repeated three times by the Priest, accompanied each time by the striking of his breast. This takes place just after the particle of the broken Host is placed in the chalice. The *Agnus Dei* is the last of the five parts of the Ordinary of the Mass that are sung by the choir or cantor at High Mass. *See pp. 48, 52.*

alb　from the Latin word *alba*, meaning white, the alb is the long white linen vestment worn by the Priest as a symbol of purity. *See p. xx.*

alleluia　from the Hebrew *Hallelu + Yah*, meaning 'let us praise the Lord.' The word alleluia is an ancient way of expressing jubilation and triumph. For this reason, it is carefully avoided during the penitential season of Lent (actually beginning with the custom of 'burying the alleluia' on the

PRIEST WEARING
ALB AND CINCTURE

feast of Septuagesima) so that it may be resurrected with our Lord in the Easter Vigil.

As a chant, the Alleluia is one of the propers of the Mass that is sung by the choir or cantor at High Mass, and takes place, along with the Gradual psalm, between the reading of the Epistle and the reading of the Gospel. *See p.12.*

altar　from the Latin *alt + ara*, meaning 'high sanctuary,' the altar is the table or block upon which we offer Christ's perfect sacrifice to God. It sits upon an elevated platform called the **predella**, at least three steps above the floor of the sanctuary. The tombs of martyrs were often used as altars in the early Church, a custom which continues today in the requirement that any consecrated altar contain first class relics of at least two martyrs. These may be enclosed in an altar stone, which is usually placed beneath the spot where the host and chalice will sit during the Mass. *See p.xxiv.*

altar cards　three cards containing the prayers of the Ordinary are used on the altar during the Mass. The largest of these cards, in the center of the altar, contains the *Gloria*, the *Munda cor meum* (recited just before the Gospel), the *Credo*, the first of the Offertory prayers, and much of the Canon. The small card on the Gospel side contains the Last Gospel, and the small card on the Epistle side contains the prayers involving water (i.e. the *lavabo*, the mixing of water and wine, and the ablutions). *See p.xxiv.*

altar boy　see *server.*

altar cloths　three cloth coverings made of fine white linen are necessary in order to celebrate Mass on an altar. The bottom two are made to fit the **mensa**, or top, of the altar. The bottommost is called the **cere cloth**, as it is waxed. This protects the linen above from the moisture of the stone altar, while also preventing any accidental spillage of the chalice from passing through. Above these two cloths is placed the main altar cloth, which is the same width as those below it, but in length it extends to the floor on either side of the altar. *See p.xxiv.*

altar rail　a railing made of wood, metal or stone which sets apart the sanctuary from the body of a church. Here the faithful may kneel to receive Holy Communion. *See entry for Church.*

altar stone　a piece of natural stone with a cavity that contains the relics of at least two martyrs. This is the most important part of any altar, without which Mass cannot be celebrated. The placement of this stone within the **mensa** of an altar is performed during the Consecration of the altar by a bishop.

amen Hebrew word meaning 'so be it.' It is typically used at the closing of a prayer or creed as a solemn way of expressing assent.

amice from the Latin word *amictus,* meaning wrap, this is an oblong vestment of fine white linen worn around the neck and shoulders, beneath the alb. Its origin was as a covering for the head, and in earlier times it was worn like a hood and laid upon the shoulders like a cowl or collar upon reaching the altar. It was then pulled back over the head when leaving the sanctuary, serving in the place of the modern biretta. *See p. xx.*

antependium from the Latin *ante + pendere,* meaning 'to hang before,' this is a decorative cloth, usually matching the color of the vestments, which hangs down from the front of the altar. *See p.xxiv.*

antiphon from the Greek word *antíphōnos,* meaning 'to sound against,' this describes a method of praying or singing in which two

ALTAR WITH ANTEPENDIUM

or more groups chant in response to another. Much of the Divine Office and parts of the Mass are chanted antiphonally; however, many of the 'antiphons' included in the propers of the Mass are merely a vestige of this practice, in which only a portion of a psalm is recited or sung. *See p.67 for a fuller description of antiphonal chant.*

apostle from the Greek word *apostolos,* meaning 'one sent,' the term apostle generally refers to one of our Lord's original Twelve Apostles; however, it is also used in reference to St. Paul and others who, like him, brought the faith to regions which had been previously unfamiliar with Christ's Gospel, as for example, St. Patrick in Ireland.

Asperges me Latin phrase meaning 'sprinkle me.' This is the *incipit,* or opening words, of the rite of sprinkling with holy water that precedes the principal Mass on Sunday. During the *Asperges,* the Priest wears a cope over the amice, alb, cincture and stole, removing it at the close of the rite and donning the chasuble before beginning the Mass. *See p.xxvi.*

aspergillum deriving from the Latin word *aspergere,* meaning to sprinkle, the aspergillum is an instrument intended for the sprinkling of holy water. *See p.xxiii.*

aspersorium deriving from the Latin word *aspergere,* meaning to sprinkle, the aspersorium is a vessel which holds the holy water used in the sprinkling of the congregation. *See p.xxiii.*

ASPERSORIUM
WITH
ASPERGILLUM

atonement the act of making reparation for our sins, in order to balance the spiritual effects of our offenses. Atonement is one of the four ends of sacrifice.

baldachinum see *canopy.*

Benedictus Latin word meaning blessed. This is the *incipit,* or opening word, for the second part of the *Sanctus.* In longer musical settings of the Mass, the *Sanctus* is divided into two movements, so as to ensure that there will be silence during the consecration. After the elevation of the Chalice, the *Sanctus* then resumes with the *Benedictus. See p.28.*

Benediction of the Blessed Sacrament from the Latin *bene + dicere,* meaning 'to speak a blessing,' this is a brief service in which the Blessed Sacrament is exposed in a monstrance for adoration by the faithful. Various litanies and hymns are sung, particularly the *Tantum Ergo* and *O Salutaris Hostia,* while the celebrant blesses the congregation, making the sign of the cross over them with the monstrance.

Blessed Sacrament one of the titles given to the Body and Blood of our Lord in the Eucharist, indicating the primacy of this Sacrament over the others.

biretta a stiff square cap with three or four ridges, topped with a tuft, worn by the celebrant while processing in and out of the sanctuary and while seated. The color corresponds to that of the cleric's cassock: black for priests, violet for bishops and red for cardinals.

bishop from the Greek word *epískopos* meaning overseer, the Bishop is considered a successor to the Apostles, one who is consecrated to the fullness of the Priesthood. He is the chief pastor of a group of churches, called a *diocese.* In addition to his power of jurisdiction, only a bishop can ordain priests, dedicate churches, consecrate altars, chalices, patens and other articles used in the Mass, and typically only bishops may confer the sacrament of Confirmation.

A Bishop vests like the Priest for Mass, except that he wears both Dalmatic and Chasuble, to show the fullness of his Priesthood; he also wears special gloves, stockings and sandals. He carries a staff called a *crosier,* and he wears a *mitre* over his skullcap, which is called a *zucchetto.*

BISHOP WEARING
PONTIFICAL VESTMENTS

breviary from the Latin word *breviarium,* meaning 'summary' or 'compendium,' the Breviary is the book which contains the prayers of the Liturgy of the Divine Office. It may be divided into four volumes corresponding to the seasons of the Church, or printed as one large volume called a *totum.* Any breviary will contain the *ordinary* for praying each hour, along with any variations to that ordinary having to do with the seasons; the *psalter,* which lays out the psalms, canticles and antiphons to be prayed at each hour; separate sections having the *propers* for the seasons of the Church, and for the feast days of the saints; and lastly the *special offices,* such as those for Our Lady, general offices for given categories of saints (i.e. Virgins, Martyrs, Confessors) and for the Dead.

After the Second Vatican Council, the Breviary was revised and published under the name *Liturgy of the Hours.* In this streamlined and simplified liturgy, Lauds and Vespers

became respectively Morning and Evening Prayer, Compline became Night Prayer, Prime was abolished and Terce, Sext and None combined into Daytime Prayer. Matins was greatly condensed into an Office of Readings and the Psalter was rearranged so that the Psalms are now read over a four-week rotation rather than a one-week rotation.

burse from the Latin word *bursa*, meaning purse, the burse is a special cover for carrying the corporal. It is made of two square pieces of cardboard, covered with fabric and bound on three sides. The outer fabric matches that of the vestments and chalice veil, while the rest is lined with linen or silk. *See p.xxii.*

candlebenches see *gradine*.

Canon from the Greek word *kanōn,* meaning 'measuring rod,' a canon is a rule or law, and refers to the unchangeable heart of the Mass during which the consecration takes place.

canopy a square covering, large enough to cover the altar and the predella, which is usually made of fabric, though in larger churches it was often created as a freestanding structure, in which case it is called a *baldachinum*. Its function, especially in these larger churches, is to protect the altar from any matter falling from a ceiling which is not accessible for regular cleaning. *See p.xxiv.*

canticle from the Latin word *canticulum*, meaning 'little song,' a canticle denotes a non-metrical verse or song taken from scripture. There are ten canticles used in the Roman Breviary: from the Old Testament are taken the Canticle of the Three Youths (Daniel 3:57), the Canticle of Isaias (Isaiah 12), the Canticle of Ezechias (Isaiah 38:10-20), the Canticle of Anna (1 Samuel 2:1-10), the Canticle of Moses (Exodus 15:1-19), the Canticle of Habacuc (Hab. 3:2-19), and the Canticle of Moses (Deuteronomy 32:1-43). The three canticles from the New Testament are the Canticle of Zacharias (Luke 1:68-79), the Canticle of the Blessed Virgin, commonly known as the *Magnificat* (Luke 1:46-55) and the Canticle of Simeon, known as the *Nunc dimittis* (Luke 2:29-32). *See p.10.*

cardinal from the Latin word *cardo*, meaning hinge, a cardinal is appointed by the pope to be his adviser and assistant in governing the Church. At one time, even a layperson could be so appointed, but in 1918, Canon law was modified to require that they be at least priests, and in 1962 John XXIII further required that they be bishops.

TRADITIONAL HAT WORN BY CARDINALS

The Sacred College of Cardinals, in addition to being the pope's supreme council, is tasked with electing in conclave a new pope from among its members in the event that the Holy See becomes vacant. Cardinals wear a red cassock and hat, after which the color and bird are named.

cassock from the Italian word *casacca*, meaning coat, the cassock is the traditional garment worn by clerics. Also known as a **soutane**, it is an ankle-length garment with long sleeves, usually belted and having a button closure. A black cassock is typically worn by all clerics from their entry to the seminary (or minor orders) through the priesthood. It is also worn by laypersons when serving at Mass, along with the surplice. A bishop's cassock is traditionally violet, the cardinal's is red, and the pope's is white. However, it is common practice for bishops and cardinals to wear instead a black cassock with buttons, piping and girdle made of violet or red, respectively. *See p. xxi.*

catechumen from the Greek word *katēchoúmenos*, meaning 'one instructed orally,' a catechumen is one who is receiving instruction in the faith in preparation for baptism. In the early Church, the catechumens were invited to join in the first part of the Mass, but were dismissed after the sermon, as the sacred mysteries of the Mass were only for the faithful.

celebrant from the Latin word *celebrans,* which means solemnizing, the celebrant is the officiating priest or bishop in the celebration of the Mass. *See p.xix.*

censer also known as a thurible, the censer is a metal vessel, suspended on chains, in which incense is burned during the celebration of Solemn High Mass, Vespers, Benediction and other solemn offices of the Church. *See p.xxiii.*

cere cloth from the Latin word *cera*, meaning wax, this bottommost of the altar cloths is made of fine white linen and impregnated with wax in order to make it waterproof. This serves the double function of protecting the altar linens from the moisture of a stone altar while also preventing any spillage of the chalice from passing through. However, its significance may also derive from the use of waxed cloth as a shroud for the dead. *See p.xxiv.*

ceremony from the Latin word *cærimonia*, meaning 'sacred rite,' ceremony refers to any external practice, or set of practices, that embody the public exercise of our faith.

St. Thomas Aquinas points out that, as man has two natures, the spiritual and the corporal, we also need two means of worship: an interior devotion to God, and an exterior expression of our adoration. It is the ceremonies of the Church, then, that help to excite in us the fervor which we would otherwise lack in our everyday lives.

chalice from the Latin word *calix*, meaning cup, the chalice is first among the sacred vessels. Lined with precious gold, it is used to hold the Precious Blood during the celebration of the Mass. *See p. xxii.*

chalice veil   a square piece of fabric made of the same

material and color as the Priest's vestments, often lined with silk, used to cover the chalice and paten while they sit upon the altar prior to the Canon and after the ablutions. *See p. xxii.*

chasuble   from the Latin word *casula*, meaning 'little house,' the chasuble is the sleeveless outer vestment worn by the celebrant at Mass. Its color is prescribed according to the seasons of the Church or the particular feast being celebrated. It is typically made of silk or other rich fabric and is sometimes heavily ornamented.

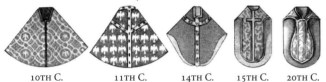

10TH C.   11TH C.   14TH C.   15TH C.   20TH C.

The early chasuble was a circle of fabric formed into an ample, flowing garment that covered the entire body and required the gathering up of the sides in order to allow the use of the arms. As this vestment became stiffer and more heavily ornamented, the assistance of the deacon and subdeacon was necessary to lift it so that the celebrant might move his arms freely, especially during the elevation of the Sacred Species. Over time, the form of the chasuble was changed in order to alleviate this problem, until it resembled a broad scapular with cutaways for the arms in front, a shape which inspired the nickname "fiddleback chasuble." This stiff cutaway vestment is properly called a Roman chasuble, while the shortened modern form of the earlier, flowing vestment is called a Gothic chasuble. *See p.xx.*

Christmastide   the season of celebration following the feast of Christmas. Liturgically speaking, this season extends 12 days, from the vigil of the Nativity (that is, Christmas eve) through the Epiphany on January 6, after which we technically celebrate ***Epiphanytide***. However, the larger season commemorating Christ's birth and hidden life extends through Epiphanytide up to the feast of the Purification (also known as Candlemas) on February 2. *See p. xvii.*

Church (building)   the major parts of a Church building are shown as labeled at right:

    a) Sanctuary
    b) Altar Rail
    c) Transept arms
    d) Nave
    e) Side aisles
    f) Narthex
    g) Sacristy

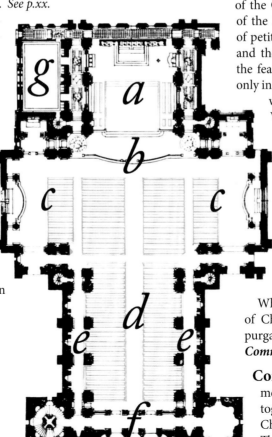

Church Militant   see *Communion of Saints.*

Church Suffering   see *Communion of Saints.*

Church Triumphant   see *Communion of Saints.*

ciborium   Latin name for the sacred vessel which contains the consecrated Hosts intended for the faithful or reserved in the tabernacle. It is shaped like a chalice but is covered to protect its precious contents. It may also be fitted with a veil. *See p.xxiii.*

cincture   from the Latin word *cingere*, meaning 'to gird,' the cincture is a girdle or belt, usually a tasseled cord, which is tied about the waist to confine the alb and the stole when the Priest vests for Mass. It is a symbol of chastity. *See p.xx.*

cleric   from the Latin word *clericus,* meaning priest, a cleric is a member of the clergy. This was once signified by receiving the tonsure, but in more modern times it denoted one who had received at least the minor orders, or had taken religious vows.

CINCTURE

In medieval England, the designation was so widespread that the term "clerk" came to mean any educated man, whether in orders or not. Today one is considered a cleric only after ordination to the diaconate or above.

collect   from the Latin word *collecta*, meaning assembly, a collect is a prayer that is intended to represent the petitions of the Church as a whole. In the context of the Mass, the Collect is a short prayer of petition that occurs between the Gloria and the Epistle. This prayer is proper to the feast being celebrated and is used not only in the Mass, but in the Divine Office as well, at Lauds, Terce, Sext, None and Vespers for the day. *See p.11.*

communion   from the Latin word *communio,* meaning fellowship, communion is the sharing together of something in common.

When we speak of the reception of the Eucharist, which allows us to actively participate in the Body of Christ, we call this ***Holy Communion***.

When we refer to the Mystical Body of Christ in His Church in heaven, in purgatory, and on earth, we call this the ***Communion of Saints***.

Communion of Saints   all the members of the Church are bound together as the Mystical Body of Christ through the grace of Baptism. This Mystical Body, also called the

74

Communion of Saints, has three aspects, just as our One God has three persons.

The **Church Militant** is that portion of the Church here on earth which must continuously struggle against temptation and sin.

The **Church Suffering** are those faithful who have departed this life in God's grace, but first must pay the temporal debt of their sins in purgatory.

(Though the guilt of sin is forgiven in the Sacrament of Penance, the effects of sin do not disappear. We must make reparation for these effects, in the same way as if we had broken a window and must replace it. If we do not complete this reparation here on earth, it must be completed in Purgatory before we can enter into the joys of Heaven.)

The **Church Triumphant** are the saints and martyrs who have completed their struggle and emerged victorious. With God and His angels, they enjoy forever the beatific vision in Heaven. *See p.42, entry for indulgence.*

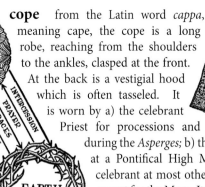

ILLUSTRATION SHOWING THE THREE ASPECTS OF THE MYSTICAL BODY OF CHRIST IN THE CHURCH.

confession   the act of recounting our sins to a Priest in the sacrament of Penance. The Commandments of the Church require that we confess our sins at least once a year, and though we are only obligated to confess all mortal sins, it is beneficial for the health of our souls to seek the graces conferred by this sacrament even for our venial sins, to strengthen us against sinful habits. *See p. 4.*

confiteor   Latin word meaning 'I confess.' This is the opening word, or *incipit*, of the prayer used at the beginning of the Mass to confess our venial sins and receive absolution. This prayer was at one time commonly used in the confessional as a part of the Sacrament of Penance. *See p. 4.*

conscience   from the Latin word *conscientia*, meaning 'knowledge within oneself,' conscience is the interior voice of reason by which we judge right from wrong. A true conscience is well aligned with the Laws of God and of the Church. We are bound to act as our conscience dictates, as long as we feel no doubt as to the rightness of our action. If our conscience is later proven to have been in error, we are not culpable, but we must then reform our future actions accordingly or we risk grave sin.

consecration   from the Latin word *consecratio*, meaning 'to make sacred,' this is the act by which a common person or thing is specially dedicated to some sacred use, as in the consecration of a bishop or church or altar.

Within the context of the Mass, the Consecration refers to the repetition of the words our Lord spoke in His Institution of the Eucharist, by which act the bread and wine undergo a *transubstantiation* and become the Body and Blood of Christ. *See pp.36-38.*

contrition   from the Latin word *conterere*, meaning 'to break something that is hardened,' contrition is sorrow for our sins. In order to receive absolution for our sins, we must sincerely repent of them and make a firm resolution to avoid them in future.

cope   from the Latin word *cappa*, meaning cape, the cope is a long robe, reaching from the shoulders to the ankles, clasped at the front. At the back is a vestigial hood which is often tasseled. It is worn by a) the celebrant Priest for processions and during the *Asperges;* b) the assistant Priest at a Pontifical High Mass; and c) the celebrant at most other solemn offices, except for the Mass. Its name in Latin is the *pluviale*, meaning raincoat, hinting as to its original function. *See p.xxi.*

corporal   from the Latin word *corporalis*, meaning 'of the body,' this most sacred of the altar linens is intended to hold the Body of our Lord. This square piece of fine white linen is placed upon the altar, atop the altar stone, and the Host and Chalice rest upon it during the Mass. It is then folded in a special way, so as to retain any particles of the Host, and kept inside the burse until it can be properly purified. *See p.xxii.*

Council of Trent   an Ecumenical Council convened by Pope Paul III in 1545 to combat Protestant heresies and to enact a counterreformation; that is, a reform of abuses from *within* the Church, rather than from without, in order that it might be strengthened and preserved.

This pivotal Council solidified the Church's teachings on issues disputed by Protestant factions, such as Original Sin, Justification and the Sacraments. The fruit of this Council included the revision and standardization of the Catechism in 1566, the Breviary in 1568, the Missal in 1570 and the Vulgate Bible in 1592. Held in the Italian city of Trento, known in Latin as *Tridentum*, its reforms are known as *Tridentine*. *See entry for Tridentine Mass.*

covenant   from the Latin word *conveniens*, meaning agreeable, a covenant is a formal agreement between two parties, which is solemnized by an oath or ritual.

Biblical examples of covenants made between God and man are that made with Abraham, in which God promised to make his descendants as numerous as the stars, solemnized through circumcision; the covenant made with Noah, in which God promised never again to destroy the earth by flood, solemnized with the sign of the rainbow; and the covenant with Moses, in which God made the Israelites His chosen people, and they agreed to keep His commandments, solemnized through the blood of sacrificial animals.

In the Latin Vulgate, the word **testamentum** is used to represent *berith*, the Hebrew term for covenant. This usage gave rise to our name for the Old and New Testaments, as the former referred to the Old Covenant (particularly that with Moses) and the latter to the New Covenant in Jesus' blood. You will notice that this term is also used when the covenant is referred to during the consecration of the wine, in the phrase *novi et aeterni* **testamenti**. *See pp.38-39.*

credence   from the Latin word *credentia*, meaning side table, a credence is a small table found near the Epistle side of the altar, on which the cruets, finger basin and towel are kept for use in the Mass.

credo   Latin word meaning 'I believe.' This is the opening word, or *incipit*, of the Nicene Creed, known in the Missal as the **Symbolum Nicænum**. *See page 16 for more information about the development of the Nicene Creed and why it is called a **Symbol**.*

CREDENCE

crosier   the common name for the Pastoral Staff conferred on bishops (and some abbots) as a symbol of their authority.

crucifix   from the Latin word *crucifixus*, meaning 'the crucified,' a crucifix is a physical depiction of our Lord on the Cross.

cruets   small vessels of glass or metal that hold the water and wine which are to be mixed in the Chalice for the Sacrifice of the Mass. They are also used for the *Lavabo* and the ablutions. *See p.xxiii.*

dalmatic   the outer vestment worn by the deacon at Mass. It is a loose-fitting garment with open sides and short wide sleeves, and is ornamented with two vertical strips called **clavi** that run from the shoulder to the hem, joined by two horizontal strips at top and bottom. It is made from the same color and fabric as the celebrant's chasuble. During seasons of penitence, it is often replaced by a **folded chasuble.**

The dalmatic is also worn under the chasuble of a bishop during the Pontifical High Mass as a symbol of the fullness of his priesthood.

Its name comes from the fact that this tunic was originally worn in Dalmatia; it was introduced into the Roman wardrobe during the reign of Diocletian (284-305 AD). *See p.xix.*

DEACON WEARING
THE DALMATIC

deacon   from the Greek word *diakonos*, meaning servant, a Deacon is one who has received the second of the major orders. His liturgical duties are to assist the celebrant and to sing the Gospel at Solemn High Mass. He may also distribute Holy Communion and confer the Sacrament of Baptism (in case of need and with permission).

Like the Subdeacon, his liturgical vestments include the amice, alb, girdle and maniple, but he also wears the stole as a symbol of the authority of his office. This is worn diagonally over the left shoulder, with the ends joined under the right arm. He then wears the Dalmatic over these. *See p.xix and the entry for Holy Orders.*

diptych   from the Greek word *diptychon*, meaning 'twice folded,' a diptych consists of two hinged tablets. In the early Church, a set of diptychs was used in the Mass: one side held the names of the living, and the other the names of the dead,

for which the Mass was to be offered. The use of these tablets during the Commemorations of the living and the dead during the Canon led these prayers to be called the Diptychs. *See pp. 32 and 42.*

ROMAN DIPTYCH

disposition   with regard to our faith, our disposition describes the extent to which we are earnest in seeking God's grace. The Sacraments are an important means of this grace, but we must clear the way for this grace to enter our souls. For example, in the sacrament of Penance, we must have contrition in order to receive absolution; likewise, when we are to receive the Eucharist, we must have a conscience clear of sin. We do well, then, to prepare for the Sacraments with an attitude of humility and reverence, and by asking God to give us the disposition necessary to receive them worthily.

Divine Office   one of the Church's three main acts of *liturgy,* or formal public worship, the others being the Mass and the Sacraments.

The Divine Office is a service of prayer and praise consisting of psalms, lessons, hymns and responsories which is somewhat similar in form to the Mass, both having been developed from the early Christian *synaxis*. Its purpose is to sanctify each day by devoting certain hours to prayer. All priests and most religious are required to recite these prayers daily, either privately or in groups.

Because the Divine Office is the ancient and universal prayer of the Church, our participation in this liturgy helps us to fulfill our purpose as members of the Mystical Body of Christ. It is also uniquely powerful as a means of aligning our own prayer intentions with those of the Church itself, which have endured through two millenia. *See pages 64-67.*

dogma   a Greek word meaning 'doctrine' or 'tenet.' The dogmas taught by the Church are the truths of divine revelation and must be believed by all the faithful.

Dominus vobiscum   Latin phrase meaning 'The Lord be with you,' the response to which is *et cum spiritu tuo*: 'and with your spirit.' This is an ancient Hebrew form of greeting that was adopted by the early Christians. It is frequently used as a liturgical responsory in the Mass (where it is repeated eight times) and in the Divine Office. *See p.6.*

Douay-Rheims Bible   the first complete English translation of the Vulgate Bible to be approved by the Church, created by scholars who had fled to the English College in Douai, France to escape the persecution of the Catholic Church in England. The New Testament portion was published in 1582, while the College was temporarily located in Reims, France, and the Old Testament portion was published in 1609, after their return to Douai.

Its creation was in response to the growing number of faulty translations then being circulated, which reinforced the views of those who opposed the authority of the Church. Therefore its creators placed the highest emphasis on accuracy, rather than beauty of language, resulting in a very reliable but sometimes infelicitous translation.

In 1750, Bishop Richard Challoner published a revised version in which he sought to remedy the awkwardness of the original Doauy-Rheims translation. Challoner's revised version is still in use today. *See pp.68-69.*

doxology   from the Greek word *doxa,* meaning glory, a doxology is a formula of praise that is usually Trinitarian in nature. The Great Doxology is the *Gloria in Excelsis Deo,* and the minor doxology is the prayer we know as the *Glory be.* However, there are other doxologies used at the end of prayers, such as "for thine is the kingdom..." after the *Our Father. See pp.10, 67.*

Ember Days   days of prayer, fasting and abstinence intended for the sanctification of each of the four seasons. The Wednesday, Friday and Saturday immediately following Ash Wednesday, Pentecost, September 14 and December 13 are set aside for this purpose.

epistle   from the Greek word *epistole,* meaning letter, the Epistles are the 21 books of the New Testament consisting of letters written by the Apostles and their successors to the leaders of the early Church.

   In the Mass, when the Epistle is read, it is generally taken from one of these letters; however, it may also be taken from the Apocalypse, the Acts of the Apostles, or the Old Testament. *See p.12.*

Epistle side   the left side of the altar (our right). It derives its name from the fact that the Epistle is read or sung from this side of the altar. *See p. xxv.*

Eucharist   from the Greek word *eukharistia,* meaning thanksgiving, the Eucharist is that Sacrament, instituted by our Lord at His Last Supper, whereby ordinary bread and wine undergo a transubstantiation and become His Body and Blood, and the food of our souls. *See entries for Blessed Sacrament, communion.*

examen   an examination of conscience made daily as a devotion, with the purpose of more easily detecting and correcting our weaknesses and faults.

exorcist   the third of the four minor orders leading to the priesthood. The duties of the exorcist, besides the authority to cast out demons, included that of pouring out the water at Mass. This office was abolished in 1972 by Pope Paul VI. Today exorcisms, when deemed necessary, are performed by a Priest. *See entry for Holy Orders.*

Extraordinary Form of the Mass   a modern name for the Tridentine Mass, first used by Pope Benedict XVI in his 2007 Motu Proprio *Summorum Pontificum,* as a way of affirming that both forms of the Mass are one Rite and equally valid, with the Pauline Mass being the Ordinary Form, and the Tridentine Mass being Extra-Ordinary. *See entry for Tridentine Mass.*

fasting   from the Old English *fæstan,* meaning 'to observe,' fasting is a form of penance in which one restricts the amount of food eaten, as a way of disciplining the body and bringing about the virtue of temperance. All the faithful between the age of 21 and 59 (with exceptions for the sick, those engaged in manual labor and pregnant or nursing mothers) are obliged to fast on the prescribed days by eating only one full meal. Two other small meals may be taken if needed, but they should not equal together the size of the full meal. Currently the Church prescribes both fasting and abstinence from meat on Ash Wednesday and Good Friday; however,

before 1966, all of the Fridays in Lent, Ember Fridays, December 7 and Christmas Eve were also included in this requirement. Fasting alone was prescribed for all days in Lent except Sundays, and on Ember Wednesday and Saturday.

   The Church also requires that we fast for at least one hour before reception of Holy Communion. During this time, water may be drunk, but not nutritive liquids like milk or juice. Before 1964, this Eucharistic fast began at Midnight. *See p.xxvi.*

figure   see *type.*

frontal   see *antependium.*

gloria   the Latin word for glory. In the context of the Mass, the Gloria refers to the **Great Doxology**, *Gloria in Excelsis Deo,* the second of the sung parts of the ordinary of the Mass. The *gloria patri,* commonly known in English as the 'glory be,' is termed the **minor doxology**. *See p.10.*

Gospel   from the Old English *godspell,* meaning 'good tidings,' the Gospels are the accounts of the life and teachings of Jesus Christ as written by the four Evangelists, Matthew, Mark, Luke and John. In the Mass, the Gospel is the culminaton of the Mass of the Catehumens, where we receive instruction from God. *See pp. xiii, 14-15.*

Gospel Side   the right side of the altar (our left), the place of honor. It derives its name from the fact that the Gospel is read or sung from this side of the altar. *See p. xxv.*

gothic vestments   a term used to distinguish between the two main styles of liturgical vestments, though it does also largely describe the style of vestments specific to the Gothic period. Gothic vestments feature a fuller, more flowing chasuble and a stole and maniple which are longer and narrower without splayed ends.

gradine   an Italian word meaning 'little steps,' the *gradine* are raised platforms at the rear of the altar, intended for the placement of candles. Also known as a **candlebench**. Reliquaries and flowers may also be placed on these ledges. *See p.xxiv.*

grace   derived from the Latin word *gratia,* grace is a gift freely given by God to Man for his eternal salvation. Our own strength of will is not sufficient to preserve us from sin without the help of God's grace; therefore we should seek always to cooperate with and increase God's grace in our souls by means of prayer, good works, and the sacraments.

   There are many forms of grace, but the basic three are:
- *Sacramental Grace*: the particular graces imparted by each of the sacraments.
- *Sanctifying Grace*: also called habitual grace, this is a permanent state of grace, given at Baptism, which infuses the soul with divine life. It makes us the adoptive sons and daughters of God, and thereby heirs to eternal life. Sanctifying grace may be lost through mortal sin, and must be restored in the sacrament of Penance.
- *Actual Grace*: the influence of God by which He assists us in doing His will. It takes its name from the fact that it is bound up with the *act* for which it was intended.

77

gradual   from the Latin word *gradus*, meaning step, the gradual takes its name from the fact that it was originally sung *from the steps* of the ambo where the epistle was sung. It was originally a full psalm, sung antiphonally between the Epistle and Gospel, but over time the psalm was shortened to include only a few lines. *See pp.12, 67, entry for alleluia.*

heresy   from the Greek word *airesis*, meaning 'sect' or 'division,' heresy is a belief that is contrary to the dogmas of the Church. By adhering to these **heterodox** beliefs, one necessarily divides oneself from the Mystical Body of Christ in the Church.

   Heresy which is the result of ignorance, rather than deliberate choice, is called **Material Heresy** and has no guilt attached. *See p.16, entry for dogma, heterodox.*

heterodox   from the Greek *heteros + doxa,* meaning 'different belief,' heterodox opinion differs from the accepted doctrines of the Church. Where such beliefs are contrary to the **dogmas** of the Church, heterodoxy may become **heresy**. *See p.16, entries for dogma, heresy.*

High Mass   see *Missa Cantata.*

holocaust   from the Greek word *holokaustos,* meaning 'burned whole,' a holocaust is a sacrifice that is entirely consumed by fire as an atonement for sin. *See p.xii.*

Holy Day of Obligation   feast days in which all the faithful are required to attend Mass and to refrain from unnecessary servile labor. In the United States, six holy days of obligation are currently observed in addition to Sundays: the Solemnity of Mary (January 1); the Ascension (forty days after Easter); Assumption of the Blessed Virgin (August 15); All Saints' Day (November 1); the Immaculate Conception (December 8); and Christmas (December 25). In the 1962 Calendar of feasts, January 1 is celebrated as the Circumcision of Jesus; the rest have not changed. *See p.xvi.*

Holy of Holies   the innermost chamber of the Temple in Jerusalem, that holiest of places where the Ark of the Covenant was kept. It was separated from the Temple proper by a veil; none but the High Priest could enter, and he but once a year, on the Day of Atonement. In the moment when Jesus died on the cross, this veil was torn in two, signifying that by His death, the way was made open to the Most Holy through Jesus' blood. *See pp. 6 and 38.*

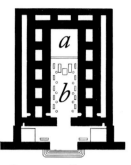

PLAN OF THE TEMPLE IN JERUSALEM, SHOWING A) THE HOLY OF HOLIES; B) THE HOLY PLACE.

Holy Orders, Sacrament of   the sacrament by which the Church bestows the authority, as well as the graces needed, to administer the sacraments and perform the duties of the priesthood.

   Currently the Church recognizes three levels within this single sacrament: the diaconate, the priesthood, and the episcopate. However, the Council of Trent defined the orders of clerics into Major and Minor Orders, each being steps leading toward the fullness of the priesthood as seen in the illustration below. The Minor Orders are **Porter**, **Lector**, **Exorcist** and **Acolyte**, and the Major Orders are **Subdeacon**, **Deacon** and **Priest**. Related to these seven are the **Tonsure**, which is not formally considered an order, and the **Bishop**, which is not seen as a separate order from the priesthood, but rather a perfection thereof.

   Of the seven orders, only the Deacon and the Priest actually receive the Sacrament of Holy Orders, which leaves an indelible mark, or **character,** upon its recipient; the ordinations of the Minor Orders and of Subdeacons are considered **sacramentals**, and Bishops are not ordained, but rather, **consecrated**. *See entry for Minor Orders.*

Holy Week   the most solemn week of the Church year, lasting from Palm Sunday until Holy Saturday, in which we recall the last days of our Lord, including His Passion and Death. *See pp.xvi-xvii.*

hosanna   Hebrew word meaning 'Save me, I pray!' However, it was commonly used as an exclamation of triumph, as found in Psalm 117:25, as well as in our Lord's entry into Jerusalem.

GRAPHIC SHOWING THE MINOR AND MAJOR ORDERS AS STEPS TOWARD THE FULLNESS OF THE PRIESTHOOD.

host from the Latin word *hostia*, meaning victim, the host is the bread we offer on the altar, which becomes Christ's Body and the perfect sacrifice.

humeral veil from the Latin word *humerus*, meaning shoulder, the humeral veil is a fringed oblong of silk approximately 3' x 8' which is worn over the shoulders like a shawl and is intended to cover the hands when carrying one of the sacred vessels. It is worn by the subdeacon at Solemn High Mass, while he holds the paten, and by the Priest when carrying the Blessed Sacrament in a monstrance. It is either white or of the same fabric as the vestments. *See p.xxi.*

hymn from the Greek word *hymnos*, meaning song, hymns are songs of praise. Liturgical hymns are those used as a formal part of worship, such as those which are proper to the hours of the Divine Office, while non-liturgical hymns are used more informally, as for example, music sung by the choir or congregation at Mass which does not belong to the propers for that Mass. *See p.10.*

in persona Christi Latin phrase meaning 'in the person of Christ.' In the Mass, the Priest serves *in persona Christi*, especially in speaking the words of the Consecration, "This is My Body." *See p.xiv.*

incense from the Latin word *incensum*, meaning 'a thing that is burnt,' incense refers both to the solid resin which is burnt, as well as the aromatic smoke it produces. The type used in the Catholic Church is typically *frankincense*, a resin obtained from the *Boswellia sacra* tree of southern Arabia. Incense used in the Mass is stored in a metal vessel called an *incense boat*, and burnt in a portable censer called a *thurible*. *See p.22.*

incense boat  the sacred vessel in which the incense used for Mass is stored; a spoon is used to place this incense in the thurible. *See p.xxiii.*

incipit Latin word meaning 'it begins.' The *incipit* is the opening word or phrase of a document, and is often used to name that document, as is the case with Papal encyclicals. Sets of Mass Propers for a given feast are also referred to by their *incipit*. *See p.8.*

indulgence from the Latin word *indulgentia*, meaning 'leniency' or 'pardon,' an indulgence is the remission of all (in the case of *plenary indulgences*) or part (in *partial indulgences*) of the temporal punishment we have deserved for our sins. Indulgences are granted by the authority of the Church from the infinite merits of our Crucified Lord.

To understand the need for indulgences, one must first properly understand the difference between guilt for sin (which is removed by means of the Sacrament of Penance) and the temporal punishment for sin, by which we must make reparation for the effects of our sin. If we break a neighbor's window, he may forgive us if we apologize, but the window remains to be replaced. It is the same way with sin: our sins create a real effect in the world, just as a ball may break a window, and we must balance that real effect by means of good works or mortification, either here on earth or in purgatory.

The usual conditions for gaining an indulgence are that one must first have the intention of gaining one, be in a state of grace (freed from the stain of sin by means of the confessional; see entry for *grace*), and fulfill the requirements of the specific indulgence sought.

An indulgence gained may be applied on behalf of a soul in purgatory if one desires. *See entry for Communion of Saints.*

intercession from the Latin word *intercedo*, meaning literally 'go-between,' intercession is the act of mediating between God and man. When we pray to the saints, it is their intercession that we are seeking, that they may offer our prayers to Him and ask for His graces and blessings on our behalf. Christ is our intercessor in the Mass, in the person of the Priest. *See p.56, entry for in persona Christi.*

introit from the Latin word *introitus*, meaning entrance, the introit is the antiphonal psalm which is sung at High Mass as the celebrant enters the sanctuary. At low Mass, it is recited by the Priest after the prayers at the foot of the altar. It is both the first of the propers, as well as the true beginning of the Mass itself; the prayers preceding it are preparatory in nature. In the early Church, an entire Psalm was sung antiphonally (*see p.67*) for the introit; however, it has since been shortened to part of a psalm. *See p.8.*

kyrie eleison Greek phrase meaning 'Lord, have mercy.' This litany, which occurs between the Introit and the Gloria, invokes three times each of the persons of the Trinity dwelling within each other. It is the first of the sung parts of the Ordinary of the Mass. *See p.8.*

Lavabo Latin word meaning 'I shall wash.' This is the *incipit*, or opening phrase, of that portion of Psalm 25 which is recited by the celebrant as he washes his fingers following the Offertory. *See p.24.*

lector Latin word for reader. The role of Lector was the second of the four minor orders. However, as the Subdeacon reads the Epistle and the Deacon the Gospel, this role was largely symbolic. Today this role is typically fulfilled by a layperson in the Ordinary Form of the Mass. *See entry for Holy Orders.*

Lent see *Quadragesima*.

litany from the Greek word *litaneia*, meaning supplication, a litany is a form of prayer which originated in Jewish worship. It consists of a series of petitions followed by a response or affirmation.

liturgical colors specific colors prescribed by the Church for the celebration of the seasons of the liturgical year and for particular feasts. See p.xviii for an in-depth discussion of these colors and their associated seasons.

liturgy from the Greek word *leitourgia*, meaning 'a public work done on behalf of a people,' liturgy refers to the formal ceremonies used in the public worship of God.

Liturgy of the Hours see *Breviary, Divine Office*.

Low Mass see *Missa Privata*.

luna (or lunette) Latin word meaning moon (or little moon). The luna is the crescent-shaped or circular receptacle which secures the Sacred Host in an upright position when it is displayed in a monstrance.

maniple from the Latin word *manipulus*, meaning a handful, the maniple is one of the sacred vestments worn by the celebrant, deacon and subdeacon at Mass. It is a band of fabric matching the chasuble, roughly three feet long and 4-5 inches wide, which is secured over the left arm by means of a concealed tie or piece of elastic. *See p. xx.*

Mass of Paul VI see *Ordinary Form of the Mass.*

Mass of the Catechumens that portion of the Mass, from the prayers at the foot of the altar up through the Creed, which was open to both the baptized faithful and those seeking baptism, called *catechumens*. The character of this part of the Mass is one of prayer, praise and instruction; it proceeds largely from the early Christian *synaxis*, which was itself based on the practice of the Jewish synagogue. *See pp.xii-xiii, 16.*

Mass of the Faithful that portion of the Mass, from the Offertory to the end, which features the sacred Mysteries of our Faith, for which only the baptized faithful were permitted to be in attendance. The character of this part of the Mass is one of oblation and sacrifice, and proceeds largely from the ceremonies of the Jewish Passover and the Institution of the Eucharist. *See pp.xii-xiii, 16, 18.*

master of ceremonies one whose role is to direct the actions of all those participating in a sacred rite, especially the Mass. He may be either a cleric or a layman; he is vested in cassock and surplice. *See p.xix.*

Melchisedech in Hebrew, the name Melchisedech means 'King of Righteousness.' He is found in the book of Genesis (14:18-20) and is referred to in the Psalms and in St. Paul as the prototype for priests: "Thou art a priest for ever according to the order of Melchisedech." His sacrifice of bread and wine is one of the types of the Eucharist mentioned in the Mass. *See p.40.*

Minor Orders The four minor orders are lower in hierarchy to the three Major Orders of Subdeacon, Deacon and Priest. One first entered the clergy by receiving the *Tonsure*. Then one received in succession the roles of *Porter*, *Lector*, *Exorcist* and *Acolyte*. The ordinations by which these roles were conferred are *sacramentals*, not sacraments, but each carries the privilege of performing an ecclesiastical function. Today these minor orders have been largely suppressed, and their roles are typically fulfilled by laymen. *See entry for Holy Orders.*

mensa Latin word meaning table. The mensa is the flat stone top of a consecrated altar.

Messiah from the Hebrew word *mashíach*, meaning anointed, the Messiah was the one promised by God to redeem Man from the sin of Adam. Prophecies of the promised Messiah pervade the Old Testament, and the fulfillment of those prophesies are the focus of the New Testament. The Greek equivalent of this Hebrew word is *Christos;* hence the meaning of the title given to Jesus.

Missa Cantata this form of the Mass is properly known as *Sung Mass*, but it is commonly called *High Mass*. For most parishes, lacking as they often do the additional ministers required for Solemn High Mass, this is the preferred form for Sunday Mass. Here, as at Low Mass, the celebrant is typically served by one or more boy servers, and all actions take place at the altar.

As at Solemn High Mass, the prescribed parts of the Mass are sung, the propers are sung by a choir or cantor, six candles are lit upon the altar, and incense may be used with permission of the Bishop. Hymns in the vernacular may be sung only at the entrance and recessional; any other nonliturgical music must be sung in Latin.

Missa Pontificale *Pontifical High Mass* is a Solemn High Mass sung by a bishop or cardinal within his own diocese. The celebration of this form of the Mass requires, in addition to the Deacon and Subdeacon, an assistant Priest, two assistant deacons and at least nine acolytes, and a seventh candle is lit upon the altar.

When presiding at a Pontifical High Mass outside his own diocese, a prelate will sing Mass from the *faldstool*, and only an assistant Priest will join the deacon and subdeacon.

Missa Privata also known as *Low Mass*, this simplified form of the Mass is the one most commonly celebrated.

At Low Mass, the Priest is typically assisted by one server. As there are no additional ministers, all the actions take place at the altar, and all parts of the Mass are spoken rather than sung. In addition, only two candles are lit and there is no use of incense. Hymns may be sung in Latin or in the vernacular at the entrance, the Offertory, during the distribution of Holy Communion, and at the recessional.

Missa Solemnis also known as *Solemn High Mass*, this is considered the standard form of the Mass, though it is the least often celebrated. All other forms of celebration of the Mass are derived from its ceremonies.

At Solemn High Mass, a Priest Celebrant presides, assisted by a Deacon (who sings the Gospel and the Dismissal) and a Subdeacon (who sings the Epistle). A thurifer and an even number of acolytes are also required, as well as a crucifer and torchbearers for processions. All these are orchestrated in their roles by a Master of Ceremonies, who is typically one of the acolytes.

The propers must be sung by the choir, or at the very least by a cantor, and incense is used several times throughout. Six candles are to be lit upon the altar, with a seventh added if the Mass is celebrated by a Bishop, in which case it is termed a Pontifical High Mass.

Missal from the Latin word *Missalis*, meaning 'of the Mass,' the Missal is the book which the Priest uses upon the altar, containing the formulas and prayers of the Mass. It includes the Ordinary and Canon of the Mass, as well as all the propers for each and every Sunday, feast day and votive Mass. Those who attend the Tridentine Mass may also have a hand Missal which helps them to follow along with the prayers of the Mass.

mitre  from the Greek word *mitra*, meaning turban, the mitre is the liturgical head covering worn by a bishop and certain prelates. It is formed of two stiffened pieces of silk or linen which are joined by a headband, with two fringed lappets that hang down in back. It is always removed when the celebrant is praying, as for example during the Collects or the Canon.

monstrance from the Latin word *monstrans*, meaning showing, the monstrance is a sacred vessel, made of precious metal and usually highly ornamented, which is used to display the Sacred Host during the Exposition of the Blessed Sacrament (as on the feast of Corpus Christi or during Benediction). It consists of a base, a stem by which it may be carried, and a crystal or glass receptacle surrounded by rays, in which the Blessed Sacrament may be placed, secured by a *lunette*. A *humeral veil* is always used by the Priest whenever carrying the exposed Host in the monstrance. *See p.xxiii.*

movable feast a feast day which does not have a set calendar day and therefore changes from year to year. The most important of these is Easter, which is always celebrated on a Sunday, but is calculated to fall as close as possible to its anniversary in the Jewish lunar calendar. Several other feasts are then calculated from this date, from Septuagesima and Ash Wednesday to the Ascension, Pentecost and Corpus Christi.

Other movable feasts include that of Christ the King, which is always the last Sunday in October, and the feasts of the Holy Name and Holy Family (usually the first two Sundays in January). *See p.xvi.*

nobis quoque peccatoribus Latin phrase meaning 'and to us sinners also.' These first words of the prayer commemorating the Church Militant and Triumphant are the only words spoken aloud during the Canon of the Mass.

oblation from the Latin word *oblatio*, meaning offering, an oblation is something which is offered to God. It may be offered as a sacrifice, in which case it is either wholly or partially destroyed, or it may be given for use toward the greater glory of God.

offertory from the Latin word *offertorium*, meaning 'place where offerings are brought,' the Offertory refers to the portion of the Mass, as well as its proper actions and prayers, in which the bread and wine are offered to God by the celebrant. This takes place immediately after the Creed and ends with the responsory of the Preface. During this time the Offertory Antiphon is sung at High Mass, and a hymn may be sung during Low Mass (or following the Offertory Antiphon at High Mass). *See pp.18-26.*

Ordinary Form of the Mass also known as the *Mass of Paul VI*, or more commonly as the *Novus Ordo* (meaning 'new order'), this is the Mass celebrated according to the Post-Vatican II Roman Missal of 1969. It is typically celebrated in the vernacular language, but may also be celebrated in Latin. This name for the Mass was instituted by Pope Benedict XVI in his 2007 Motu Proprio *Summorum Pontificum*, as a way of affirming that both forms of the Mass are one Rite and equally valid, with one being the Ordinary Form by which it is celebrated, and the other being Extra-Ordinary.

Ordinary of the Mass the unchanging framework of the Mass, into which the interchangeable *propers* are fitted. In most Missals, this Ordinary is found toward the center of the book, with the propers for the Seasons of the Church in front, and the propers for the feast days of saints in back. *See pp.xv, 8.*

ostensorium see *monstrance.*

pall from the Latin word *pallium*, meaning 'cloak' or 'covering,' the pall is a stiffly starched square of linen used to cover the chalice at Mass, in order to protect the consecrated species. It may be stiffened by inserting a piece of cardboard between two pieces of linen, and it may be decorated on the upper side, but the side touching the chalice should be plain.

PALL COVERING
THE CHALICE

Pasch an Anglicized version of the Hebrew word *Pesach*, the Pasch is the ancient celebration of the Passover.

 The Passover lamb was a *type* for Christ, the Lamb of God. By the blood of the Passover lamb, the Israelites were saved from the Angel of Death; by shedding His Blood for us on the Cross, our Lord fulfilled the Passover, and by rising in triumph from the dead, He freed us from the death of sin through Adam.

For this reason, in the early Church, Christ's Crucifixion was termed *Pascha crucifixionis* and His Resurrection, *Pascha resurrectionis*. Over time, the celebration of Easter came to be known as the Pasch, and its season of celebration as Paschaltide. This name for Easter can be found in various forms in nearly all Western languages except English and High German. *See p.48, entry for Passover.*

Paschaltide Paschal as an adjective comes from the Latin *Paschalis*, meaning 'of the Pasch.' Thus Paschaltide is the season of celebration following Easter. This season extends from Holy Saturday through vespers of the Saturday following Pentecost. During this period, the *Vidi Aquam* is sung in place of the *Asperges Me* at the beginning of Mass, alleluias are added in several places during the liturgy, and the *Regina Coeli* is recited at the usual times of day, in place of the *Angelus*.

Passiontide the two weeks leading up to the Easter Vigil, including both *Passion Week* and *Holy Week*. During this time, all crosses, statues and images (except those of the Stations of the Cross) are covered with an unadorned veil of violet fabric. In the Liturgies of the Mass and the Divine Office, the *doxologies* are also omitted.

Passion Week   not to be confused with Holy Week, Passion Week is the penultimate week in Lent, from Passion Sunday through Palm Sunday. During this week, the Church brings its focus upon the suffering and death of our Lord in preparation for the events of Holy Week. For this reason, the doxology *Gloria Patri* is omitted from the Mass and the daily office until the Easter Vigil Mass.

Passover   the Jewish celebration of their deliverance from slavery in Egypt. In preparation for the final plague, the Hebrews were to sacrifice an unblemished lamb and paint its blood upon the lintel and doorposts of each home, that the Angel of Death might "pass over" that house. That night, they were to be ready to travel, with sandals upon their feet and bread that was unleavened due to haste.

Our Lord made it clear in His celebration of the Passover meal with His disciples before He died, that His sacrifice was the true fulfillment of the Passover: that the blood of the lamb which would set us free was indeed His Blood; that our daily bread, come down from Heaven, without which we would have no life within us, was His Body. *See entry for Pasch.*

paten   from the Latin word *patena*, meaning dish, the paten is a plate made of precious metal, usually made specifically to fit atop the chalice without sliding.

PATEN ATOP
THE CHALICE

The host is kept on the paten until the Offertory, when it is laid upon the corporal until after the Our Father; then it is broken and mingled with the Precious Blood. During this time, at Solemn High Mass, the paten is held by the Subdeacon, using the *humeral veil*.

It is said that the custom of holding the paten in this way arose from the period when the *Sancta*, a reserved piece of the Host from a previous Mass, was kept upon the paten until it was placed in the Chalice. For further discussion of this practice, see the entry for *Sancta*.

penance   from the Latin word *pænitentia*, meaning repentance, penance may refer to: a) the sacrament by which our sins are forgiven (*see confession*); b) the necessary sorrow we must have for our sins; or c) the prayers, reparation, or good works imposed by a Priest in the confessional as a satisfaction for sin.

perfect contrition   from the Latin word *contrītiō* meaning grief, perfect contrition is a sincere and heartfelt sorrow for our sins that arises from a true love of God and horror of offending Him, rather than fear of the punishment of sin (in which case our contrition is termed **imperfect**). An act of perfect contrition, joined with the desire for the Sacrament of Penance, is sufficient to restore the sanctifying grace lost through mortal sin. Imperfect contrition, on the other hand, is sufficient for absolution when joined to the Sacrament of Penance.

petition   from the Latin word *petitio*, meaning request, petition is the principal form of prayer, in which we beg God to grant us His graces and blessings. Petition is one of the four ends of sacrifice.

Pontifical High Mass   see *Missa Pontificale.*

porter   this lowest of the minor orders is technically considered the doorkeeper of the church, though in practice this role was typically fulfilled by the sexton or sacristan. These minor orders were abolished by Pope Paul VI in 1972. *See Holy Orders, Minor Orders.*

preces   the plural form of the Latin word *prex*, meaning prayer. This term is used to refer to pairs or groups of versicles and responses found in the Liturgies of the Mass and the Divine Office. *See p.67.*

predella   an Italian word meaning platform, the predella is the raised platform upon which the altar sits, typically approached by at least three steps. It is also known in English as the ***foot-pace***. The server should not kneel on the predella while serving at low Mass. *See p.xxiv.*

priest   from the Greek word *presbyteros*, meaning elder, a priest is an ordained minister and mediator between Man and God. His primary function is to lead divine worship, particularly in its highest form: *sacrifice*. He is also given the authority to perform all those liturgical duties (including the administration of the sacraments) not reserved to bishops. *See Holy Orders.*

propers   from the Latin word *proprium*, meaning 'particular to,' the propers of a given Mass are those parts which are changeable according to the day or feast being celebrated. These include the Introit, the Collects, the Epistle, Gradual and Alleluia (or Tract), the Gospel, the Offertory Antiphon, the Secret, the Communion Antiphon and the Postcommunion prayer. There may also be a proper Preface, and certain Masses have a Sequence following the Alleluia.

At High Mass, the following propers *must* be sung: the Introit, Gradual and Alleluia (or Tract), the Sequence (if applicable), the Offertory Antiphon and the Communion Antiphon. *See p.xv, 8.*

psalm   from the Greek word *psalmos*, meaning 'a tune played with a stringed instrument,' the Psalms are poetic compositions that were intended to be sung in the functions of the Jewish Temple and later in the Synagogue. They form the cornerstone and model of all prayer in the Christian heritage, even among non-Catholics, and as such, they are the backbone of the Liturgies of the Divine Office as well as the Mass. The Church holds most to have been written by King David, though there has been disagreement over their authorship throughout the millenia of their existence, as some contain inscriptions attributing them to other authors.

It should be noted that the numbering of the Psalms in the Catholic Douay-Rheims Bible differs from that found in most English-language Bibles. This is because the Douay-Rheims derives its numbering from the Latin **Vulgate**, which is itself based on the 2nd century BC **Septuagint**. The King James Version (upon which most English Bibles are based) instead derives its numbering from a 16th century Hebrew text. *See pp.2, 10, 12, 18, 67-70.*

Purgatory   from the Latin word *purgatorium*, meaning cleansing, purgatory is that state in which the faithful departed remain in order to be purified, while there still remains upon them the stain of sin. This may be due to venial sins for which the soul has not offered an act of perfect contrition or received

absolution; it may also be due to grave sins which have been remitted, but for which there remains a temporal debt to be paid. See the entries for *Communion of Saints* and *indulgence* for a further discussion of temporal debt for sin.

Purification of the Blessed Virgin Mary this feast, celebrated on February 2, commemorates the 40th day after Christmas, when the ritual purification of our Lady after childbirth would have been complete, and her child, Jesus, presented in the Temple at Jerusalem. Accordingly, it also brings to a close the season of Christmas. This feast is popularly called **Candlemas** due to the blessing of candles which takes place before Mass. *See p.xvii.*

purificator an oblong linen cloth, folded in three sections lengthwise, which is used by the celebrant to dry the chalice, as well as his fingers, after the ablutions. Because it, like the corporal and pall, contain some trace of the Sacred Species, the rubrics direct that they be specially washed by one in major orders before being handled by a layperson. *See p.xxii.*

pyx from the Greek work *pyxis*, meaning box, a pyx is a small, round metal vessel in which the Blessed Sacrament may be safely kept and carried by a priest in his visits to the sick.

Quadragesima the Latin word for fortieth, and name for the forty days which in English we call Lent. This season of penitence, lasting from Ash Wednesday until Holy Saturday (excluding Sundays), recalls the sufferings of our Lord and prepares us for the joy of Easter.

In the ancient Hebrew faith, forty was the number of purification, calling to mind the forty days of the flood, the years spent wandering in the desert, and the days Moses spent with our Lord on Mt. Sinai. This number is also found in the New Testament: our Lord spent forty days fasting in the wilderness before entering into His ministry.

During Quadragesima, we likewise discipline our wills through fasting and abstinence. Purple vestments are worn (except on *Laetare* Sunday, when they are lightened to rose), the organ is not played, and the *Gloria* and *Alleluia* are omitted from the Mass, with the Tract taking the place of the latter. There is also a proper Preface.

The weekday Masses during Quadragesima take precedence over most other feasts; a notable exception to this rule in Ireland and America is the feast of St. Patrick. *See p.xvii, entries for fasting and abstinence.*

Quinquagesima the Latin word for fiftieth, Quinquagesima represents the fiftieth day before Easter, and is celebrated on the Sunday immediately preceding Ash Wednesday. See the entry for *Septuagesima* for further information on this practice. *See p.xvii.*

relics from the Latin word *reliquiae*, meaning remains, relics are the remains of the saints and belong to three classes: *First class* includes the body of a saint or some part thereof. *Second class* includes any object intimately related to that saint, and *Third class* is anything which has been touched to the body of a saint.

Veneration is given to relics strictly as an extension of the honor we accord to those who were temples of the Holy Spirit in this life, in much the same way that we cherish souvenirs of those we love in this life.

As members of the mystical Body of Christ, it is fitting that we in the Church Militant should seek the help of the saints, who, as part of the Church Triumphant, may intercede for us with God. *See entries for Communion of Saints, intercession.*

reliquary a vessel, usually of precious metal, in which the relics of the saints may be kept and/or displayed. *See p.xxiii.*

responsory the Anglicized version of the Latin word *responsorium*, meaning 'an answering.' A responsory is a group of versicles, greetings, or prayers intoned by the celebrant in a liturgy, each of which has a response which is to be spoken or sung by the server, choir or congregation. This can be as simple as the "*Dominus Vobiscum*," or it can be a litany such as that preceding the Preface. *See pp.xxv, 67.*

ORNATE 14TH C. RELIQUARY

reverence from the Latin word *reverentia,* meaning awe or respect, reverence is that virtue by which we show honor to persons of dignity or sacred places. We owe reverence to all those who represent God's authority on earth, whether civil (our leaders), religious (the clergy), supernatural (the saints) or natural (our parents and teachers). Likewise we owe reverence to those manifestations of our God here on earth, especially in the Mass, where He comes to us in the Sacrament of the Eucharist.

rite from the Latin word *ritus,* meaning 'a religious custom or ceremony,' a rite in its simplest sense refers to the prescribed words and actions that constitute a religious ceremony, from the rite of Baptism to that of Burial.

However, in a larger sense, *Rite* may also refer to a complete system of such liturgies and practices, as used by particular groups within the Church. Many of these Rites derived from the varying practices which developed in isolated geographical areas during the Middle Ages; however, most of these variants were abolished when the Council of Trent codified the Mass as we now know it.

The Rite established at Trent is called the Latin (or Roman) Rite and it is the one most widely used. Eight others are considered licit by the Church: the Armenian, Byzantine, Chaldean, Coptic, Ethiopian, Malabar, Maronite and Syrian. Within these rites are different **usages** as well, many of which are proper to various monastic orders, including the Ambrosian, Mozarbic, Gallican, Sarum, Benedictine, Carthusian and Dominican usages.

Rogation days from the Latin word *rogatio,* meaning entreaty, the Rogation Days are the Monday, Tuesday and Wednesday immediately preceding Ascension Thursday. During these days, also called the **Lesser Litanies**, the Church invokes God's protection and blessing of the harvest. Each day features a procession, during which the litany of the Saints is chanted, followed by the Rogation Mass. Another more ancient Rogation day, called the **Greater Litanies**, was celebrated on the Feast of St. Mark, April 25.

Roman vestments   a term used to distinguish between the two main styles of liturgical vestments, rather than to describe a style of vestments specific to Rome. At the time that the Tridentine rite fell out of use, Roman vestments were more common, but are rarely seen now except in parishes where the Latin Mass is said. The Roman style chasuble is stiffer and often heavily ornamented, with open sides like a scapular, and the stole and maniple usually have splayed ends.

rubrics   from the Latin word *ruber,* meaning red, the rubrics are directions which govern the actions performed in a given ceremony. These are traditionally printed in red to distinguish them from the text of the liturgy. *See p.xxv.*

sabaoth   Hebrew word meaning armies. As found in the *Sanctus,* '*Dominus Deus Sabaoth*' is one of the ancient titles given to God, describing His might: He is the 'Lord God of Hosts'—hosts in this case meaning armies, specifically the heavenly armies of angels.

Sabbath   from the Hebrew word *shabát,* meaning rest, this was the seventh day of the week, upon which God commanded that His people rest from their labors as He did, and turn their thoughts to those things which are holy. From this word springs the name for Saturday in many languages.

St. Paul was instrumental in transferring the observance of this holy day to Sunday, the first day of the week, as this was the day on which our Saviour rose from the dead.

sacrament   from the Latin word *sacramentum,* meaning 'a sacred pledge,' a sacrament is a visible sign, instituted by Christ, through which the Church confers sanctifying grace upon the soul of one who is properly disposed to receive it.

The Council of Trent defined seven sacraments to have been instituted by Christ. These are (in the order shown in the illustration at left): Matrimony, Holy Orders, Extreme Unction, Penance, Holy Eucharist, Confirmation and Baptism.

Baptism and Penance are both considered sacraments of the dead, being conferred on those who are spiritually dead due to sin. The remaining sacraments are those of the living and it is imperative that they be received in a state of grace. *See entries for grace, disposition.*

THE SEVEN SACRAMENTS SHOWN SPRINGING FROM THE PIERCED SIDE OF OUR LORD.

sacramental   any rite, object or action which is used by the Church, in imitation of the Sacraments, as a means for the faithful to obtain a spiritual good in proportion to the disposition of the individual.

Sacramentals are divided into six classes:
- *orans,* or prayers, such as the Our Father or the Divine Office;
- *tinctus,* or dipping, such as the use of holy water or oil for anointing;
- *edens,* or eating, of blessed foods;
- *confessus,* or confession, such as the *Confiteor*;
- *dans,* or alms, which are bestowed in the name of the Church; and
- *benedicens,* or blessings, the largest class, which includes any consecrations or blessings of persons or places (*i.e.* kings, abbots, churches, homes), as well as blessed items (*i.e.* candles, palms, ashes, medals, scapulars, etc.)

See p.4, entry for disposition.

sacrifice   from the Latin *sacra + faciens,* meaning 'to make holy.' Considered the purest form of worship, a sacrifice differs from an oblation in that a precious gift is surrendered fully to God and more or less destroyed in the process. *See pp.x, xii, 26, 34, 38, 40.*

Sancta   Latin word meaning Holy. In the ancient Church, during the breaking of the Host, a third piece, called the *Sancta,* was kept reserved until the next Mass. It was then placed in the Chalice along with the piece broken from the newly consecrated Host. In this way, the unity and continuity of the Sacrifice of the Mass was emphasized.

At times, the *Sancta* from the Mass of a Pope or Bishop might be shared with other churches. In such cases, it was called the *Fermentum,* Latin for leaven. Like any fermented food which requires a portion of the previous batch as a culture, the fermentum demonstrated the "spiritual leaven" shared amongst all the faithful through the Mass. It is believed that this practice gave rise to the holding of the paten by the subdeacon from the Offertory until the breaking of the Sacred Host, as this particle would remain on the paten during that time. *See p.46.*

sanctuary   from the Latin word *sanctuarium,* meaning 'holy place,' the sanctuary is that part of the Church in which the High Altar is located, usually enclosed by the **altar rails**. There, in the center of the altar, rests the **tabernacle**, where our Lord resides in our midst. When we are in view of the sanctuary, we should maintain reverence in the presence of our Lord. *See entry for Church.*

sanctuary lamp   also called an **altar lamp**. At least one lamp must be kept burning near the altar when the Blessed Sacrament is kept reserved in the Tabernacle, to remind us of His presence. It is usually suspended by a rope or chain, and most have a red glass covering, though this is not required. Its use derives from the lamp kept burning perpetually before the tabernacle in the book of Exodus. This lamp traditionally burns only pure olive oil, but a pure beeswax candle may be substituted. *See p.xxiv.*

84

Sanctus Latin word meaning holy. The *Sanctus* is the fourth of the sung parts of the Ordinary of the Mass, sung at the culmination of the Preface, as a transition to the Canon. It is a hymn composed of the song of the Angels from Isaiah 6:1-3, and the *Benedictus* from Matthew 21:9. *See p.28.*

secret from the Latin word *secernare*, meaning 'to set apart,' the Secret is one of the proper prayers of the Mass, said over the offerings immediately before the Preface. It takes its name from the fact that it is the only prayer of the Mass in collect form (that is, one meant to *collect* our intentions as a congregation) that is spoken silently. The Secret is directly related to the proper Collect and Postcommunion prayers for each Mass. *See p.26, entry for collect.*

Septuagesima Latin word meaning seventieth. Septuagesima represents the seventieth day before Easter. This feast is celebrated three Sundays before Ash Wednesday (though this is not in fact the seventieth day before Easter). These seventy days are meant to represent the seventy years of the Babylonian Captivity, in remembrance of which some in the early Church began this anticipated period of Lenten fasting.

The larger Season of Septuagesima is a 2½ week period of solemnity separating the joy of Christmastide from the Penitence of Lent. Beginning on Septuagesima Sunday, purple vestments are worn, and in the Mass, the *Gloria* is omitted and the *Alleluia* replaced with the Tract. *See p.xvii, entry for alleluia.*

Septuagint from the Latin word *septuaginta*, meaning seventy, this was the first complete Greek translation of the Hebrew Bible, and takes its name from the seventy-two scholars charged with its completion in the 2nd century BC. This translation is known to have been used by the Apostles and the Evangelists. *See p.68.*

server a layman or boy who fulfills the duties of an acolyte, most often at Low Mass. When serving at the altar, they wear the *cassock* and *surplice*, garments which were originally proper to the minor clergy.

The main duties of the server at Mass are to make the responses, to ring the bell, to move the Missal when required, and to assist the celebrant at the Offertory, *Lavabo* and ablutions. *See p.xix, entry for acolyte.*

sequence from the Latin word *sequentia*, meaning 'a following out,' the Sequence is a hymn that had its origins in the adding of words to the long series of notes sung on the final syllable of the Alleluia—thus it was literally a "following out" of the chant. At the height of their use, in the Middle Ages, there were proper sequences for each feast, but now only five have been retained. *See p.12.*

Sexagesima Latin word meaning sixtieth. Sexagesima represents the sixtieth day before Easter, and is celebrated two Sundays before Ash Wednesday. *See entry for Septuagesima.*

shekinah from the Hebrew word *shakhan*, meaning 'to dwell,' the Shekinah is the name for the presence of God dwelling among men, as manifested in the cloud and the pillar of flame that led the Israelites through the wilderness. Once the Ark of the Covenant had been made, this presence

took its place upon the throne (also called the *mercy seat*) as noted in Exodus 40:32-33: "a cloud covered the tabernacle, and it was filled with the brightness of the Lord's presence; nor could Moses enter the tabernacle that bore record of the covenant, so thick the cloud that spread all about it, so radiant was the Lord's majesty; all was wrapped in cloud." From this time, only the high priest could enter that veiled sanctuary after careful preparation. In Solomon's temple, the home of the Ark was known as the *Holy of Holies*, but as the Ark was lost at the time of the Bablyonian Captivity, the Holy of Holies in the Second Temple was empty. *See p.22.*

sin from the Old English word *synn*, meaning 'injury' or 'crime,' sin is any act that is in defiance of God's law. By putting our own will and pleasure before our duty to obey God, we offend Him and effectively refuse His friendship and graces. We should always try to repair this relationship with God by seeking the sacrament of Penance, or if this is not available, by at least making an act of *perfect contrition*.
There are two main types of sin:
1. *Original Sin* is the state of sin into which every human creature is born as a result of Adam's sin, which robbed us of God's *sanctifying grace*.
2. *Actual Sin*, on the other hand, are those acts we commit by choice, by omission, or by our complicity in others' sins. The seriousness of actual sins depends on the gravity of the act and the degree to which we were deliberate in our intent:
   • *Material Sin* is an act that is committed involuntarily, or as a result of ignorance of God's law. For these we are not culpable.
   • *Mortal Sin* is so called because it deprives us of the sanctifying grace that gives our souls life. This can only be restored through the sacrament of Penance, or through an act of perfect contrition. Three things are necessary to make a sin mortal:
     1. *It must be a serious matter;*
     2. *We must be fully aware that our act is gravely sinful;*
     3. *We must freely choose to commit the act anyway.*
   • If any of these three is lacking, our act is considered a *venial sin*.

Solemn High Mass see *Missa Solemnis.*

soutane see *cassock.*

stole from the Greek word *stolē*, meaning garment, the stole is a band of silk, approximately 4 inches wide and 8 feet long. It is worn by those clergy of the rank of deacon or above when administering the sacraments, as a symbol of the authority of their office. Its color matches that of the other vestments, and while its more ancient form (as worn with "Gothic" vestments) is narrow and straight, its style as worn with "Roman" vestments is wider and has splayed ends.

A deacon wears the stole over the left shoulder, joined under the right arm; a priest wears it around the neck and crossed at the waist; and a bishop wears it in similar manner, but uncrossed. *See p.xx.*

subdeacon the lowest of the Major Orders, his ordination is considered a sacramental, being similar to the Sacrament of Holy Orders, but not imprinting an indelible mark. At Mass, the subdeacon vests in amice, alb, cincture, maniple and tunicle, and his duties are to sing the Epistle, to bring the sacred vessels to the altar, and to hold the paten from the Offertory until the breaking of the Sacred Host. *See p.xix, entry for Sancta.*

surplice a white tunic made of linen or cotton. It is shorter than the alb, is never belted, and has wide sleeves. It is the official vestment of the minor orders, though it is also worn (along with the cassock) by laypersons when serving at Mass. *See p.xix.*

SERVER
WEARING
CASSOCK
AND SURPLICE

symbol from the Greek word *symbolon,* meaning token, symbol may refer to a physical representation of a thing or idea, such as the symbols for the various sacraments shown on page 84, or it may refer to a summary of the dogma of one's faith, as in the **Nicene Creed**. *See p.16.*

synagogue from the Greek word *synagogé,* meaning assembly, the synagogue is the name for the meeting place (*beit knesset* in Hebrew) where the Jews gathered to pray and receive instruction in the sacred scriptures. This was an ancient practice which became more important during the time of the Babylonian Exile, when worship in Jerusalem was impossible, and the faithful sought an alternate means of continuing the practice of their faith.

After Christ's death the Apostles continued to worship largely in the manner they were accustomed, first in the synagogues, then in their own gatherings. Thus the practices of the synagogue formed the basis the early *Synaxis,* which in turn gave rise to the Liturgies of the Mass and the Divine Office. *See p.xii, 12, 64.*

synaxis like the word synagogue, this word derives its meaning from the Greek word for assembly, and denotes the early Christian gatherings which were similar in form to the practices of the synagogue. *See p.64.*

synod from the Greek word *synodos,* meaning meeting, a synod is an ecclesiastical assembly convened to discuss matters pertaining to the faith or the practice thereof.

tabernacle from the Latin word *tabernaculum,* meaning tent, the tabernacle is the compartment located at the center of a traditional altar, in which the Blessed Sacrament is kept reserved under lock and key. It may be made of wood, stone or metal, and is covered by a veil of gold, silver, white, or of the same color as the vestments. Inside it is lined with silk or precious metal and a folded corporal is kept on its floor.

Its name calls to mind the tent which sheltered the Ark of the Covenant during the years the Israelites spent wandering in the wilderness, and in which the presence of God, called the **Shekinah**, was said to dwell. *See p.xxiv.*

Tanakh the body of Jewish scripture is referred to by this acronym, formed from the first letter of each of its parts:

1. the **Torah:** Also called the **Pentateuch**, these are the Books of Moses. Both Jewish and Christian tradition is unanimous in acknowledging Moses as the author of these first five books of the Bible, evidenced most strongly by Jesus' words to the Pharisees in John 5:46: "For if you did believe Moses, you would perhaps believe me also; for he wrote of me."
2. the **Nevi'im:** The writings of the prophets, including Joshua, Judges, Samuel, Kings, Isaiah, Jeremiah, Ezekiel and the Twelve minor prophets, form the second main division of the Hebrew bible.
3. the **Ketuvim:** This category of writings include the Psalms, other poetical books such as Proverbs, the Song of Songs and Ecclesiastes, as well as various Chronicles ranging from Ruth and Esther to Daniel and Esdras.

Taken together, these comprise more or less what we call the Old Testament. *See p.68.*

Tenebrae Latin word meaning darkness. Tenebrae is a simplified version of Matins and Lauds (hours from the **Divine Office**; *see pp.65-66*) for Holy Thursday, Good Friday and Holy Saturday. Matins are the vigils of the night, and Lauds are usually prayed at dawn, but on these three days they are said together on the previous evening, hence the entire service takes place in darkness.

TENEBRAE
HEARSE

Matins is a service of three nocturns, each having three psalms with antiphons, as well as three lessons with responsories. Lauds is a service having five psalms with antiphons.

After each one of these fourteen psalms is read or chanted, one of fifteen candles on a special holder called a **hearse** is extinguished until only one is left. This is then hidden behind the altar while Psalm 50 and the final prayers are said; at this point, a great noise is made using clappers or books, representing the earthquake that took place at the moment of Christ's death. The single candle is returned to the hearse and all depart in silence.

thanksgiving one of the four ends of sacrifice, it is worth noting that the word *Eucharist* derives from the Greek word for thanksgiving. It is our solemn duty as members of the Mystical Body of Christ to give thanks to God for the gifts that he bestows upon us. *See pp.x, 54.*

thurible an Anglicization of the Latin word *thuribulum,* meaning censer. *See entry for censer.*

thurifer The acolyte or server who is responsible for the thurible (censer) during sacred ceremonies. *See p.xix.*

tonsure from the Latin word *tondere,* meaning 'to shear,' the tonsure was the sacred rite by which a young man first entered the clerical order. Typically a circular portion of the scalp was shaved and the young man was invested with the surplice. At one time, this was a

separate ceremony, performed when a young man first offered himself to God's service, but later it was joined to the ordination ceremony upon receiving the first of the minor orders. It was, in fact, the practice of maintaining the tonsure among clerics that led to the wearing of the skull cap, called the *zuchetto,* in order to keep the head warm. *See entry for Holy Orders.*

torchbearer   any acolyte or server charged with carrying candles during liturgical functions or processions. *See p.xix.*

tract   from the Latin phrase *in uno tractu,* meaning 'in one movement,' referring to the method by which this chant is sung (as distinguished from those which are sung antiphonally). The Tract is usually part of a psalm which takes the place of the Alleluia in penitential Masses (*i.e.* from Septuagesima through Easter, Masses for the Dead). *See p.12.*

tradition   from the Latin word *traditio,* meaning to surrender or deliver over, tradition refers to the collected teachings of the Church which have not come directly from sacred scripture but are nevertheless considered to be divine revelation as handed down from the Apostles or inspired by the Holy Spirit. An example of such a teaching is that of the Assumption of the Blessed Virgin Mary: though the story of this event is not found in the Bible, it has been handed down from the Apostles, who were present at her death.

transubstantiation   from the Latin *trans + substantia,* meaning literally 'change of substance,' this term explains what takes place when a valid celebrant speaks the words of the Consecration at Mass: the bread and wine, though their appearance, feel and taste remain the same, are truly and wholly changed in substance to the Body and Blood of Christ. The very deliberate show of reverence for the consecrated Host at Mass helps to establish the truth of this doctrine in the minds of the faithful.

Tridentine Mass   This name for the Mass comes from *Tridentum,* the Latin name for the city of Trent. At the Council of Trent, the varied practices for the celebration of the Mass that had developed over the centuries in different regions were normalized and brought, as much as possible, in line with the most ancient codices, in order that the Liturgy of the Mass might be celebrated in all places according to one rite. This was especially important as a way of safeguarding the liturgy from any erroneous doctrine or practice, especially in places where Protestant teaching was strong.

Upon the completion of the Tridentine Missal in 1570, the Papal Bull *Quo Primum* was issued, decreeing, "it shall be unlawful henceforth and forever throughout the Christian world to sing or to read Masses according to any formula other than that of this Missal published by Us."

This form of the liturgy was used until 1969, when it was supplanted by the Mass of Paul VI, a product of the Second Vatican Council. The Tridentine Mass is now commonly referred to as the "Extraordinary Form of the Mass," following the verbiage of the Motu Proprio *Summorum Pontificum* of Benedict XVI, as a way of reaffirming its validity while at the same time distinguishing it from the more widely celebrated Pauline Mass, which he termed the "Ordinary Form." *See p.xi, entry for Council of Trent.*

tunicle   the outer vestment worn by the subdeacon at Mass. Though it is meant to be shorter than the deacon's *dalmatic,* with narrower sleeves and only one horizontal strip (or none) joining the *clavi,* it is now rarely distinguishable. It is made from the same color and fabric as the celebrant's chasuble. Like the dalmatic, it is often replaced by a folded chasuble during seasons of penitence. *See p.xix, entry for dalmatic.*

type   from the Greek word *typos,* meaning 'model' or 'impression,' a type in the scriptural sense is a person or event which, though existing in its own right, also is intended by God as a foreshadowing to be fulfilled by its **antitype**.

Many types for Jesus can be found in the Old Testament, ranging from the priest Melchisedech to the blameless Joseph, to Jonah, who was brought back from the belly of the whale. The Passover is both a type and a precursor of the Mass. *See p.40.*

versicle   from the Latin word *versiculus,* meaning 'little verse,' a versicle is an exclamatory line, typically taken from a psalm, which is meant to be answered by a server, choir or congregation. *See pp.xxv, 67.*

Vespers   Latin word meaning evening. Vespers is the sixth of the canonical hours of the Divine Office, prayed in the evening "at the lighting of the lamps." Along with Lauds, which is prayed at dawn, it is the most solemn of the hours. It was once common for the faithful to return to church on Sunday evenings to participate in this service.

The revision of the Breviary after the Second Vatican Council simplified Vespers and renamed it "Evening Prayer." *See pp.64-66, entries for breviary, Divine Office.*

vestments   from the Latin word *vestimentum,* meaning clothing, vestments are special garments worn by the clergy during the liturgics and other ceremonies of the Church, or when they are performing the duties of their office. The wearing of specific vestments in the exercise of worship was first commanded by God in Exodus 28:2: "And thou shalt make a holy vesture for Aaron thy brother for glory and for beauty." *See pp.xix-xxi.*

Vidi aquam   Latin phrase meaning 'I saw water.' This is the *incipit,* or opening phrase, of the Antiphon which takes the place of the *Asperges me* at the beginning of the Mass during Paschaltide.

Vulgate   the full Latin name for this version of the Bible is *Vulgata Editio,* meaning 'Popular Edition.' This refers to St. Jerome's translation of the Bible into the Latin language, which was then the language commonly spoken among Christians. It was declared by the Council of Trent to be free from errors of doctrine or morals, and therefore the only authentic version for public use.

Devotions for Confession

(Adapted from *Forgive Us our Trespasses* by Mother Mary Loyola)

Four things are necessary in order to make a good confession:

1. We must heartily pray for grace to make a good confession.
2. We must carefully examine our conscience.
3. We must take time and care to make a good act of contrition.
4. We must resolve by the help of God to renounce our sins and to begin a new life for the future.

1. We must pray for grace to make a good confession.

Because this is an important work and we can do no good work without the help of God's grace. Because it is sometimes difficult to tell our sins. And because prayer is the means fixed by God for getting His help. "*Ask,*" He says, "*and you shall receive.*" You may say one of the hymns to the Holy Spirit, or:

Prayer for Help

I BELIEVE that there, behind the tabernacle door, is the Judge of the living and the dead, before Whom I shall have to appear when I die, to give an exact account of my whole life. I believe that He will have to judge me then with strict justice, that there will be no time for confession and contrition then. O my Judge and my Saviour, now while I have time, help me to find out my sins and to confess them with true sorrow, that I may stand without fear before You in the terrible hour of Judgment.

Holy Mary, Mother of God, pray for me a sinner now and at the hour of my death. Amen.

2. We must carefully examine our conscience.

If you go to confession frequently and examine your conscience every night, preparation for the Sacrament of Penance becomes very easy. You come to it with the work half done. Set to work briskly the minute you get into church, beginning at once with the first of the four points. Follow some order in the arrangement of what you have to say—the ten commandments of God; the six precepts of the Church; the seven deadly sins; or—to cover the same ground in another way—your duties (I) to God; (II) to your neighbour; (III) to yourself. Your sins will thus remain in your memory, and when your examination is finished you will be able to leave them quietly and turn to your next point. Without an orderly arrangement, examination of conscience becomes difficult and wearisome, and you will be running after your sins instead of thinking how to get rid of them. Ten minutes given to it in a business-like way is enough for an ordinary confession. Give the rest of the time, another ten minutes, to your contrition.

When we have not been to confession for some time, and even in our preparation for our weekly confession, we may sometimes find it useful to recall the places we have been in, and the persons we have met. This helps us to remember our sins. Any circumstance that changes the kind of sin and makes it much worse, *e.g.,* striking a parent, stealing anything belonging to a church, must be mentioned; and as far as we can, we should say the number of times a sin has been committed.

By the law of God we are bound to confess every mortal sin once, and be absolved for it once. We are not bound to confess our venial sins, but it is well to do so. A good practice is to pick out two or three of the chief and try to be sorry for them. This is better than spending much time in trying to remember them all.

The Ten Commandments of God

1. I AM THE LORD THY GOD, Who brought thee out of the land of Egypt, and out of the house of bondage. Thou shalt not have strange gods before Me. Thou shalt not make to thyself a graven thing, nor the likeness of anything that is in heaven above, or in the earth beneath, nor of those things that are in the waters under the earth. Thou shalt not adore them, nor serve them.
2. Thou shalt not take the name of the Lord thy God in vain.
3. Remember to keep holy the Sabbath day.
4. Honor thy father and thy mother, that thou mayest be long-lived upon the land which the Lord thy God will give thee.
5. Thou shalt not kill.
6. Thou shalt not commit adultery.
7. Thou shalt not steal.
8. Thou shalt not bear false witness against thy neighbor.
9. Thou shalt not covet thy neighbor's wife.
10. Thou shalt not covet thy neighbor's goods.

The Six Commandments of the Church

1. To hear Mass on Sundays and holy days of obligation.
2. To fast and abstain on the days appointed.
3. To confess at least once a year.
4. To receive Holy Eucharist during the Easter-time.
5. To contribute to the support of our pastors.
6. Not to marry persons who are not Catholics, or who are related to us within the fourth degree of kindred, nor privately without witnesses, nor to solemnize marriage at forbidden times.

The Seven Deadly Sins, and the Opposite Virtues

1. Pride . . . . Humility.
2. Greed . . . . Generosity.
3. Lust . . . . Chastity.
4. Anger . . . . Meekness.
5. Gluttony . . . . Temperance.
6. Envy . . . . Brotherly love.
7. Sloth . . . . Diligence.

A Form of Examination of Conscience

(I) Duties Towards God.

- **Confession.** How long is it since my last? Did I do the four things by way of preparation? Did I leave out anything I ought to have told? Did I take time and care to make a good act of contrition? What was my purpose of amendment like? Did I say my penance carefully?
- **Communion.** Did I take the time to prepare for our Lord's visit? Did I thank Him for coming to me?
- **Prayers.** When I kneel down to pray do I remember that I am going to speak to God, and make at least a good start? Do I say my prayers in a hurry, or looking about all the time? Have I said my morning and night prayers, and without willful distractions? Have I examined my conscience at night and made a real act of sorrow for my sins? Have I laughed or talked in church, or shown any irreverence during Mass or Benediction? Have I done anything to distract others at prayer? How do I listen to sermons or catechism? Have I said grace before and after meals as I ought?
- Have I done or read anything likely to injure my faith?
- Have I spoken with disrespect of God, or of holy things? Have I said bad words?
- Have I stayed away from Mass on any Sunday or Holy day of Obligation? Have I been late on these days, or inattentive?

(II) Duties Towards my Neighbour.

- Have I disobeyed parents, or anyone else in authority over me? Have I provoked them, or shown disrespect in word or manner? Have I caused them great sorrow, or not helped them when they were poor, or old, or sick? Have I done what I was told at once, or been angry, or answered back? Have I been obstinate, sulky, or impertinent when told of my faults? Have I deceived my parents or those who are over me?
- Have I been in a passion? or kept up bad temper for a long time? Have I struck any one or quarrelled? Have I called people names, or in other ways provoked them? Have I wished harm to anyone? Have I refused to forgive? Have I given bad example to anyone by word or conduct? Or shared in any sin by proposing it, defending it, or in any other way? Have I done anything to spite my parents, teachers, or companions?
- Have I prevented others from studying, or working, or in any way doing their duty?
- Have I given unnecessary trouble to parents or superiors?
- Have I stolen anything, or kept what did not belong to me, without trying to find the owner? Have I destroyed, wasted, or willfully damaged things? Have I paid back anything I owed?
- Have I told lies, or got others to tell them? (*A lie of excuse that does not harm another is a venial sin.*) Have I told any lie that I knew would be the cause of harm to another? (*This is calumny, and may be a mortal sin. If I have sinned by calumny, detraction, or theft, I must repair as well as I can the harm I have done, and ask my confessor's advice how to do it.*) Have I made known any one's secret faults? (*This is detraction.*) Have I injured my neighbour's character by speaking ill of him, or listened willingly to uncharitable conversation? Have I judged anyone rashly, that is, thought ill of him without sufficient cause? Have I made others quarrel, or made mischief by tale-bearing?

  (*Note: Tale-telling to make mischief, or out of spite, is wrong. But if you know of any immodest conduct or conversation carried on, you must at once make it known to your parents, or those in authority, and not fear to be called "tell-tale." If you neglect to do this, you may become answerable for such sins by concealment.*)

(III) Duties Towards Myself.

- Have I done anything wrong, by thought, word, or deed, against purity or modesty? Have I got others to do wrong? Have I gone with bad companions? Have I read bad books, or given them to others?

  (*Note: A bad thought which is not willful is no sin, but not to try to put away the bad thought, to take pleasure in it, to consent to it—this is a sin.*)
- Have I been vain of my abilities, my person, or my dress? Have I despised others? Have I been jealous of others, or vexed when my companions were praised?
- Have I been greedy? Have I, without leave, eaten meat on Friday, or on any day when it is forbidden?
- Do I rise promptly in the morning, or am I lazy?
- Have I been idle at my lessons? Have I stayed away from school or kept others away?
- Have I, through curiosity, read letters or anything I ought not to have read? What about the duties and occupations of my daily life—how have they been done—conscientiously, or carelessly?
- Have I done anything else that I ought to confess? What is my chief fault, from which most of the others come—pride, anger, sloth, or what? Am I trying to conquer it?

3. We must take time and care to make a good act of contrition.

This is the chief part of our preparation, without which all the rest is worse than useless. Have we gathered together every sin we have committed?— not one will be forgiven without **contrition**. And on the other hand, should any sin, even a grievous one, be forgotten after sufficient care, our act of contrition, which would include that and every other grievous sin if we remembered it, would blot it out.

Now what is this contrition that we must have? The catechism says it is "*a hearty sorrow for our sins, because by them we have offended so good a God, together with a firm purpose of amendment.*" Notice that true sorrow looks two ways—backwards, to hate sin in the past; and forwards, to avoid it in the future.

The best motive for sorrow is God Himself—to be sorry for God's sake, because He is infinitely good and deserving of all love, and because by sin we have displeased and disappointed Him Whom we love. This **perfect contrition** is so pleasing to God, that it gets forgiveness at once for all guilt, mortal or venial, even before confession and absolution. If sufficiently intense, it remits all punishment too, eternal and temporal. It remits more or less, according to our dispositions. **Imperfect contrition**, called also **attrition**, is supernatural sorrow, but chiefly for our own sake, because we have lost heaven, or deserved hell or purgatory. Though less perfect than the other, it is good and put into our hearts by the Holy Ghost. It will forgive venial sin and remit a part of the temporal punishment, and is sufficient when joined with confession and absolution for the forgiveness of mortal sin.

See how necessary contrition is: it almost seems to be the one thing necessary. We simply must have it. Now how are we to get it? The catechism says *"by earnestly praying for it, and by making use of such considerations as may lead us to it."* The sorrow of our will is in our power; we can and must give it Him. Like all good things it must come from Him, but He has promised that all who ask shall receive and all who seek shall find. We will ask for it with all our heart, and we will seek for it by thinking over some of the things which will move us to it. This is our part; if we do it, God will come in and do His.

MY GOD, give me true sorrow for having offended You. I must come to You for it. I cannot get it by myself. But I know You want to give it to me more than I want to have it. I know there is nothing You are so pleased to give. You tell me to ask and I shall receive, to seek and I shall find, to knock and it shall be opened to me. I am asking, seeking, knocking now. Give me what I need—perfect contrition for all my sins, sorrow for them because they have offended You Who are so good. Grant me what I ask, through Jesus Christ our Lord.

4. We must resolve by the grace of God to renounce our sins and to begin a new life for the future.

Remember we have to make a **purpose of amendment.** Now a purpose is not a mere passing wish, it is a strong intention or determination, it is the making up of our mind about something. Clearly, then, it needs time and thought. This purpose, as has been said, is really part of our act of contrition, for *there can be no true sorrow for the wrong we have done unless we intend not to do it again.* The purpose of amendment we are bound to have is a firm determination to avoid all mortal sin and the proximate occasions of mortal sin. Let us see what these are.

When we have fallen into sin we must look back to see what was the occasion. Any circumstance leading to sin is called an **occasion of sin.** It may be proximate or remote. A **proximate occasion** is one which usually leads us into sin. A **remote occasion** is one in which we sometimes, though seldom, commit sin. Persons, places, and things may all become occasions of sin, some to one person, some to another. Certain things, such as bad companions, improper conversations, and bad books, are always proximate occasions of sin. Should there be any person, place, or thing which, no matter what we do, always leads us into mortal sin, we are bound to keep away from it at any cost. Our Lord says, *"If thy hand, or thy foot scandalize thee,"*—that is, if something you care for as much as hand or foot, leads you to commit sin—*"cut it off and cast it from thee. It is better for thee to go into life maimed or lame, than having two hands or two feet to be cast into everlasting fire."* (Matt. 18.)

We should of course resolve to avoid venial sins too, and if we have these only to confess, we should pick out one at least, and make a firm resolve about that. If you cannot make up your mind what to choose, think what our Lord would advise, and you will make a good choice.

Our natural character lays us open to the same temptations, and the routine of our daily life brings round the same occasions. And therefore it is not surprising if we take the same faults to confession again and again. What we have to do is to lessen the number; to rid ourselves of them by degrees; to turn occasions of sin into occasions of victory; thus, as St. Augustine says, using them as steps by which to climb up to heaven.

We do not make a purpose of *transfiguration*—to become all at once entirely different from what we were—but a purpose of *amendment*. Mending is a gradual and a laborious process, whether it be the mending of a stocking or of a man-of-war. No one expects it to be done all at once. If God is patient with us, and willing to wait whilst we mend, why should we be so impatient with ourselves!

In a few minutes you will be confessing your sins before Almighty God and the grandees of the court of heaven. Think how ashamed you would be if you had to confess them before your father and mother, brothers, sisters, schoolfellows. Should you feel less shame to confess before God, the Holy of Holies; before Blessed Mary, conceived without sin; before angels and saints, standing without spot before the great white throne? The sense of shame does us good and helps us to sorrow. Think, too, that all that heavenly court looks down lovingly upon you, and is praying for you, and rejoices to see you purifying your soul in the Precious Blood to be ready for their company some day.

It happens, however, sometimes, that we have to wait, not a few minutes, but a long time at the confessional, and that having finished our preparation, we begin to look about and get distracted. This is a pity. If we like, we may say our rosary then, or read some of the pages of this book. These will not distract us, but on the contrary, will help us to make a good act of contrition when our turn comes to go in.

Form for Confession

1. Kneeling down in the confessional make the sign of the Cross:

In the name of the Father, and of the Son, and of the Holy Ghost.

2. Ask a blessing:

Bless me, Father, for I have sinned.

3. Say how long it has been since your last confession:

It has been ___ weeks since my last confession.

4. Tell your sins in the way you can remember them best. Say how often or about how often you have done them. If you are nervous or afraid, ask the Priest to help you. At the end say:

For these sins and all the sins of my past life, I am truly and heartily sorry, especially for the sin of (say which sin).

5. After confessing your sins, *leave them.* Do not begin to think if you have told all. Whatever you have forgotten is forgiven. Listen attentively to the advice of your confessor. Then, while he gives you absolution, renew your act of sorrow as if you were kneeling at the feet of Jesus and He Himself were absolving you.

If you have restitution to make, whether of good name or of anything else, and do not know how to do it, or if on any other point you want to know what you ought to do, ask your confessor's advice about it.

Now recite the Act of Contrition:

O my God, I am heartily sorry for having offended Thee, and I detest all my sins because I dread the loss of heaven and the pains of hell, but most of all, because they have offended Thee, my God, who are all good and deserving of all my love. I firmly resolve, with the help of Thy grace, to confess my sins, to do penance, and to amend my life. Amen.

6. When the Priest says the words of absolution: "*I absolve thee from thy sins, in the name of the Father, and of the Son, and of the Holy Ghost,*" bow down your head, make the sign of the Cross and say:

Amen.

7. The Priest will dismiss you, saying "*Go in peace, your sins are forgiven.*" Say:

Thank you, Father.

8. Come out of the confessional, and go to your place with your eyes cast down. Say your penance right away.

Thank God very heartily for the Precious Blood that has been applied to your soul and has cleansed it from all its stains. Say some psalm or hymn or prayer in thanksgiving.

Thanksgiving: Psalm 102

BLESS THE LORD, O my soul, and let all that is within me, bless His holy name. Bless the Lord, O my soul, and never forget all He hath done for thee. Who forgiveth all thy iniquities; Who healeth all thy diseases. Who redeemeth thy life from destruction; Who crowneth thee with mercy and compassion. Who satisfieth thy desire with good things: thy youth shall be renewed like the eagle's.

The Lord doth mercies, and judgment for all that suffer wrong. He hath made His ways known to Moses: His wills to the children of Israel. The Lord is compassionate and merciful; long-suffering and plenteous in mercy. He will not always be angry; nor will He threaten forever. He hath not dealt with us according to our sins; nor rewarded us according to our iniquities.

For according to the height of the heaven above the earth: He hath strengthened His mercy towards them that fear Him. As far as the east is from the west, so far hath He removed our iniquities from us. As a father hath compassion on his children, so hath the Lord compassion on them that fear Him. For He knoweth our frame; He remembereth that we are dust: Man's days are as grass, as the flower of the field so shall he flourish.

For the spirit shall pass in him, and he shall not be: and he shall know his place no more. But the mercy of the Lord is from eternity and unto eternity upon them that fear Him: And his justice unto children's children, to such as keep His covenant, and are mindful of His commandments to do them. The Lord hath prepared His throne in heaven: and His kingdom shall rule over all.

Bless the Lord, all ye His angels: you that are mighty in strength, and execute His word, herkening to the voice of His orders. Bless the Lord, all ye His hosts: you ministers of His that do His will. Bless the Lord, all His works: in every place of His dominion, O my soul, bless thou the Lord.

HAIL, JESUS! hail, who for my sake
Sweet Blood from Mary's veins didst take
   And shed it all for me;
Oh, blessed be my Saviour's Blood,
My life, my light, my only good,
   To all eternity.

To endless ages let us praise
The Precious Blood, whose price could raise
   The world from wrath and sin;
Whose streams our inward thirst appease,
And heal the sinner's worst disease,
   If he but bathe therein.

O sweetest Blood, that can implore
Pardon of God, and heaven restore,
   The heaven which sin had lost:
While Abel's blood for vengeance pleads
What Jesus shed still intercedes
   For those who wrong Him most.

O to be sprinkled from the wells
Of Christ's own Sacred Blood excels
   Earth's best and highest bliss:
The ministers of wrath divine
Hurt not the happy hearts that shine
   With those red drops of His!

Ah! there is joy amid the saints
And hell's despairing courage faints
   When this sweet song we raise:
Oh, louder then, and louder still,
Earth with one mighty chorus fill,
   The Precious Blood to praise!   *—Faber.*

Prayers in Preparation for Holy Communion

Psalm 129

Out of the depths have I cried to thee, O Lord; Lord, hear my voice: let thy ears be attentive to the voice of my supplications.

If thou, Lord, shouldest mark iniquities, O Lord, who shall stand? But with thee is forgiveness, that thou mayest be feared.

I trust in the Lord, my soul trusts in His word. My soul waiteth for the Lord more than sentinels wait for the dawn:

More than sentinels wait for the dawn, let Israel wait for the Lord: for with the Lord there is mercy, and with Him is plenteous redemption. And he shall redeem Israel from all his iniquities.

Prayer of St. Ambrose

O loving Lord Jesus Christ, I a sinner, presuming not on my own merits, but trusting in Thy mercy and goodness, with fear and trembling approach the table of Thy most sacred banquet. For I have defiled both my heart and body with many sins and have not kept a strict guard over my mind and my tongue. Wherefore, O gracious God, O awful Majesty, I a wretched creature, entangled in difficulties, have recourse to Thee, the font of mercy: to Thee do I fly that I may be healed, and take refuge under Thy protection. And I ardently desire to have Him as my Savior, whom I am unable to withstand as my Judge.

To Thee O Lord, I show my wounds, to Thee I lay bare my shame. I know that my sins are many and great, on account of which I am filled with fear. But I trust in Thy mercy, of which there is no end. Look down upon me, therefore, with the eyes of Thy mercy on me, who am full of misery and sin, Thou Who wilt never cease to let flow the fountain of mercy.

Hail, Victim of Salvation, offered for me and for all mankind on the tree of the Cross. Hail, noble and precious Blood, flowing from the wounds of my crucified Lord Jesus Christ and washing away the sins of the whole world. Remember, O Lord, Thy creature, whom Thou hast redeemed with Thy Blood; I am grieved because I have sinned, I desire to make amends for what I have done.

Take away from me, therefore, O most merciful Father, all my iniquities and sins, that, being purified both in soul and body, I may worthily partake of the Holy of Holies. And grant that this holy oblation of Thy Body and Blood, of which, though unworthy, I purpose to partake, may be to me the remission of my sins, the perfect cleansing of my offenses, the means of driving away all evil thoughts and of renewing all holy desires, the accomplishment of works pleasing to Thee, as well as the strongest defense for soul and body against the snares of my enemies. Amen.

Prayer of St. Thomas Aquinas

Almighty and eternal God, behold, I approach the sacrament of Thine only-begotten Son, Our Lord Jesus Christ. I approach as one who is sick to the physician of life, as one unclean to the fountain of mercy, as one blind to the light of eternal brightness, as one poor and needy to the Lord of heaven and earth.

Therefore I beseech Thee, of Thine infinite goodness, to heal my sickness, to wash away my filth, to enlighten my blindness, to enrich my poverty, and to clothe my nakedness, that I may receive the Bread of Angels, the King of Kings, and the Lord of Lords with such reverence and humility, with such contrition and devotion, with such purity and faith, with such purpose and intention, as may conduce to the salvation of my soul. Grant, I beseech Thee, that I may receive not only the sacrament of the Body and Blood of our Lord, but also the fruit and virtue of this sacrament.

O most indulgent God, grant me so to receive the Body of Thine only-begotten Son, Our Lord Jesus Christ, which He took of the Virgin Mary, that I may be found worthy to be incorporated with His mystical body and numbered among His members.

O most loving Father, grant that I may one day contemplate forever, face to face, Thy beloved Son, Whom now on my pilgrimage I am about to receive under the sacramental veils; Who lives and reigns with Thee in the unity of the Holy Spirit, God, world without end. Amen.

Act of Faith

O my God! I firmly believe that Thou art one God in three Divine persons, Father, Son, and Holy Ghost; I believe that Thy Divine Son became man, and died for our sins, and that he will come to judge the living and the dead. I believe these and all the truths which the Holy Catholic Church teaches, because Thou hast revealed them, who canst neither deceive nor be deceived.

Act of Hope

O my God! relying on Thy infinite goodness and promises, I hope to obtain pardon of my sins, the help of Thy grace, and life everlasting, through the merits of Jesus Christ, my Lord and Redeemer.

Act of Love

O my God! I love Thee above all things, with my whole heart and soul, because Thou art all-good and worthy of all love. I love my neighbor as myself for the love of Thee. I forgive all who have injured me, and ask pardon of all whom I have injured.

Prayers of Thanksgiving After Holy Communion

Thanksgiving after Communion

I thank Thee, Eternal Father, for giving me, as the food of my soul, the Body and Blood of Thy Only-begotten Son, Our Lord Jesus Christ. May this Divine Food preserve and increase the union of my soul with Thee. May it purify me by repressing every evil inclination. Grant that it may be to me a pledge of a glorious resurrection on the last day.

Anima Christi

Soul of Christ, be my sanctification;
Body of Christ, be my salvation.
Blood of Christ, fill all my veins;
Water from Christ's side, wash out my stains.
Passion of Christ, my comfort be.
O good Jesus, listen to me.
In Thy wounds I fain would hide
Ne'er to be parted from Thy side.
Guard me should the foe assail me;
Call me when my life shall fail me.
Bid me come to Thee above
With Thy saints to sing Thy love
World without end. Amen.

Adoro Te
(Hymn of St. Thomas Aquinas)

O GODHEAD hid, devoutly I adore Thee,
Who truly art within the forms before me;
To Thee my heart I bow with bended knee,
As failing quite in contemplating Thee.

Sight, touch, and taste in Thee are each deceived;
The ear alone most safely is believed.
I believe all the Son of God has spoken:
Than Truth's own word there is no truer token.

God only on the Cross lay hid from view,
But here lies hid at once the manhood too:
And I, in both professing my belief,
Make the same prayer as the repentant thief.

Thy wounds, as Thomas saw, I do not see;
Yet Thee confess my Lord and God to be.
Make me believe Thee ever more and more,
In Thee my hope, in Thee my love to store.

O Thou, memorial of our Lord's own dying!
O living bread, to mortals life supplying!
Make Thou my soul henceforth on Thee to live;
Ever a taste of heavenly sweetness give.

O loving Pelican! O Jesu Lord!
Unclean I am, but cleanse me in Thy Blood:
Of which a single drop, for sinners spilt,
Can purge the entire world from all its guilt.

Jesu! whom for the present veiled I see,
What I so thirst for, oh, vouchsafe to me:
That I may see Thy countenance unfolding,
And may be blest Thy glory in beholding. Amen.

Suscipe of St. Ignatius Loyola

TAKE, O LORD, and receive my entire liberty, my memory, my understanding and my whole will. All that I am and all that I possess You have given me: I surrender it all to You to be disposed of according to Your will. Give me only Your love and Your grace; with these I will be rich enough, and will desire nothing more.

Prayer of St. Bonaventure

PIERCE, O most Sweet Lord Jesus, my inmost soul with the most joyous and healthful wound of Thy love, with true, serene, and most holy apostolic charity, that my soul may ever languish and melt with love and longing for Thee, that it may yearn for Thee and faint for Thy courts, and long to be dissolved and to be with Thee.

Grant that my soul may hunger after Thee, the bread of angels, the refreshment of holy souls, our daily and supersubstantial bread, having all sweetness and savor and every delight of taste; let my heart ever hunger after and feed upon Thee, upon whom the angels desire to look, and may my inmost soul be filled with the sweetness of Thy savor; may it ever thirst after Thee, the fountain of life, the fountain of wisdom and knowledge, the fountain of eternal light, the torrent of pleasure, the richness of the house of God.

May it ever compass Thee, seek Thee, find Thee, run to Thee, attain Thee, meditate upon Thee, speak of Thee, and do all things to the praise and glory of Thy name, with humility and discretion, with love and delight, with ease and affection, and with perseverance unto the end.

May Thou alone be ever my hope, my entire assurance, my riches, my delight, my pleasure, my joy, my rest and tranquility, my peace, my sweetness, my fragrance, my sweet savor, my food, my refreshment, my refuge, my help, my wisdom, my portion, my possession and my treasure, in whom may my mind and my heart be fixed and firmly rooted immovably henceforth and for ever. Amen.

Petitions of St. Augustine

O LORD JESUS, let me know myself, let me know Thee,
And desire nothing else but only Thee,
Let me hate myself and love Thee,
And do all things for the sake of Thee,
Let me humble myself, and exalt Thee,
And think of nothing else but Thee,
Let me die to myself and live in Thee,
And take whatever happens as coming from Thee.
Let me flee from myself, and turn to Thee
That so I may merit to be defended by Thee.
Let me fear for myself, let me fear Thee,
And be amongst those who are chosen by Thee.
Let me distrust myself, and trust in Thee,
And ever obey for the love of Thee.
Let me cleave to nothing but Thee,
And ever be poor for the sake of Thee.
Look upon me, that I may love Thee;
Call me that I may see Thee
And forever possess Thee. Amen.

Thanksgiving After Communion
(St. Thomas Aquinas)

I GIVE THEE THANKS, O holy Lord, Father Almighty, Eternal God, that Thou hast vouchsafed, for no merit of my own, but of the mere condescension of Thy mercy, to satisfy me, a sinner and Thine unworthy servant, with the Precious Blood of Thy Son our Lord Jesus Christ. I implore Thee, let not this Holy Communion be to me an increase of guilt unto my punishment, but an availing plea unto pardon and forgiveness. Let it be to me the armor of faith and the shield of good will. Grant that it may work the extinction of my vices, the rooting out of concupiscence and lust, and the increase within me of charity and patience, of humility and obedience. Let it be my strong defense against the snares of all my enemies, visible and invisible; the stilling and the calm of all my impulses, carnal and spiritual; my indissoluble union with Thee the one and true God, and a blessed consummation at my last end. And I beseech thee that Thou wouldst vouchsafe to bring me, sinner as I am, to that ineffable banquet where Thou, with the Son and the Holy Spirit, art to Thy saints true and unfailing light, fullness and content, joy for evermore, gladness without alloy, consummate and everlasting bliss. Through the same Jesus Christ our Lord. Amen.

Prayer before a Crucifix

BEHOLD, O kind and most sweet Jesus, I cast myself upon my knees in Your sight, and with the most fervent desire of my soul I pray and beseech Thee that Thou wouldst impress upon my heart lively sentiments of Faith, Hope and Charity, true repentance for my sins and a firm purpose of amendment, while with deep affection and grief of soul I ponder within myself and mentally contemplate Thy five most precious wounds, having before my eyes that which David spoke in prophecy of Thee, O good Jesus: *they have pierced my hands and feet, they have numbered all my bones.*

Bibliography and Reading List

The many things you have learned in this book came from some of these books.
If you would like to learn more, we highly recommend reading these.

Know Your Mass
by Fr. Demetrius Manousos, O.F.M. Art by Addison Burbank. Published in 1954 by Guild Press, Inc.

My Catholic Faith: A Catechism in Pictures
by Rev. Louis LaRevoire Morrow. Originally published in 1949 by My Mission House,
Reprinted in 2000 by Sarto House.

How to Understand the Mass
by Dom Gaspar Lefebvre. Illustrations by Jos. Speybrouck. Originally published in 1937,
Reprinted in 2006 by Catholic Authors Press.

The Mass Explained to Children
by Maria Montessori. Originally published in 1932, Reprinted by Roman Catholic Books.

The Ceremonies of the Roman rite described
by Adrian Fortescue. Published in 1920 by Burns, Oates and Washbourne.

Calvary and the Mass
by Bishop Fulton Sheen.

The Heart of the Mass
Originally published in 1954 under the title *The Treasures of the Mass*.
Reprinted in 1997 by Sarto House.

How Christ Said the First Mass
by Rev. James Luke Meagher, D.D. Published in 1908 by the Christian Press Association Publishing Co.

Teaching Truth by Signs and Ceremonies
by Rev. James Luke Meagher, D.D. Published in 1882 by Russell Brothers.

Explanation of the Prayers and Ceremonies of Holy Mass
by Dom Prosper Gueranger, Abbot of Solesmes.
Translated by Rev. Dom Laurence Shepherd, St. Mary's Abbey, Stanbrook, 1885.

Holy Mass
by Mother Mary Loyola. Originally published in 1927,
Reprinted in 2010 by St. Augustine Academy Press.

Mass and the Sacraments
by Fr. John Laux, M.A. Published in 1934 by Benziger Brothers.

The Mass and Vestments of the Catholic Church
by Rt. Rev. Monsignor John Walsh. Published in 1916 by Benziger Brothers.

A General and Critical Introduction to the Study of Holy Scripture
by Andrew Edward Breen, D.D. Published in 1897 by John P. Smith Printing House.

The Catholic Encyclopedia
Available online at http://www.newadvent.org/cathen/

Propers for the Mass can be found at many sites online. One we recommend is *Una Voce* of Orange County:
http://www.uvoc.org/Propers.html

Bookmarks

It is not unusual to lose your place during the Mass, especially since much of it is in reverent silence. If this should happen, listen and watch for the clues in this chart to help you find the right page. ***Keep in mind that the sides of Christ's altar are determined by <u>His</u> Right and Left, not ours.*** See page xxv for an explanation of the sides of the altar.

Volume of Celebrant's Voice	Location of Celebrant	R L	Actions of the Celebrant or Ministers ❀ Sounds, Gestures and Other Cues ❀	Part of Mass	See Page #
normal	foot of the altar		The Celebrant bows low to recite the *Confiteor*, then the server or ministers do likewise.	**Confiteor**	5
raised	center of altar		At High Mass, the *Kyrie* is sung by the choir. At Low Mass, it is recited aloud by the Priest.	**Kyrie**	9
raised	center of altar		At High Mass, the Celebrant intones, "*Gloria in Excelsis Deo*," followed by the choir.	**Gloria**	11
raised	left side of altar (our right)		At High Mass, the Subdeacon reads the Epistle. At Low Mass, the Priest reads the Epistle aloud.	**Epistle**	13
raised	right side of altar (our left)		At High Mass, the Deacon reads the Gospel. At Low Mass, the Priest reads the Gospel aloud.	**Gospel**	15
raised	center of altar		At High Mass, the Celebrant intones, "*Credo in unum Deum*," followed by the choir. All kneel at the words "*Et incarnatus est*."	**Credo**	17
normal	left side of altar (our right)		The Celebrant pours wine and a drop of water into the Chalice.	**Mixing of Water and Wine**	21
normal	both sides of altar		At Solemn High Mass, the Celebrant will incense the offerings, the altar, and all those present.	**Incensing**	23
normal	left side of altar (our right)		The Celebrant washes his hands.	**Lavabo**	25
raised	center of altar		The Celebrant turns to the people with his hands raised in front of his body.	**Orate Fratres**	27
raised	center of altar		As we approach the Preface, a responsory is sung (or spoken at Low Mass), ending with the phrase, "*Dignum et Justum est*."	**Preface**	29
raised	center of altar		At High Mass, the choir sings the *Sanctus*.	**Sanctus**	29
silent	center of altar		The Celebrant imposes his hands over the offerings, symbolizing the placing of our sins upon the sacrificial Lamb.	**Hanc Igitur**	35